/ 2 5

AWAKENING LOVE

At long last, spirituality is returning to medicine and psychology for a simple reason: healing is impossible without taking the spiritual side of life into account. Drs. Demetry and Clonts give clear, compelling instructions on how to contact our spiritual dimension and allow it to flower in our life.

Larry Dossey, M.D., author,
Reinventing Medicine and *Healing Words*

Awakening Love is a superb guide to new perceptions! Spiritual teachers will welcome such practical techniques for healing our little-understood human nature.

As we venture deeper into the convergence of science and spirituality, the biblical words of the Master can be heard with new ears. If we grasp the remarkable wisdom teachings, blended with biblical parables we all know, we will have new tools for living life. The insights are not only transforming, but prepare one for inner inspiration from one's dreams and impressions.

Likewise, I applaud the lucid explanation of elementals and their power in a world saturated with addiction. So many cravings tear at humanity, it is gratifying that two physicians and healers address the causes of our collective emotional pain and trauma. Most people never become aware of elementals, those "little inner beings" which create bondage to our lower nature. Despite sincere, conscious efforts to change, many experience failure, which exhausts hope.

Recalling Master Jesus as the great healer, new realizations emerge as we discover the hidden meanings of his words. And all of us who fell in love with the teacher, Daskalos, will rejoice in this treasure inspired in his name. *Awakening Love* provides a new guide to comprehending our own higher dimensions, thus freeing us to swim again in divine love.

Carol E. Parrish-Harra, Ph.D.,
Dean, Sancta Sophia Seminary,
author, *Adventure in Meditation*

AWAKENING LOVE

THE UNIVERSAL MISSION

Spiritual Healing in Psychology and Medicine

Nicholas C. Demetry, M.D.

&

Edwin L. Clonts, M.D.

Blue Dolphin

Published by Blue Dolphin Publishing, Inc.
P.O. Box 8, Nevada City, CA 95959
Orders: 1-800-643-0765
Web: www.bluedolphinpublishing.com

ISBN: 1-57733-075-7

Library of Congress Cataloging-in-Publication Data

Demetry, Nicholas C., 1950–
    Awakening love : the universal mission : spiritual healing in
psychology and medicine / Nicholas C. Demetry & Edwin L. Clonts.
        p. cm.
    Includes bibliographical references and index.
    ISBN 1-57733-075-7
        1. Spiritual healing. 2. Enneagram. 3. Chakras. 4. Atteshlis,
Stylianos, 1912–1995. I. Clonts, Edwin L., 1950– II. Title.

BL65.M4 D385 2000
29.3′1—dc21

                                                                00-050793

Cover design: Image- Elan Sun Star
Digital Magic- Shane Johnson
Sunstock
P O Box 1087, Kailua Hawaii 96734
www.sunstock.com
sunstar@sunstock.com

Printed in the United States of America

10   9   8   7   6   5   4   3   2

*Dedicated to the memory of
Stylianos Atteshlis, also known as Daskalos*

ACKNOWLEDGMENTS

We wish to gratefully acknowledge Helen Palmer and Dr. David Daniels for their inspiring coursework and books on the Enneagram that have motivated us to continue our exploration of personality. We thank Patricia Hayes, whose enthusiastic teaching and penetrating insights encouraged us to deepen our study of the energy body and its chakra centers and to apply this knowledge in our clinical practice and writing.

We thank Beth Cunningham for graciously volunteering to serve as our book agent, Maria Demetry for her tireless supportive contributions, and Donna Overall for her poetry. We deeply appreciate the enduring patience, flexibility, and spiritual dedication of Paul Clemens and the Blue Dolphin staff.

Nick expresses his deepest, heartfelt gratitude to all his Greek-American family members and ancestors for their courageous spirit and open-hearted generosity—"Yasoo"! "Me Agape"! Ed thanks his own ancestry for their courageous spirit and his family for his early spiritual education, which eventually developed into this book.

CONTENTS

WHO AM I?

Source without beginning or end
Never changing
Awakened heart! Warmth, joy, laughter
I am that I am
Grace shining its smiling face
      on Itself, for Itself, and within Itself
Language of silence speaks
To be still is to know everything!

Nick Demetry
Lucknow, India, 1993

TOPIC AREAS OF INTEREST
IN THIS BOOK

Breaking down the barriers between psychology and religion—All chapters

Bridging the Bible to alternative spirituality—Introduction, Chapters I, II, IV, VI, VII, IX

Understanding the essential unity of the world religions—Introduction, Chapters I, IV, VII

How thoughts and attitudes impact our lives—Chapters II, IV, V, VI, VII, IX, Appendix III

New paradigms for understanding addiction—Chapters II, III, IV, V, VI

Discovering your personalty type and its spiritual needs—Chapters III, V, VII, Appendix I

Understanding the process of transformation—Chapters VI, VII, Appendix II

Guiding spiritual principles for transformation—Chapter VII

Parenting and spiritual development of children—Chapters III and IV

Exercises for self-healing and spiritual growth—Chapters VII and VIII

Case studies which illustrate the process of healing and spiritual growth—Appendix II

Science and spirituality—Appendix III

INTRODUCTION

Mental health and spirituality have a recognized connection. This connection is being explored actively by psychotherapists and spiritual seekers alike. Some psychotherapists are integrating spirituality into their practices in creative and intimate ways. They often work in the context of Jungian and transpersonal psychology or even in the broad realm of "alternative spirituality" such as attitudinal healing. They look to those who have established effective links between the psychology of the inner life and the transcendent principles and practices of spirituality. One such link, the discipline of psychosynthesis, was established by psychologist Roberto Assagioli to join the technologies of Western psychology and Eastern spirituality.

Other therapists prefer to avoid direct work with the transcendent, yet recognize that the happiness and function of their clients are somehow improved by a spiritual faith. Most therapists would at least support spirituality as a core component of the treatment of chemical dependency and other addictions. Few healers would totally discount or ignore the possibility that the quality of one's inner life is affected by a transcendent realm.

Mainstream religion, which provides the context in which most people strive for the transcendent, has yet to be integrated with psychology and personality theory in any cohesive way. The primary obstacle to such a synthesis lies in the impossibility of joining integrated domains of human understanding with the many sectarian and sometimes conflicting dogmas of religion. Yet every religion is striving in its own way for the universal, so there must be some tangible and commonly acceptable way of viewing

1

mainstream religious experience so that it can connect meaningfully with modern-day psychology.

The authors have discovered that one key to solving this dilemma lies in a direct study of the life and teachings of Jesus. In Jesus it is not difficult to see the workings of a master healer and advanced psychotherapist, even when we look for understanding through the veil of history and human bias in the most traditional rendition of his life, the King James Bible. Though Jesus lived nearly 2000 years before Sigmund Freud and the giants of twentieth-century psychology, Jesus demonstrated that he understood the mind and emotions just as keenly as he understood the spirit of man. Jesus might indeed be called a founding father of psychospiritual healing.

The authors arrived at this conclusion by different routes, finally joining in common purpose under the inspiration of the late Stylianos Atteshlis, better known as Daskalos (i.e., teacher, in Greek). Daskalos lived most of his life on Cyprus. He was a mystic, a healer, an artist, an educated man and thinker, a brother and guide. Though he taught within a Christian context and modeled his life after Jesus, he taught the conceptual as well as the experiential basis for the spiritual unity of the world's great religions. He viewed life in unified terms and did not separate spirituality from any realm of human experience. Above all, Daskalos awakened within his students the remembrance of what real love is, that love is all, and what it means to be a real human being living a life of love.

In April 1994 we had a private meeting with Daskalos and told him of our immediate plans to sail from Cyprus to the Isle of Patmos, where the Apostle John was exiled and received the book of Revelation. Daskalos responded that Father Yohannan (John) would be with us. It was on this trip to Patmos that our idea to write this book was conceived. Daskalos died later the following year.

In memory and appreciation of Daskalos' inspiration, we are integrating collective religious philosophy, individual spiritual experience, and modern-day psychology in this book. Traditionally, these realms have often lain splintered in separate places within the human psyche, hindering the quality and progress of our lives. Daskalos showed that one key to the process of healing this separation lies in the understanding of personality. We have found that this link is clarified and validated by the theories of Enneagram personality type and the structure of the energy body and its chakra centers. Along with the life and teachings of Jesus, these models serve as powerful, instructive maps for our journey.

Through years of work in psychiatry and family practice, we have discovered that the Parable of the Prodigal Son describes the transformative journey of every man and woman back to love. We offer personal accounts of dialogue with Daskalos, practical healing exercises to support our synthesis, and case histories from clinical practice (in Appendix II). We will demonstrate the harmony between Jesus' teachings and those of masters from other world religions in the process. We will focus on Jesus because of his familiarity as the central religious figure of Western civilization, knowing fully well that spiritual teachers from various traditions could be presented in the same manner. Chapters I–III and Appendix I help the reader identify his or her personality type and Chapters IV–VI the area(s) of core wounding of the personality. Chapters VII-IX guide the transformation and healing of the personality and its wounds.

For those who have been raised within a Christian tradition, this book may provide a bridge between one's personal psychology and those roots. For those raised outside the Christian faith, it can illustrate a way of thinking about one's own religion in such a way as to make it more accessible as a guide to personal inner growth and psychospiritual transformation. This book is intended in any case to make the reader's own religion more real in his or her life, even as it promotes the essential spiritual unity of all the world's great religions within the single family of humanity. It is written not only for health professionals, but for all people wishing to better the quality of their lives.

Above all, we wish to pay a tribute to love as the unifying element of ourselves and all creation. The practical application of the material and exercises is to remove the blocks that hold us from love and reawaken the remembrance of love in our hearts, allowing us to walk the same joyful paths in our daily lives as have the saints of the ages.

1

A SYMBOL OF HEALING

The Bible refers to "the true Light, which lighteth every man that cometh into the world." (John 1:9) God freely shares with us his own divine nature, the "true light," so as to make us his beloved Sons and Daughters by grace at the time of our creation. This innermost spirit gift, which Jesus expressed so beautifully in the flesh, is sometimes called "the Christ." The word "Christ" is derived from the Greek *Christos,* which means "the Anointed." "The Christ Self" is therefore one appropriate name for our higher spirit Self, which establishes our truest identity forever as children of divine light.

Through our Christ Self we all are all ONE for eternity, equal in grandeur, perfection, love, and mystery. For this reason, the mission to know oneself as love incarnate is the same in essence for every soul. Through our personality forms, however, we experience a host of fears, imperfections, inequalities, and separation. Our resources—material, cultural, educational, emotional, family—vary in innumerable ways. For these reasons, the specific path back to Self-knowledge is absolutely unique for each soul as well.

Healing must involve the universal as well as the particular nature of human design; the formless as it interacts with form, the eternal as it interacts with the temporal, and the boundless as it relates to the bounded. Healing must take into account the descent of spirit into flesh and the ascent of flesh back to spirit, as well as the activity of the multiple intervening dimensions. This mysterious interplay between the Son of God (the Christ Self) and the Son of Man (the human nature) produces a progressing entity

4

known as the *soul*. True healing, therefore, is soul work. Any step the soul takes toward expanded awareness of its Christ nature, however small, is a genuine step on the path of healing.

The following symbol is now offered to depict this process of healing:

The circle is the symbol of wholeness, or atonement. It represents the oneness, perfection, and eternal nature of our Christ Self. It reminds us that all is God, and that in our Christ nature we are already healed. The interlocking triangles of the hexagram represent the soul, because they depict the descent of spirit into matter and the ascent of matter back to spirit. The cross represents the present-day personality, figuratively crucified by its limitations in the world of form, awaiting healing and resurrection.

This symbol is the central figure of the Symbol of Life used by the late Stylianos Atteshlis, though it is altered slightly by interlocking the triangles fully. According to Daskalos, the Symbol of Life was used by Origen, the great third-century Bishop of Alexandria. The interpretation we have given the above symbol for the purposes of this book, however, does not reflect the identical meaning of this symbol within the context of the entire Symbol of Life as taught by Daskalos. We have sought a more psychological interpretation for our readers.

By design, we also use this symbol to depict a separate, yet related process of collective healing. The cross, having been given various esoteric meanings, is most generally known as the symbol of Christianity. It refers in Christian theology to the redemption and salvation afforded by the death of Jesus.

The hexagram has been used as an ornamental and magical symbol since ancient times. In general it has tended to symbolize the union of opposites, such as spirit and body (the soul), heaven and earth, essence and substance, fire and water, the male and female aspects of deity. During the Middle Ages its use was widespread throughout various Christian, Jewish, and Islamic circles. Daskalos, in particular, uses the hexagram as the symbol of the soul, though he appears to use interlocking and non-interlocking triangles interchangeably for this purpose.[1]

The hexagram did not come to be associated specifically with Judaism until the nineteenth century. Known as the Magen David, or "Star of David," it eventually came to be the emblem on the Israeli flag. In 1921 the Jewish philosopher Franz Rosenzweig offered an interpretation of the Star of David in his classic work, *The Star of Redemption*. He showed how the star symbolizes the collective soul task of the Jewish people. Like the task of Christianity, he showed the Jewish task to be one of redemption, of consciously bringing God into creation in a manner consistent with their understanding of God's revelation to them.

The cross, as the symbol of Christianity, within the Star of David, the symbol of Judaism, and their enclosure by a circle denote the essential spiritual unity of all major world religions. The redemption of which Christianity and Judaism speak is equivalent to healing, because it is the process of bringing spirit to embodiment in matter and making them one in purpose. It is the enlivening of creation with love and joy, expanding her possibilities endlessly.

Jesus' teachings contain universal truths that resonate beautifully with the words of spiritual masters from all the world's great religious traditions. Therefore a subtheme of "pan-ecumenism" inexorably follows and runs throughout this book. The word "religion" comes from the Latin *religio*, which means "to bind together." Religion will actually succeed in binding all people together to the extent that it promotes a universal experience of the heart and spirit. Mere beliefs about spirit, or dogma, can never accomplish this great task. Beliefs about spirit will inevitably be held by thinking individuals and are useful to the extent that they in fact promote genuine and shared religious experience. The substitution of religious concepts for religious experience, however, creates nothing more than conceptual experience and useless disharmony.

It is those "religions of the mind" that have historically promoted so much division, even bloodshed, and often with the best of intentions. The very word "religion" has become a pejorative in some circles, connoting that which is formalized, dogmatized, socialized, and oppressive. This is the source of the wariness that often leads people today to distinguish "religion" from "spirituality" and make a point of saying, "I'm spiritual but not religious." They are making a statement in favor of direct personal experience of the transcendent outside the context of institutional structure or pressure. Many adhere to the eclectic modern trends of "New Age" or "alternative spirituality."

Still, the world's great religions have an enormous reservoir of good will and well-earned wisdom. They profit from the loving devotion and deep loyalty of many millions. Their contribution to human spiritual and social progress far outweighs any historical errors. There is no reason they cannot join, along with credible alternative movements, in a common mission to promote love and brotherhood among all peoples of the world, regardless of their religious philosophies. The examples of Jesus and the masters of many wisdom traditions can show us the way to truly "bind together" in the light and unity of spirit.

The process, as always, begins with the individual and now bears further exploration. The life and teachings of Jesus and his apostles will be used as a model to understand the process of healing and spiritual transformation for all of us.

II

THE NATURE OF
HUMAN DESIGN

General Domains of Human Experience

A grand overview of healing and its purpose has been considered. Now it is appropriate to take a closer look at the nature of human design and the role it plays in our earth experiences.

The three functions of human experience are thought, feeling, and action. The thinking function expresses itself through the higher virtues of wisdom and truth. The feeling function expresses itself through the higher virtues of love, empathy, and devotion. The kinetic function expresses itself through the higher virtues of right action, the right use of will through the proper use of power for physical manifestation. The body is often "dissected" esoterically into the three corresponding centers of these functions—the head, the heart, and the belly. Every person tends to gravitate primarily toward one of these energetic levels of experience.

This particular model of the body can be illustrated by using a metaphor of Jesus' apostles as the Body of Christ and Jesus as the perfect Christ light at their center. The apostle Thomas represents the "head" of this body, John the "heart," and Peter the "belly."

Thomas was the intellectual, the scientist, the skeptic who needed the confirmation of observable evidence before he would accept a phenomenon as fact. In spite of the numerous eyewitness accounts of Jesus' resurrection by trusted associates, he did not believe until he had seen the risen Jesus with his own eyes and touched his body. Jesus responded by saying, "Thomas, because thou hast seen me, thou hast believed: blessed are they that have not seen, and yet have believed." (John 20:29) Thomas has come to be known as "Doubting Thomas" through the centuries.

Many educated members of modern society would see Thomas' scientific "head" orientation as the most reliable model for living. Science is by nature open-minded, because it is based on the premise that the current knowledge about a phenomenon is not necessarily all there is to know and that more might be discovered by further observation. Even in religious circles, the "head" energy often predominates. Professed followers of Jesus can be found who display the tolerant and open-minded, yet skeptical world views that one associates with the "Thomas" perspective. These are the ones who are most likely to grasp the many-sided nature of Jesus' teachings.

Jesus' gospel, while many-sided, was above all a gospel of love. The experience of the Christ light within pervades one's whole being, but is truly centered in the heart. Spontaneous loving kindness and charitable service arise from those whose hearts are awakened by the Christ.

The Bible refers to the apostle John as "the disciple whom Jesus loved." While it is highly unlikely that Jesus had favorites, it is probable that John received this designation because he was the lone apostle at the cross when Jesus died and because he wrote so extensively about love in his later epistles. The following passage exemplifies John's "heart" perspective:

> Beloved, let us love one another: for love is of God; and every one that loveth is born of God, and knoweth God. He that loveth not knoweth not God; for God is love. (I John 4:7-8)

John's lofty ideal of divine unconditional love is a goal of many of Jesus' followers. Few perhaps achieve this pinnacle of soul experience, but many have grown beyond measure and enriched the lives of those they touch merely by holding the goal in their hearts.

The belly symbolically is the realm of power, achievement, sexuality, and divine instinctive intelligence. Those who are drawn to the belly center are motivated by the lessons around power and appropriate action. They are the ones who feel the challenge to ground spiritual abstractions into concrete realities in the physical realm. They are the movers and shakers and builders of the world, driven more by instinct than intellect. According to Daskalos, this is the domain through which the Holy Spirit guides us through the maze of life.[1]

Among the apostles Peter most strongly embodies the "belly" domain, as Jesus made evident when he said, "Thou art Peter, and upon this rock I will build my church." (Matthew 16:18) Peter did in fact become the leader of the early Christian church in Jerusalem after Jesus' death. Peter was a forceful and dominating personality who tended to act spontaneously and decisively on instinct, if not always wisely. An example is this episode in the Garden of Gethsemane, which occurred after officers of the chief priests and pharisees approached Jesus to arrest him:

> Then Simon Peter having a sword drew it, and smote the high priest's servant, and cut off his right ear. The servant's name was Malchus. Then said Jesus unto Peter, "Put up thy sword into the sheath: the cup which my Father hath given me, shall I not drink it?" (John 18:10-11)

The historical missionary zeal and social activism of Jesus' followers attest to the force of the "belly" domain of experience in religious life the past 2000 years. Within the realm of religious activism, it has always been easy to spot both the divine strength and the human folly that characterized Peter.

The Personality and Its Shadow: An Overview

Creation exists for the manifestation of truth and beauty by Spirit in time and space. Our bodies were designed to be a direct link between Creator and creation, the agents of conscious co-creation with God if we so choose. Our bodies have not only a physical, but also an emotional and mental structure that interact to produce a unique expression. For the purposes of this book, that emotional/mental expression will be defined as personality. This is only a practical and functional definition; it must be acknowledged that personality is really too mysterious to be defined, though certain aspects of it can be observed and described. While change- less in the sense that I am always uniquely *me*, that present-day expression of me must be purified and refined to serve as a manifestation of love and an agent of creation.

Like the physical body that is composed of organs with healthy as well as unhealthy cells, so too the personality as a whole has its own functioning "organ" structures. These organ structures, which regulate circumscribed domains of experience, are called *chakras* in Eastern metaphysical thought and will be discussed in depth in a later chapter. The chakras contain their own "cellular" building blocks. These have been termed *elementals* by Daskalos. Like physical cells, which can be healthy or unhealthy, i.e. cancer- ous, the elementals can be either positive or negative in nature. The positive elementals are called *thought-desires,* or virtues. They are pure thought forms created by the higher mind under the inspiration of spirit. The negative elementals are called *desire-thoughts* and are the substrates of addiction consciousness. They are emotional thought forms which enslave the mind.[2]

The Bible refers to these negative elementals as demons, or unclean spirits. They each have an "inflated" and "deflated" aspect, much like a puffer fish. They tend to pose as opposites, but are in effect the same creature and have essentially the same effect on the mind. Some examples would include: timidity vs. foolhardiness, vanity vs. self-disparagement, self-indulgence vs. self-denial, laziness vs. "workaholism," domination vs submission. In any given social context, of course, one aspect might be more functional than the other. Sometimes it may be difficult to distinguish an inflated "demon" from a genuine virtue in a person on the basis of external behavior alone. Generous behavior, for instance, can either arise virtuously and spontaneously out of a sense of abundance, or egocentrically, out of a desire to "get" or control. It is worth remembering that Judas betrayed Jesus with a kiss.

Negative elementals result from the choice to derive primary identity from the material plane with its illusions of separation, fear, vulnerability, and death. These elementals then enslave the personality to the extent we continue to energize and multiply them by our choices of thought, emotion, and action. Identification with this complex of negative elementals is sometimes called egotism. This is the manner we experience the shadow of which Carl Jung spoke. The problem of egotism will be discussed from various perspectives throughout the book.

Returning to the metaphor of the apostles of Jesus as the Body of Christ, it is clear that Judas represents the shadow within this body. Judas was eventually consumed with the elementals of greed, fear, pride, and the lust for power. Judas is an extreme example of how destructive the shadow can be when one fully identifies with it.

The self-destructive cult best characterizes the shadow of modern religious life and has received a lot of media attention. These cults function under a spiritual facade, but are actually characterized by fear and isolation. They are generally dominated by a charismatic individual who takes charge of the group's thought processes to enhance his or her feeling of control. The individual group member must give up personal integrity and any sense of self-determination in return for the comfort of the group's acceptance.

These shadowy elements can be seen in nearly every religion to some degree, because they exist within every individual. So pervasive is the shadow in our world that it often becomes the dominating element of the personality. The shadow gives the separated individual a sense of uniqueness by virtue of taking a particular size, shape, and location in the personality. In truth it has no cosmic reality at all; it is merely the absence of the Christ light in awareness.

The personality so heavily identified with that which is not real is termed by Daskalos the "present-day personality," or alternatively, the "present personality self" or "temporary personality."[3] The present-day personality, "overshadowed" by egotism, may be attracted to this illusion of specialness. In reality, this illusion creates so much suffering that the personality is figuratively crucified. The cross is therefore used as a symbol of the crucified present-day personality.

The enlightened personality, on the other hand, is one who identifies with who he or she IS. As love incarnate, manifesting the beauty and wonder of Christ in creation, this personality has achieved the sublime and ever-unfolding purpose for which it was created. While growing forever in love, wisdom, and power as part of an eternal soul, this personality, which Daskalos calls the permanent personality, also knows itself as a unique being who never changes identity.[4] When the personality identity is joined with its Christ Self, the enlightened one can say with the same assurance as Jesus, "Before Abraham was, I Am." (John 8:58) At such a level of consciousness, the personality and the soul cannot be meaningfully distinguished, because the personality has achieved the actual expression of soul virtues in time and space.

Before resurrection and ascension of the personality can occur, its shadow elements, or negative elementals, must be brought to the light of Christ in awareness for healing. The Bible refers to this process as repentance. In modern times we are more likely to call it psychotherapy. However we term the process, the shadow can be a potent instigator of transformational change when used to show us just where forgiveness is needed on our path to atonement. The Judas in oneself can therefore be one's guide to love and freedom, or one's destroyer, depending on how we relate to him. The choice for life or death, as always, is our own.

Vices and Virtues

To better understand the nature of the shadow and its influence on the personality, it is helpful to look at some of the more common manifestations of the shadow. The "seven deadly sins" of the Christian tradition—namely anger, pride, envy, greed, gluttony, lust, laziness—as well as the vices of fear and dishonesty are useful ones for the present purpose of illustration. These vices, or negative elementals, are defined as follows:

1. **Anger**—An emotionally aggressive, or "fight" response to a perceived threat.
2. **Pride**—"Noble egotism." A demon disguised as an angel of light.
3. **Dishonesty**—Intentional inconsistencies among thoughts, emotions, words, and actions, arising from fear of truth.
4. **Envy**—A painful sense of discrepancy between oneself and others, elevated to a sense of great longing and missing.
5. **Greed**—An unwillingness to let go of what one possesses out of a sense of lack. The state of being possessed by one's possessions.
6. **Fear**—The emotional "flight" response to a perceived threat.
7. **Gluttony**—A hunger for pleasurable experiences as a means to escape a perceived threat.
8. **Lust**—An exaggerated need for consumption with the desire to dominate and control, a desire arising out of a sense of vulnerability.
9. **Laziness**—Becoming neglectful of the essential task of focusing and revitalizing, especially as related to oneself. Self-deadening and self-forgetting.

As darkness can only be eliminated by light, the corresponding virtue, or positive elemental, needed to replace each of the previous vices is listed and defined below:

1. **Tranquility**—The acceptance of the divine purpose.
2. **Humility**—The awareness of being sustained by grace
3. **Truthfulness**—A consistency of thought, feeling, and action, resulting from the trust that one's efforts are a reflection of God's will.
4. **Equilibrium and Stability**—The state of mind resulting from the awareness of the divine presence in all things.
5. **Nonattachment**—The ability to experience life at its fullest while holding on to nothing.
6. **Valor**—Faithful action in the face of adversity, arising from awareness of the invulnerable nature of one's core spirit reality.
7. **Commitment**—Maintaining a steady course of action to meet one's higher goals. The drive to "keep on keeping on."
8. **Surrender**—To "let go and let God."
9. **Purposeful Action**—Action arising out of self-understanding.

Although these vices and virtues seem fairly clear and are easily recognized as defined above, their manifestations within the human personality are more subtle. In healing, we are challenged to recognize the elemental vices within the personality and transform them into virtues.

Looking back through history, it is possible to find within early Semitic religious traditions age old approaches to this challenge. The Enneagram is one such ancient system of understanding ourselves in this way. It will be used to examine the origin of the present-day personality types and their transformation into Self-aware souls with spiritual purpose.

III

MANIFESTATIONS OF THE PRESENT-DAY PERSONALITY

The Enneagram

The word Enneagram is derived from the Greek *ennea*, meaning "nine," and *grammes*, meaning "points." It is a nine-pointed star diagram that can be used to describe nine different personality types and their interrelationships. It also provides us with a method to study ourselves, our negative elementals, and how we can best transform our human weaknesses into strengths and virtues. By so doing, we can place ourselves into closer relationship with God and our Christ Self.

While the origins of the Enneagram remain somewhat obscure, it is known that it was widely used among the Sufis, a mystical Islamic movement of the eighth century and beyond. It is also notable that the Enneagram has strong similarities to the mystical Jewish teaching, the Kabbalah. Recently however, Andreas Ebert of Germany's Ecumenical Enneagram Association has offered new evidence that the roots of the Enneagram most likely lie in the tradition of a third- and fourth-century ascetic Christian movement, the Anachoretins, or Anchorites. They are more commonly known as the Desert Fathers and Mothers. The Sufis arose 300 years later in the same geographical area and displayed striking similarities to the dress, teachings, ascetic lifestyle, and spiritual practices of the earlier Anachoretins. [1]

The Anachoretins moved into the Egyptian desert in order to confront their demons, or vices, and deeply contemplate God in an undistracting environment. Evagrius Ponticus, the first major writer among these ascetics, developed a list of these vices. Eventually, Pope Gregorius I reduced this list to the Church teaching of the Seven Deadly Sins. These seven vices and the two additional ones presented in the previous chapter came to be the vices associated with the Enneagram.[2]

A number of excellent and detailed books on the Enneagram, notably those by Palmer, Bennett, Riso, Ebert and Rohr, have been published within the past ten years. For the purposes of this book, the presentation of Enneagram theory will be limited. The teachings of Jesus will be emphasized for instruction in the transformation of the nine personality types.

The structure of the Enneagram consists of a triad interlocking with a hexad to form a nine-pointed star, which is enclosed by a circle, as illustrated:

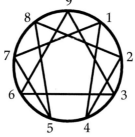

According to the teachings of Pythagoras (570-500 B.C.), the numbers contained within this structure are highly significant. Pythagoras taught that all creation is literally number and that the numbers one through ten each contain within themselves a divine Law stating some fundamental relationship between matter and spirit.[3]

The triad within the Enneagram represents the Law of Three. According to Pythagoras, the Law of Three is the resolution of the tension between thesis and antithesis.[4] Daskalos, reflecting this understanding, taught in a private session that the triangle represents oneness within duality and offers us the instruction to be one in the spirit/soul while in the context of the world's duality. The Law of Three, therefore, is the fundamental experience of the evolving personality.

The hexad represents the Law of Six. The Law of Six, according to Pythagorean theory, is the process of creating which anticipates the union with divine perfection.[5] Within the hexad can be identified a movement through seven stages of transformation toward this divine reunion (1—7—5—8—2—4—1). The Law of Three evolving through each of the seven stages constitutes the transformational process of the personality and its eventual reunion with the soul.

Within the same hexad can also be found a movement in the opposite direction, away from the awareness of unity with God into duality and conflict (1—4—2—8—5—7—1). This movement away from the awareness of God's presence, followed by the seven progressive stages to reunion with God, will be presented allegorically through the Parable of the Prodigal Son in a later chapter.

The life stages of Jesus offer another example of this seven-stage process of reunion with God:

1. In the beginning was the Word.
2. Birth (The Word made flesh)
3. Baptism
4. Transfiguration
5. Crucifixion
6. Resurrection
7. Ascension

The ascension, or final reunion with the Father, gives rise to the completion of the soul's cycle. The Law of Nine, according to Pythagoras, is the completion of the human journey and the expression of all human knowledge. The arithmetic sums $8+1, 7+2, 6+3$, and $5+4$ contain all the number Laws, establishing the completeness of nine.[6] The Enneagram, therefore, represents the completion of the soul's incarnational experience, which ensues upon the soul's ascension and reunion with God.

The circle represents the Law of One, which expresses the final and ultimate unity underlying the diversity of All That Is.[7] The nine points of the Enneagram, as used in the context of personality theory, represent the nine personality types. The origin of the present-day personality and its further differentiation into these nine types will now be presented.

Origin of the Present-Day Personality: The Fall

The animal kingdom commonly displays various types of instinctive intelligence that lie well beyond ordinary human ability. Many people, especially those from Earth traditions of spirituality, consider humans and animals to be of equal value in God's creation. Humans possess one ability, however, that distinguishes them from the animal kingdom. This is the capacity of self-awareness and self-observation, known since the days of Sigmund Freud as the ego. Even at purely physical levels of awareness and at low levels of intelligence, humans maintain this capacity to be aware of an individuated ego identity. Ego appears to be an innate function of the human mind and a distinguishing feature of the human personality.

At the advancing levels of consciousness which the human mind was designed to achieve, however, the personality also has the capacity for identification with its inner Christ Self. This Christ consciousness is experienced as a wondrous connection with All That Is, for the Christ Self is a pure spirit fragment of divinity. Daskalos refers to the Christ Self as the "Spirit-ego-self," or alternatively, "the Holy Monad" to emphasize its individualized nature. This high spiritual level of Self-observation occurs through a reflecting function of the higher mind, sometimes called the "super-conscious." Like a mirror which must be cleaned to reflect clearly, Daskalos says this higher mind must be cleansed by forgiveness to reflect the Christ Self clearly to the Self-observer.[8] The Apostle Paul referred to this process when he wrote, "Let this mind be in you, which was also in Christ Jesus." (Phillipians 2:5)

The awakened personality is a self-aware soul that knows itself as an individualized, spirit-embraced, multidimensional entity, evolving through the progressive experience of its own divine and perfect nature. Only at the dimmest levels of awareness does the personality experience crucifixion. Tragically, this has been the predominant level of human awareness throughout history.

Jesus, in the most profound and dramatic teaching example of all time, rendered crucifixion and death meaningless. Why then do we continue to perpetuate our own crucifixion by identifying ourselves so exclusively with an isolated ego form, denying our Christ Self?

The Biblical story of Adam and Eve in the Garden of Eden offers an allegorical explanation of this fall of awareness that occurred in the dawn of human history and persists to this day. In the Garden where they were created, Adam and Eve lived in harmony with God. God warned them not to eat of the "tree of the knowledge of good and evil" in the Garden, or they would die. The serpent tempted Eve by saying, "For God doth know that in the day ye eat thereof, then your eyes shall be opened, and ye shall be as gods, knowing good and evil." (Genesis 3:5) Eve, and then Adam, yielded to this temptation and ate from the tree. They immediately felt ashamed of their nakedness and were then ejected from the Garden by God, who said. "For dust thou art, and unto dust shalt thou return." (Genesis 3:19)

Each of us is Adam or Eve. The temptation of the serpent to eat the forbidden fruit and "be as gods" represents the temptation of one's ego to identify primarily with itself in the world of form and rule over the world as a "god." Through this false identification which denies our spiritual Source, we try to "create ourselves in our own image." Rather than accept our uniqueness and wholeness as created by God, we yield to the ego's temptation to feel a sense of uniqueness and power by being that which is *not* God.

The ego creates and maintains this grandiose and illusory false self by creating a veil of negative elementals, which in turn blocks its view of its true Christ Self. The act of setting oneself apart from God, creation, and one's own true nature is inherently frightening, so these negative elementals are all fear-based. Every act of hurt and death by this present-day personality is some type of response to the god of fear which now rules it. The ego, in its fundamental dissatisfaction, seeks to remedy its emptiness through addictive searching.

This process of the Fall which we continuously reenact can be shown symbolically. The individual human soul is by nature like Adam or Eve in the Garden of Eden, whole and Self-aware within the circle of atonement (see Chapter 1), and is depicted below:

Circle of Atonement

The ego's decision to identify exclusively with its individual body and separate itself from the Garden of God-consciousness is depicted below:

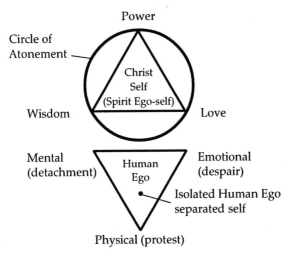

The illusory nature of the process is indicated by the placement of the bodily form outside the circle of atonement, where nothing can exist in reality.

The veil of negative elementals projected by the self-observing ego to block its view of its true Self is the shadow of the present-day personality. The unhealed personality, separated by shadowy illusions and crucified in its pathetic attempt to "play god," is symbolized below:

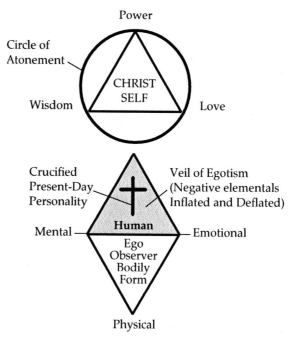

This daily process of separation, by which we break contact with our Source and try to play god, is more a result of forgetting and ignorance than of evil intent. How else is it possible to explain our choice for crucifixion and death over life and freedom? Examination of the process of separation of infant from parent after birth can help us better understand the primal emotions that we feel when separated from the awareness of our Creator's presence.

A Model of the Fall: Infant-Parent Separation

The original "forgetting," or separation, takes place as we enter the world of form after birth. At first we do not perceive ourselves as separate from our parents; we are our parents. Awareness of ourselves as being separate individuals is a gradual and necessary first step in the process of gaining a unique soul identity. This separation may occur prematurely, with psychological readiness, or too late; it may occur with love or with judgment, with safety or with fear. The manner in which the separation occurs will in many ways determine who we think we are when we realize we are no longer them.

In our culture many infants are experiencing separation from their parents before they are psychologically ready. Michael Trout, director of the Infant-Parent Institute, an organization dedicated to promoting infant mental health, has written and spoken on evolutionary societal changes and their profound impact on the newborn. In the paper titled "The All American Infant: At Odds with Its Evolution," he explains archaeological and cross-cultural evidence that infants have experienced almost continuous physical contact with their parent and sibling caregivers for the first few years of life for millions of years—until now.[9]

Our breakdown in family structure often results in lack of extended family support and increased financial pressures. It may be impossible for one or both parents to be home with their infants during the critical early bonding time. Early separation and subsequent incomplete bonding has become increasingly prominent as a source of core wounding in our society. These early emotional wounds may well be one contributing factor to our fall of awareness of God. In any case, a study of the infant's psychological wounds after premature separation from the parent reveals the nature of the primal emotions we all feel when we are separated from our Creator in consciousness.

Researchers John and James Robertson have found that reaction to early separation arises in three phases: Protest, Despair, and Detachment. Protest is exhibited in the child's refusal to accept a substitute for the mother, in tearful and violent crying or in cranky and stubborn behavior. Despair is marked by moaning, quiet weeping, and sad facial expressions, i.e. depression. Detachment occurs from several days to about one week from the onset of separation, when the child begins to become seemingly unemotional, taking on an "I don't care" attitude. Bowlby and Robertson explain: "The detachment response is a shut-down of loving feelings—and it deals with loss in a number of ways: It punishes the person for having left. It serves as a masked expression of rage, for intense and violent hatred is one of the chief responses to being abandoned. And it also can be a defense, which can last for hours, or days, or a lifetime—a defense against the agony of ever loving and ever losing again. Absence makes the heart grow frozen, not fonder."[10]

These three primary consequences of early separation are strikingly similar to the three core areas of woundedness in Enneagram theory of personality types. The triad of points 8-9-1 are thought to be wounded primarily in the "action center" with the resulting passion of anger (Protest). The 2-3-4 triad have their wounding primarily in the "feeling center" with the resulting passion of grief (Despair). The 5-6-7 triad are wounded primarily in the "thinking center" with the resulting passion of fear (Withdrawal). These three centers correspond to the belly, heart, and head of the metaphorical Body of Christ presented in Chapter 2. To avoid any misconception that these centers have precise anatomic correlation or significance, anatomic terms will not be used further in reference to them.

Whatever may have led to the separation of the personality and its subsequent emotional wounds, it must develop a strategy to survive its delusional predicament. Each of the nine personality types of Enneagram theory tend to organize themselves around a particular survival strategy that is fairly predictable. On a deeper level, the soul is working to transform its present-day personality into a corresponding entity of true survival value. Thereby does it experientially achieve the particular phase of Self-awareness for which it incarnated and come to know itself as love.

Again it is evident that the flawed present-day personality, our "inner Judas," can be appreciated rather than despised when viewed from a higher perspective. The nature of the soul's epic journey of "Judas redemption" will be further clarified by examining the particular paths of three primary soul types.

The Soul Types

Three primary soul types can be derived from an understanding of the transforming virtues of the Enneagram triads: The Angelic Souls, The Heroic Souls, and The Philosophic Souls. These soul types are represented by Peter, John, and Thomas respectively in the metaphorical Body of Christ. Each individual personality type, as it comes to express its associated virtues, may be understood as a particular expression of its associated soul type. Until the personality achieves this lofty soul purpose, the soul must utilize the temporary survival strategy the unhealed personality has devised. The soul types, their purposes, and the three primary survival strategies with which each soul type works will be discussed.

For the reader's clarification, the present-day personality traits and tendencies of each of the nine separated, or false, selves will be presented in accompanying charts in Appendix I that summarize Enneagram theory of each. Note that the personality strengths as well as the personality weaknesses of any given personality type can represent egotistical qualities of a separated self. These are the "inflated" and "deflated" aspects of negative elementals previously discussed. The "strengths" do, by and large, promote more harmonious functioning in the world and higher self-esteem than the "weaknesses." Whether any given trait is ego-based or spirit-based depends on the motivations and spiritual progress of the individual, as discussed in Chapter 2. The reader is invited to identify his or her own personality type from the charts if possible. A contemplative exercise will be given below for each Enneagram type to illustrate the way that personality experiences its world and to further aid the reader in his or her process of self-identification.

The Angelic Souls

Enneagram Figure (1)

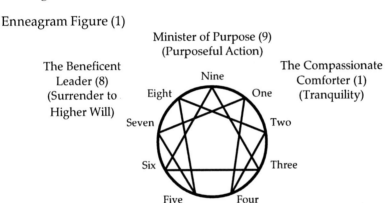

The Angelic Souls are typically associated with the higher virtues represented by the "action center" triad 8-9-1. They are the divine ministers of God and express the idealized qualities of the apostle Peter in the world. They are named according to these particular aspects of the Christ consciousness they express in the world:

Type 8 [The Beneficent Leader]—Innocence, surrender to truth, gentleness, effective leadership.

Type 9 [Minister of Purpose]—Harmony and purposeful action

Type 1 [The Compassionate Comforter]—Tranquility, serenity, perfection, tolerance.

—Separated Angelic Souls

Enneagram Figure (2)

The Neglected Self (9)
(Laziness)

The Controlling Self (8)   Nine   The Critical Self (1)
(Lust)   Eight   One   (Self-righteous
                                                                 Anger)
                   Seven   Two

                      Six   Three

                         Five   Four

Angelic Souls who have separated from their Source experience anger as the primary consequence of this separation. Their core wounding is in the domain of doing. These separated Angelic Souls express through the personality three different strategies for survival. Defined according to these strategies, the personality types might be called The Controlling Self, The Neglected Self, and the Critical Self and are discussed below:

Type 8 [The Controlling Self]—Sets up its own system of justice to defend its innocence and vulnerability. It goes to war to defend itself, i.e. externalizes anger, and becomes confrontational with others to assure the protection of its vulnerable wounded inner child. (See Chart 1, Appendix I)

Exercise for Type 8
- Close your eyes, focus your breath and attention on your solar plexus.
- Imagine yourself as the chief executive of a large company.
- You are addressing a large audience of workers about some recent changes in the company's structure and policies.
- As you come to the podium, you feel your solar plexus energy expand to encircle the whole room and people in it.
- Instinctively, you feel the sources of support and sources of challenge to you in the room.
- Your intent is to take command and control any sources of challenge that may arise against you.
- You love this power and rush of energy you get when you take charge and overcome the opposition.

Type 9 [The Neglected Self]—Denies ever having left heaven and refuses to accept its incarnation. It maintains harmony at all costs, avoiding anger and other disharmonious emotions by numbness and self-forgetting. (See Chart 2, Appendix I)

Exercise for Type 9

- Close your eyes, focus your breath and attention on your solar plexus.
- You're in college and will graduate upon completion of your dissertation.
- You've been procrastinating for six months and have only six weeks left to complete the project.
- On your way to the typewriter, you get a call from a friend who needs help finishing their garden. It's absolutely necessary it be done before their pool party next month. You spend this time actively helping out, missing classes here and there to help them meet their deadline.
- Afterwards, your spouse's mother gets ill and needs daily care.
- You volunteer every afternoon with her and cook for your spouse at night.
- Too exhausted to work on *your* project at night, you watch TV until bedtime to "zone out." Two weeks are left to finish your project. You suddenly realize that your professor will be very disappointed in you if you don't complete it and graduate.
- Somehow, through your own efforts, you manage to finish it.
- Looking back, everything got done OK after all.

Type 1 [The Critical Self]—Splits into the dichotomy of good and evil. It fights the notion of evil by denying it within itself. It seeks to regain the perfection of the angelic realm by becoming perfect in the world. (See Chart 3, Appendix I)

Exercise for Type 1

- Close your eyes and focus your breath and attention in your solar plexus.
- You're sitting at the dinner table with your family. You begin to grow irritated as you realize your food is not warm enough. As you look up, you notice your spouse looking tired and not responding enthusiastically toward you in the way it "should" be.
- You also notice out of the corner of your eye a small stain on the rug from a plate dropped earlier by your young son on the way to the kitchen.
- You think to yourself, "I should stop criticizing everything. I should stop blaming their imperfections. I should, I should be kinder. Maybe I'm not a good parent or spouse."
- Let go of this critical attitude and gently come back where you were.

Angelic Souls desire above all to learn about the nature of power so that they may return to the power of the Holy Spirit. Their goal is to transform the fire of anger into the fire that acts to ground the life of the Spirit in the world and sustain it. Jesus knew that inner spiritual power must transform the personality before power can be effectively externalized, as illustrated in these words to his followers before Pentecost:

> And, being assembled together with them, commanded them that they should not depart from Jerusalem, but "wait for the promise of the Father, which," saith he, "ye have heard of me. For John truly baptized with water; but ye shall be baptized with the Holy Ghost not many days hence. . . . But ye shall receive power, after that the Holy Ghost is come upon you: and ye shall be witnesses unto me both in Jerusalem, and in all Judea, and in Samaria, and unto the uttermost part of the earth." (Acts 1:4,5,8)

The following passage describes the descent of the Holy Spirit to these followers, now empowered Angelic Souls, at Pentecost:

> And when the day of Pentecost was fully come, they were all with one accord in one place. And suddenly there came a sound from heaven as of a rushing mighty wind, and it filled all the house where they were sitting. And there appeared unto them cloven tongues like as of fire, and it sat upon each of them. And they were all filled with the Holy Ghost, and began to speak with other tongues, as the Spirit gave them utterance. (Acts 2:1-4)

The Heroic Souls

Enneagram Figure (3)

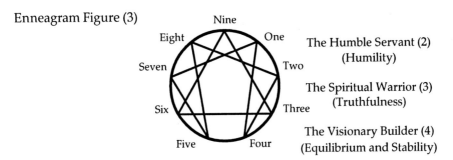

The Humble Servant (2)
(Humility)

The Spiritual Warrior (3)
(Truthfulness)

The Visionary Builder (4)
(Equilibrium and Stability)

The Heroic Souls are typically associated with the higher virtues represented by the "feeling center" points 2-3-4 and express the virtues associated with the apostle John. They are named according to those spiritual values they express:

Type 2 [The Humble Servant]—Humility, empathy, freedom, willfulness, desire to serve selflessly

Type 3 [The Spiritual Warrior]—Hope in action, optimism, leadership, practicality, dynamism.

Type 4 [The Visionary Builder]—Equilibrium and stability, passionate idealism, creativity, empathy, defender of individuality.

—Separated Heroic Souls

Enneagram Figure (4)

The Sacrificing Self (2)
(Pride)

The Success-Driven
Self (3)
(Dishonesty)

The Melodramatic Self (4)
(Envy)

Heroic Souls who have separated experience sorrow as the primary consequence of the separation. They are driven by the desire to attain the oneness of love. The survival strategy of the separated Heroic Souls is to strive for the love and acceptance of others through various ideals and images of human heroism rather than seeking the ever-present love of God directly within themselves. The 2-3-4 triad might be observed as The Sacrificing Self, The Success-Driven Self, and The Melodramatic Self. They display the strategies below:

> **Type 2** [The Sacrificing Self]—Seeks to gain love and approval through caretaking others and blocking oneself from receiving. Through pride in the role of the selfless martyr, it attempts to avoid the pain and sorrow of the original separation from love. (See Chart 4, Appendix I)

Exercise for Type 2

- Close your eyes and focus on your heart center.
- Think of a person that is important to you that needs your love.
- Focus all your attention on this person.
- Feel what they are feeling and become aware of what they need.
- Let yourself fulfill that need they have and continue to fulfill their every need and desire.
- Allow yourself to feel totally responsible for them.
- Imagine their demands getting greater and greater for your attention, your having less and less time for yourself and your own responsibilities.
- You begin to think it would be nice if they could just occasionally say or do something that makes you feel appreciated, yet you're afraid to ask them for what you need. Maybe they'll go away from you, and you'll lose your connection with them altogether.
- Feel your anger rising as you attempt to push it down, because you need to be needed to feel good about yourself.
- Making an excuse to yourself, you think, "They'll never make it without me. Look at how much I do for them!"

> **Type 3** [The Success-Driven Self]—Seeks to gain love and approval through performance and through successful accomplishment of tasks, suspending the emotions. Thereby does this industrious warrior avoid the pain of separation from love. (See Chart 5, Appendix I)

Exercise for Type 3

- Close your eyes and visualize this life scenario:
- Your boss has given you a big project to accomplish. Your image, reputation, and promotion at work are at stake. It's absolutely necessary for you to succeed at it.
- You envision your goal, feel the drive to accomplish it building in your emotions. Your energy goes into "hyperdrive" as you identify the most practical and efficient way to do it.
- Things are going well for you, and then a stumbling block appears in your way. Things slow down. You become physically tense. You become short-tempered and impatient with those working with you to get the job done. Your impatience turns into outright anger when they act all too human. Your focus is on results and accomplishment, not human relations.

Type 4 [The Melodramatic Self]—Seeks to merge with the love of God through searching and longing for an unobtainable or special love object. This noble romantic dramatizes both the passion for the love object and the tragedy of its unobtainability. In so doing, the four avoids the pain of its true sense of separation from God and fails to seek directly the love of God within. (See Chart 6, Appendix I)

Exercise for Type 4

- Close your eyes and bring your attention to your heart.
- Remember a time when your life felt so special, so blessed and so sweet, where love surrounded your every breath.
- Hold this connection, this completeness, and beautiful fullness of perfection in your heart, when you felt totally open and vulnerable to life. Magnify this feeling until your heart feels it's about to burst at the seams.
- Feel all this, the cherished memories and moments, are suddenly taken away. You can't understand what happened. Your heart is broken and empty.
- Aching in your heart's pain, you recall with bittersweet tears the memories that made it so special and complete. You feel the desire to search once again for this connection, to regain this longed-for and lost original love object, situation, or experience.

The goal of the Heroic Souls is to return to God's unconditional love and to learn the lessons of love. In the end it is to demonstrate that they themselves are the Christ love which Jesus himself demonstrated as a conscious Son of God. Jesus' Parable of the Lost Sheep, quoted below, is a good reminder to the Heroic Souls that God forgets no one in his love:

> If a man have an hundred sheep, and one of them be gone astray, doth he not leave the ninety and nine, and goeth into the mountains, and seeketh that which is gone astray? And if so be that he find it, verily I say unto you, he rejoiceth more of that sheep, than of the ninety and nine which went not astray. Even so it is not the will of your Father which is in heaven, that one of these little ones should perish. (Matthew 18:12-14)

The Philosophic Souls

Enneagram Figure (5)

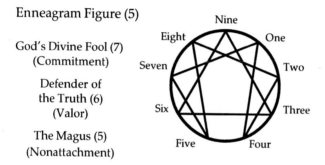

God's Divine Fool (7)
(Commitment)

Defender of
the Truth (6)
(Valor)

The Magus (5)
(Nonattachment)

The Philosophic Souls are represented by the "thinking center" points 5-6-7 and are represented by the apostle Thomas in the Body of Christ. They are named below according to the higher virtues of the Christ mind they express in the world:

Type 5 [The Magus]—Scholarly, insightful, knowing, calm, respectful, objective, open-minded, nonattached

Type 6 [Defender of the Truth]—Independent thinking, sensitive to their environment and to others, protective of the less fortunate, fair and loyal, courageous

Type 7 [God's Divine Fool]—Resourceful, imaginative, inventive, optimistic, playful and humorous, able to envision multiple options and strategies, yet committal and enduring

—Separated Philosophic Souls

Enneagram Figure (6)

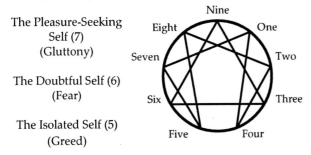

The Pleasure-Seeking
Self (7)
(Gluttony)

The Doubtful Self (6)
(Fear)

The Isolated Self (5)
(Greed)

Philosophic Souls who have separated from their Source experience fear as the primary consequence of the separation. Ultimately this is the existential fear of non-being of which theologian Paul Tillich wrote. This fear makes it difficult if not impossible to perceive the abundance of God's creation made manifest out of his absolute infinite beingness. This constant threat of scarcity and annihilation acts to block the expression and actualization of their knowledge and understanding. They often substitute intellectual pursuits for the pursuit of God's absolute wisdom and the direct knowledge of pure being.

The separated Philosophic Souls express through the personality their own distinct strategies of survival, and are observed according to these strategies as The Isolated Self, The Doubtful Self, and The Pleasure-Seeking Self.

Type 5 [The Isolated Self]—Out of the belief it is impoverished, it attempts to hoard knowledge, time, space, energy, and privacy. Fearing it will lose the little it has, it withdraws from intrusion rather than claim the abundance arising from the inner life of the Spirit. (See Chart 7, Appendix I)

Exercise for Type 5

- Bring your attention to your head center.
- Imagine yourself withdrawing all your attention into your thoughts, cutting off all connection with your body, sensations, and feelings.
- You live in your mind. Sense the expansion of your thoughts, the glory of the knowledge you hold. What a relief it is for you to live in this secret place, unruffled by all the unnecessary events outside your mind.
- Here in the palace of your mind, you can view all events with detachment and non-involvement.
- How safe it is here and how very private, for here you are finally alone in your own confined space!

Type 6 [The Doubtful Self]—Becomes hypervigilant and overly skeptical, attempting to gain security in a world that is basically menacing rather than finding the absolute security of the invulnerable Christ Self within. (See Chart 8, Appendix I)

Exercise for Type 6

- Bring your attention to your head center.
- You're working for a boss you just can't figure out. What are his motives for you?
- One moment he's frowning at you and at another moment he's smiling at you. When he looks at you and tells you you're doing a good job, you wonder, "Is he telling me the truth, or is he thinking and feeling something else that he doesn't want to reveal to me? I've done all my work well, I guess? Maybe he's going to fire me because I was out of work for a day last week with the flu. Yesterday, I saw another secretary leaving his office laughing and glancing at me."
- "Are they talking about me behind my back? What or who can I really trust, anyway?"
- Continuing to feel at conflict about what is really happening, uncertain about what to say or do to clear up the matter, feel the worry created over your doubt about the situation.

Type 7 [The Pleasure-Seeking Self]—Uses pleasure-seeking and multiple options to avoid pain, fear, and feelings of entrapment. Seeks multiple experiences in the world to avoid the pain of feeling separated from God. The pain is disguised for a time by the sensory pleasure of these experiences. (See Chart 9, Appendix I)

Exercise for Type 7

- Close your eyes and bring your attention to your head center.
- It's your junior year in college and you're in an exchange program abroad. You want to see and do everything! New languages to speak, people to meet, places to visit! So many options to keep open! "Maybe I can go to Italy next weekend, or even to Greece on our school holiday."
- You've just reached your 8 AM class and your professor is a year away from his retirement. He's talking about the agriculture of the Medieval period. As you sit in your old wooden chair, you begin to feel restless and bored. How many things can you think about to bring you pleasure to end your pain and boredom? Imagine the sunny afternoon, a bike ride, an ice cream cone, a glass of wine with a friend. Can you hold your fantasies and continue to keep track of what's going on in class?

The Philosophic Souls seek the life-giving connection with the abundance, certainty, and totality of God. They will ever be reassured to remember these words of Jesus, "I am come that they might have life, and that they might have it more abundantly." (John 10:10)

The nine personality types of Enneagram theory have only been summarized for the purposes of this book. Interested readers can find depth analyses of these personality types in any number of books, as noted previously. (A summary chart for each personality type can be found in Appendix I.)

IV

STRUCTURE OF THE PRESENT-DAY PERSONALITY
Its Chakras and Elementals

Human design, through its physical, emotional, and mental structures, has been shown to manifest nine personality types according to Enneagram theory. When the personality is separated in awareness from its Source, each of these unhealed present-day personalities develops a survival strategy through which the soul must work for a while. Sooner or later the separated personality opens to the Christ light within and can be said to be "saved," because it has purposefully created the conditions by which true healing can occur. This personality proceeds to create positive elementals, or virtues, to replace the negative elementals, or "demons," that onetime enslaved it. On its own unique path to enlightenment, or atonement, this personality becomes one with the spirit of its own soul and gains experiential knowledge of itself as a particular aspect of love incarnate.

Each of the nine personality types can be shown to have not only a core survival strategy, but also the option of moving in a general way toward higher integration, further disintegration, more introversion or extroversion. These general energetic trends will be presented in a later chapter that discusses the healing process. Three soul types can be derived from the triads of Enneagram theory (8-9-1, 2-3-4, 5-6-7), expressing themselves predominantly through the general domains of action, feeling, or thinking respectively. As noted previously, these domains do not have any precise correlation with the human anatomy.

Every personality, regardless of its type, also has a "microstructure" of chakras and elementals through which its broad energetic trends are expressed. These have been compared to the organs and cells of the physical body and do have an actual anatomic location in relationship to the physical body. While the physical organs regulate and control particular physical functions, the chakras regulate broader experiential functions as well as having an effect on the physical organs in their domain. The nature and general function of the chakras and their associated elementals will now be discussed in some depth. Finally, interassociations between the various chakras will be discussed. (Illustrative cases from clinical practice will be presented in Appendix II.)

The Seven Chakras

"Chakra" is a Sanskrit word meaning "wheel" and has usually been understood as a circular energy vortex through which cosmic energy travels to successively denser levels of creation. Within the human personality each chakra forms an energetic connecting link between the Christ Self and the mental, emotional, and physical bodies at a particular level of experience. The chakras are located close to the vertebral column, ranging from the top of the head to the tip of the coccyx. Much like a prism refracts white light into the colors of the rainbow, each chakra refracts cosmic energies into a "color" or vibration which is specific to it. Traditionally, Eastern philosophy recognizes seven major chakras and numerous minor ones. The seven major chakras govern seven major realms of psychospiritual experience and can be shown to correlate with seven stages of development within the personality. Whereas activity occurs in all chakras at every stage of personality maturation, each chakra is given a particular focus at a particular chronological age in the maturation of childhood and youth. Once again the esoteric "Law of Seven" is demonstrated as Spirit manifests through each of us.

Each chakra, in its particular state of health or dis-ease, reflects what one believes to be true about oneself at that level. When a person comes to know himself or herself as the Christ, as did Jesus, the chakras are fully open and functioning optimally as designed. Virtuous thought forms comprise the "cellular" structure of all these chakras, resulting in unified, free, and joyful personality expression and experience at every level. But when a chakra reflects the self-concept of a separated personality, the movement of spirit's love and light through that chakra is blocked by negative elementals. This blockage is most likely to occur at the particular age of developmental focus for that chakra and may manifest itself as physical, emotional, or mental disorders within the domain of that chakra. For this reason the chakras are useful centers for obtaining feedback about one's well-being at each domain.

In "The Parable of the Unclean Spirit," it is probable that Jesus was referring to separation, or disease, at the chakra level:

> When the unclean spirit is gone out of a man, he walketh through dry places, seeking rest, and findeth none. Then he saith, I will return into my house from whence I came out; and when he is come, he findeth it empty, swept and garnished. Then goeth he, and taketh with himself seven other spirits more wicked than himself, and they enter in and dwell there: and the last state of that man is worse than the first. (Matthew 12:43-45)

The original "unclean spirit" is the thought form with which all negative elementals resonate. It is the core thought beneath every "unclean spirit" because it says, "I am separate from God." When projected by a man, it finds only "dry places" and no rest outside of the man, because there is no place in creation which is truly separate from God. Being a meaningless thought form, it can only return to the illusory home of its creator, the present-day personality of the man. This is the only place where it can be revitalized. Finding the home empty of virtues, the unclean spirit is free to bring back seven spirits which resonate with itself, "spirits more wicked than himself." These spirits then occupy the seven "rooms" of the house, leaving the creator of the negative elemental even worse off. These seven rooms are the seven chakras of the present-day human personality.

Each chakra, as noted previously, reflects a belief about oneself within a particular domain of experience. The core elemental, "I am separate from God," is expressed within each of the seven major domains of self awareness, or chakras, by a corresponding "unclean spirit," as listed below:

Psychospiritual Domain	"Unclean Spirit"
1. Self-Image	"I am unworthy to exist."
2. Inner feelings	"I am vulnerable to others."
3. Self-Concept	"I am helpless."
4. Self-Nurturing	"I suffer."
5. Self-Expression	"I must lie to get what I want."
6. Self-Perception	"I see only imperfection in myself."
7. Higher Purpose	"I have no higher purpose in life."

To clarify and illustrate the nature of the problems produced for a person by the presence of these "unclean spirits," the chakras will be examined one by one. The process of personality maturation will be discussed as it relates to the domain of each chakra and an illustrative biblical example of separation given for each.

The 1st (Root) Chakra [Self-Image]

The first chakra is located at the tip of the spine and governs issues around physical self-preservation. These issues include survival, security, and safety, as well as primal erotic and procreational urges. This domain is the primary focus of development at ages 0-3 years. This is the time when the self-observing ego emerges within the personality, i.e. when the child gains the ability to "see himself."

During the first few months of life the infant does not distinguish himself from his surroundings of caregivers. The mere presence of physical tension such as hunger or cold, produced by a biological need, seems to automatically bring relief from his surroundings.[1] If parented normally, this infant is receiving the first assurance from the universe that he can trust the very fact of his existence and is worthy to exist.

By 8 months of age the child clearly distinguishes parents from others and perceives that these are the particular ones that relieve his tensions.[2] Any separation from these special beings brings anxiety. Soon thereafter he achieves the skills to stand and walk, acquiring the means to actively cut himself off from his mother's body. The "No!" of the toddler naturally follows as he begins to assert the independence of the budding ego.[3]

Among a host of mental and social achievements, the child acquires two important skills between age 18 months and 3 years which greatly augment his ability to master his world and bring pleasurable relief of biological tensions: language and toilet training. The magical words "I want" can produce the most amazing sensual experiences and relief of discomfort. The mere image created mentally by a word like "puppy" can bring great pleasure in and of itself, even if the object of longing is not literally present.[4] When control of bowels and bladder are gained, the toddler has at his command the ability to understand as well as pleasurably relieve these distinct sensations. The heavy emphasis on toilet training leads the toddler to focus considerable attention on the actual anatomic location of the first chakra.

By age 3 the child has solidly acquired among his many skills that most distinctive characteristic of a human being, ego self-awareness.[5] He has announced to the universe in many ways, "I exist!" What this young ego sees when he observes himself at this juncture is fundamental to what he will see for a long time to come. If his early biological, emotional, and intellectual needs have been met in such a way as to promote normal development, he sees himself as valued and safe in the world. If he has experienced normal bonding, consistent affection, and healthy touch, he sees himself as loving and deserving of love. The foundation of a "healthy ego" has been laid.

If his infantile needs have not been consistently met, it can be very difficult to perceive the deeper love of the Christ Self within as he matures and see himself as the unique child of God that he is. The ground is laid for the creation of a core sense of unworthiness and self-doubt and a passion of shame. Feeling unworthy to exist, he creates many associated elemental thought forms, such as:

"I don't deserve love."
"I'm too poor to be accepted."
"I can't let you know me, because if you did, you couldn't love me."
"I'm ashamed of who I am."
"I'm unable to love."
"The universe has forgotten me."
"No one accepts me for who I am."
"I'm always misunderstood."
"No one respects me."

They try to compensate for these feelings by acquiring, keeping, and controlling material possessions, by becoming addicted to material things. Physical problems within the realm of the first chakra may occur, including the sacrum and coccyx (tailbone), anus, and genitals.

The Biblical story of Zaccheus illustrates the problem of blockage in the first chakra by negative elementals:

> And Jesus entered and passed through Jerico. And, behold, there was a man named Zaccheus, which was the chief among the publicans, and he was rich. And he sought to see Jesus who he was; and could not for the press, because he was little of stature. And he ran before, and climbed up into a sycamore tree to see him: for he was to pass that way. And when Jesus came to the place, he looked up, and saw him, and said unto him, "Zaccheus, make haste, and come down; for today I must abide at thy house."
>
> And he made haste, and came down, and received him joyfully. And when they saw it, they all murmured, saying, That he was gone to be guest with a man that is a sinner. And Zaccheus stood, and said unto the Lord; "Behold, Lord, the half of my goods I give to the poor; and if I have taken any thing from any man by false accusation, I restore him fourfold."

And Jesus said unto him, "This day is salvation come to this house, for so much as he also is a son of Abraham. For the Son of man is come to seek and to save that which was lost." (Luke 19:1-10)

As chief publican, the Jew Zaccheus was employed by the despised Roman rulers of Israel to collect taxes from their Jewish subjects. Viewed as traitors to their own people, publicans were social outcasts who were able to survive only by Roman protection. They were not only paid quite handsomely for their unpopular services, but were given leeway by the Romans to extort money beyond the actual taxes and pocket the difference without fear of prosecution. Zaccheus was one such wealthy cheater whose whole existence was preoccupied with physical self-preservation and accumulation of material possessions. Undoubtedly he felt profoundly ashamed of his very existence beneath the veneer of his physical security. It could not have helped his self-image to be so short of stature that he had to climb a tree to even get a glimpse of Jesus.

One can only imagine the surprise that Zaccheus must have felt when the famed teacher Jesus stopped amidst the throng and announced that he was going to spend the night with Zaccheus! Zaccheus' surprise could have only been equaled by the contempt Jesus' enemies must have felt for Jesus by his so doing. The drama concluded in a still more startling manner when Zaccheus announced to the crowd his intention to give half of his goods to the poor and pay back fourfold all those he had cheated.

The story of Zaccheus and Jesus offers a vivid and touching example of the consequences of separation or blockage at the first chakra level as well as the result when connection to the Source is restored by forgiveness. Having experienced that one IS everything, where is the need to have or hold onto anything outside oneself—even to one's own physical body? What cannot be given away freely where it is needed, knowing that limitless resources for any of one's own needs lie within the abundance of the Christ Self within?

The 2nd (Sacral) Chakra [Inner feelings]

The second chakra is located in front of the spine at the level of the lower abdomen and is generally considered the emotional center of the personality. It holds and governs feelings around one-on-one relationships, including sexuality in the context of a relationship. It is the realm of "boundary issues," as termed by psychologists. This is to say that it is the center where the soul experiences itself both as unique, or "bounded," in relationship to others and intimately connected to others, or "without boundaries," simultaneously. This paradoxical truth of relationships, this divine dichotomy, arises from the paradoxical nature of the soul itself—Son of Man and Son of God. Human relationships therefore pose a complex and interesting challenge to the soul, with many potential perplexities and pitfalls along the way. Development of optimal second chakra function is deeply satisfying to the soul, however. The passion of creative life force fuels the will and charges the personality. The personality is able to give and receive love fearlessly, freely, and appropriately.

The psychospiritual domain of the second chakra is the primary focus of development at ages 3-7 years. This is the period when the newly established ego takes its first venture into the process of self-observation and self-discovery. Having established the fact that "I exist," the child begins the lifelong process of discovering "Who I am." The nature of "I" at this stage is learned primarily from one's relationship to that which is "not I," namely the nuclear family. Though mental development is proceeding at a fast pace, this process of self-discovery is occurring primarily on a feeling rather than intellectual level. How the child feels about herself is determined primarily by her emotional relationship with her parents. She needs a feeling of emotional safety, a loving parent to soothe her hurts and calm the fears which arise from her vivid imagination and magical thinking.[6]

The emotional relationship between parent and child is largely determined by the way the parents feel about her activity and respond to it. Up until age 3, activity had been devoted largely to achieving independence from the parent. Now, according to developmental psychologist Erik Erikson, playful activity and initiative are occurring for their own sake and are very important in the life of the child.[7] It is of course her parents that teach her what is "good," or lovable, behavior and what is "bad," or unlovable, behavior. Children desire their parents' esteem at this age because it is so crucial to how they feel about themselves. Their behavior is now more easily shaped by parental expectations. Proper discipline should be age-appropriate and directly connected to the undesirable behavior. It leads the child to feel a sense of healthy but transient remorse which prevents repetition of the hurtful behavior.[8] Children are also gaining the capacity for identification, i.e. the ability to "feel themselves into the situations of others," according to child psychoanalyst Selma Fraiberg. "How would you feel if you were that child?" becomes a useful teaching tool.[9] They are able to share and enjoy working cooperatively as well.

All of these gains are moving the child from the center of the world to a proportionate position within humanity as a whole. The crowning achievement of the "second chakra" stage of development is the emergence of conscience. Conscience develops when the choices for right and wrong in relationship to others come from within rather than from outer controls.[10] With the dawn of conscience comes the ability to appreciate the concepts of personal choice and responsibility and also the capacity to acquire genuine moral values and true empathy.

An important aspect of learning "who I am" at this stage is the discovery of "who I am as a boy" or "who I am as a girl." Boys and girls learn about gender differences by mutual comparison and sex play. They first discover pleasurable sensations in the genital area at this age. Distinctive male and female behavior results not only from genetic differences but also that desire to live up to parental expectations regarding these differences. Attitudes toward one's body and one's sexuality tend to reflect parental attitudes as well.

Given the complexity of the child's learning about herself in relation to others at this stage, it is not difficult to see how fear and guilt can arise if normal learning does not occur within the family. If the child is neglected, abandoned or does not receive normal affection, she feels afraid and unlovable. Poor discipline can lead to particular problems at this age. If the child's normal initiative is stifled repeatedly by harsh discipline or inappropriate negativity, she develops destructive guilt, a "subconscious inner Gestapo" which sees evil in her most normal behavior and overinhibits or even paralyzes the personality. If she is under-disciplined, she may lack self-control and empathy, growing up with the expectation that others should tolerate all sorts of bad behavior from her if they really love her. If her parents are unhappy, she may hold herself responsible. If she is taught that her body is "bad" or undesirable in any way, she may feel guilt and fear around sexual feelings and relationships in later life. If she is wounded by overt sexual abuse, the pain will be intensified. Adult or culturally conditioned experiences may also cause blockage at the second chakra.

Whatever the cause, separation at this level of awareness blocks the free flow of love to and from another person. Love is conditioned by that which feels safe to the separated self. The person creates numerous elementals related to the "unclean spirit" which says, "I am vulnerable to others." The following are examples of such elementals:

"No one can get close to me."
"Love endangers my well-being and attracts hurt and pain."
"I feel insecure."
"It's scary to be by myself."
"I mistrust everybody."

"I don't know if I can love or have what I want in a relationship."
"It is not safe to commit to a relationship."
"No one loves me enough to put up with me."
"I can't be myself in a relationship without hurting the other person."

Those separated from the Christ Self at the second chakra level often attempt to escape their fear and pain by the addictions of sex, drugs, thrill-seeking, and excitement. Physical disorders may manifest in the region of the reproductive organs, bladder, small and large intestines, and lumbar vertebrae (low back).

The Biblical story of "The Woman at the Well" illustrates the problem of blockage or separation at the second chakra level:

> Then cometh he (Jesus) to a city of Samaria, which is called Sychar, near to the parcel of ground that Jacob gave to his son Joseph. Now Jacob's well was there. Jesus therefore, being wearied with his journey, sat thus on the well: and it was about the sixth hour. There cometh a woman of Samaria to draw water: Jesus saith unto her, "Give me to drink." (For his disciples were gone away unto the city to buy meat.)
>
> Then saith the woman of Samaria unto him, "How is it that thou, being a Jew, askest drink of me, which am a woman of Samaria? for the Jews have no dealings with the Samaritans."
>
> Jesus answered and said unto her, "If thou knewest the gift of God, and who it is that saith to thee, Give me to drink; thou wouldest have asked of him, and he would have given thee living water."
>
> The woman saith unto him, "Sir, thou hast nothing to draw with, and the well is deep: from whence then hast thou that living water? Art thou greater than our father Jacob, which gave us the well, and drank thereof himself, and his children, and his cattle?"
>
> Jesus answered and said unto her, "Whosoever drinketh of this water shall thirst again: But whosoever drinketh of the water that I shall give him shall never thirst; but the water that I shall give him shall be in him a well of water springing up into everlasting life."
>
> The woman saith unto him, "Sir, give me this water, that I thirst not, neither come hither to draw."
>
> Jesus saith unto her, "Go call thy husband and come hither."
>
> The woman answered and said, "I have no husband."
>
> Jesus said unto her, "Thou hast well said, 'I have no husband': For thou hast had five husbands; and he whom thou now hast is not thy husband: in that saidst thou truly."
>
> The woman saith unto him, "Sir, I perceive that thou art a prophet. Our fathers worshipped in this mountain; and ye say, that in Jerusalem is the place where men ought to worship."
>
> Jesus saith unto her, "Woman, believe me, the hour cometh, when ye shall neither in this mountain, nor yet at Jerusalem, worship the Father. Ye

worship ye know not what: we know what we worship: for salvation is of the Jews. But the hour cometh, and now is, when the true worshippers shall worship the Father in spirit and in truth: for the Father seeketh such to worship him. God is a Spirit: and they that worship him must worship him in spirit and in truth."

The woman saith unto him, "I know that Messiah cometh, which is called Christ: when he is come, he will tell us all things."

Jesus saith unto her, "I that speak unto thee am he."

And upon this came his disciples, and marvelled that he talked with the woman: yet no man said, "What seekest thou?" or, "Why talkest thou with her?" (John 4:5-15, 21-27)

While alone with Jesus at the well, this Samaritan woman showed her feeling of vulnerability by saying, "How is it that thou, being a Jew, askest drink of me, which am a woman of Samaria?" This separation at the second chakra resulted in this case from prevailing cultural influences, possibly acquired in early childhood. Blockage is also implied on a more personal level by her succession of husbands, suggesting she may have had considerable difficulty with interpersonal relationships.

To fully appreciate the woman's discomfort, it must be understood that it was considered improper in that day for any self-respecting man to even speak to a woman in public, especially to a woman considered immoral. Women were considered to be innately inferior to men spiritually.[11] (By noting this woman's marital and sexual history, Jesus made it clear he was aware of her supposed immorality without either condemning or condoning her behavior.) It was still worse for a Jew to speak to any Samaritan. The Jews were deeply prejudiced against Samaritans because of long-standing historic antagonisms.[12] The Jews and Samaritans had no dealings with each other.

When Jesus' apostles arrived on this scene of Jesus speaking so intimately with a Samaritan woman, they stood in stunned silence. (. . . No man said, What seekest thou? or, Why talkest thou with her?) What was even more amazing was the content of Jesus' conversation with her. This is the first recorded instance in the Gospels of Jesus openly pronouncing to anyone that he was the Deliverer of prophecy. This woman's fear had potentially prevented her from receiving Jesus message of salvation, because she was alone with him. By speaking directly and intimately with her about himself, as well as about God, Jesus succeeded in bringing healing to the woman on the second chakra level where it was needed as well as giving her the greater message of spiritual salvation.

While Jesus' mission appeared to be strictly spiritual and not cultural or political, he did not hesitate to break openly with backward social mores if necessary to bring spiritual healing to particular individuals. Undoubtedly it was because of such bold and startling personal example as the one above that led the early Jewish Christian converts to accept women and gentiles as spiritual equals. As might be expected, the early Christians eventually reverted to their historic prejudices against women. Jesus' example, however powerful, was simply too far ahead of his time. We find it encouraging to note that Jesus' teachings of equality between men and women are at long last coming to pass, to the benefit of everyone.

The 3rd (Solar Plexus) Chakra [Self-Concept]

The third chakra is located in front of the spine in the area of the solar plexus and governs issues around self-esteem, work, and social values. It is generally considered the power center of the personality, allowing a person to be "in the world" while drawing from a Power that is not "of the world." The third chakra is the psychospiritual domain of primary focus from ages 7-12, the grade school years. Freud called these years prior to puberty the latency period. During this time the child further expands his conception of "who I am" by exploring his place in relationship to the world outside his family. According to Erikson, every culture in the world provides some sort of systematic instruction to its youth at this age to prepare a child to be a worker and provider. Erikson summarizes the tasks of the latency period as follows:

> He has experienced a sense of finality regarding the fact that there is no workable future within the womb of his family, and thus becomes ready to apply himself to given skills and tasks, which go far beyond the mere playful expression of his organ modes or the pleasure in the function of his limbs. He develops a sense of industry—i.e., he adjusts himself to the inorganic Principles of the tool world. He can become an eager and absorbed unit of a productive situation. To bring a productive situation to completion is an aim which gradually supersedes the whims and wishes of play.[13]

How the child thinks about himself at this stage tends to be related to how he views his competency in the schoolroom, the sports field, and the peer social scene. He feels a need to prove himself and needs support for his accomplishments. The danger at the "third chakra stage" lies in the possibility of developing a sense of inferiority and inadequacy. Perhaps his family life doesn't prepare him for school or support his learning. Perhaps he is prepared but the school in some way fails him. Perhaps social class, intellectual or physical endowments, or racial prejudice work to his disadvantage.

Whatever the disadvantage, he may come to think of himself as helpless in relationship to an overpowering society and react with chronic anger.[14]

Without correction of this early defect in self-esteem, it may be all but impossible to sense the true power of the Christ Self within. As they reach adulthood, those separated at the third chakra level often try to compensate for their feelings of inadequacy by controlling, proving, or phony behavior. They may become addicted to work, or "workaholic," as a way of escaping their pain, while finding no real joy in their accomplishments or appreciating how their work is contributing to the greater good. They often feel victimized and therefore justified in pushing for what they want without regard to the rights or feelings of others. They may become thoughtless conformists who are easily exploited. They create many negative elementals derived from the belief they are helpless, which may include:

"I need you to do it for me."
"I can't take care of myself."
"My success depends on you."
"My survival depends on you."
"I do what I'm told."
"I must fight to succeed."
"It makes me angry to be such a victim."
"Nothing comes easy in my life."
"I feel helpless to change my life."
"I own those I love."
"Everyone takes advantage of me."

On a physical level, the third chakra influences most of the major organs of digestion and purification. These include the liver, gall bladder, stomach, pancreas, spleen, kidneys, and adrenal glands. The upper lumbar vertebrae are also influenced. Disease in any of these organs or the low back tends to reflect a disturbance in the third chakra.

This Biblical story of King Herod and the Wise Men illustrates a case of profound separation at the third chakra level:

> Now when Jesus was born in Bethlehem of Judea in the days of Herod the king, behold, there came wise men from the east to Jerusalem, Saying, "Where is he that is born King of the Jews? for we have seen his star in the east, and are come to worship him."
> When Herod the king had heard these things, he was troubled, and all Jerusalem with him. And when he had gathered all the chief priests and scribes of the people together, he demanded of them where Christ should be born.

And they said unto him, "In Bethlehem of Judea: for thus it is written by the prophet, And thou Bethlehem, in the land of Juda, art not the least among the princes of Juda: for out of thee shall come a Governor, that shall rule my people Israel."

Then Herod, when he had privily called the wise men, inquired of them diligently what time the star appeared. And he sent them to Bethlehem, and said, "Go and search diligently for the young child; and when ye have found him, bring me word again, that I may come and worship him also."

When they had heard the king, they departed; and, lo, the star, which they saw in the east, went before them, till it came and stood over where the young child was. When they saw the star, they rejoiced with exceeding great joy. And when they were come into the house, they saw the young child with Mary his mother, and fell down, and worshipped him: and when they had opened their treasures, they presented unto him gifts; gold, and frankincense, and myrrh. And being warned of God in a dream that they should not return to Herod, they departed into their own country another way.

And when they were departed, behold, the angel of the Lord appeareth to Joseph in a dream, saying, "Arise, and take the young child and his mother, and flee into Egypt, and be thou there until I bring thee word: for Herod will seek the young child to destroy him." When he arose, he took the young child and his mother by night, and departed into Egypt: And was there until the death of Herod: that it might be fulfilled which was spoken of the Lord by the prophet, saying, Out of Egypt have I called my son.

Then Herod, when he saw that he was mocked of the wise men, was exceeding wroth, and sent forth, and slew all the children that were in Bethlehem, and in all the coasts thereof, from two years old and under, according to the time which he had diligently inquired of the wise men. Then was fulfilled that which was spoken by Jeremy the prophet, saying, In Rama was there a voice heard, lamentation, and weeping, and great mourning, Rachel weeping for her children, and would not be comforted, because they are not. (Matthew 2:1-18)

Ego separation or egotism, as previously noted, may be considered a futile attempt to "play God." Typically this attempt is made in a subtle, or less than fully conscious way. King Herod shows no such subtlety, however, in this rather extreme example of third chakra separation. He takes the ancient Hebrew prophecy of a coming messiah seriously enough to perceive a future threat to his political control of Judea. Feeling helpless before God out of superstitious fear, he decides to "outsmart" God by murdering all the baby boys in Bethlehem who might one day fulfill the prophecy. Today we might call Herod the ultimate "control freak," though his tragic and absurd actions are not really so farfetched when compared with that of some well-known twentieth-century tyrants.

So many people trip over this matter of personal power because they do not understand the real nature of power. God rules a vast universe by the power of love. Likewise must we rule our personal universes by love, because all true power is derived from love. True power is "power with," not "power over," and puts an end to victimhood. True power increases as one shares it and diminishes as one attempts to disempower others. True power is gentle; weakness is imperious. True power is exercised with ease and joy, because it allows one to be a success in the world by being oneself. Only weakness puts on airs and struggles against one's true nature. A great leader exercises power effectively by recognizing and promoting the nobler inclinations of his or her group. A demagogue weakens everyone by appealing to the lowest common denominator of the group consciousness. Much wisdom and experience is required for the personality to appreciate and live the paradoxes of power.

All true and lasting success in society arises from the limitless power of the Christ Self within and the desire to share the power of love in the world. The appearance of achievement to compensate for feelings of helplessness is a function of the present-day personality trying to survive with a closed third chakra. Worldly success, achieved naturally and instinctively through an open third chakra by connection with the Holy Spirit, is a high soul function. The paradox for such a high-achieving and spiritually advanced personality is that it cares not at all for this success which it may so naturally and easily acquire. Because this soul is working in the angelic realm of divine ministry, it can as easily give up worldly recognition as it can accept it. The choice is always according to the Will of God, for the Will of God and the will of a soul of true Power are one and the same.

The 4th (Heart) Chakra [Self-Nurturing]

The heart chakra is located in front of the spinal column at about the level of the physical heart. It is generally considered the love center of the personality, reflecting the presence of both human and divine love in one's life. On a physical level, it tends to reflect the health of the heart, lungs, bronchial tubes, breasts, diaphragm, major vessels of circulation, the chest wall, and the thoracic spine.

In spite of the fact that the heart chakra is "only number 4," the heart chakra is the highest chakra. This is so because it is situated at the very center of the soul's experience, and is therefore the center of personality unification. The heart reflects equally the "Son of Man" and the "Son of God" and is the center which navigates the soul through the endless perplexities created by this profound dichotomy. The heart receives both the divine wisdom of the Father "above" and the divine instinctual intelligence of the Holy Spirit "below." An open heart is boundless, yet must constantly contrive a way to satisfy the legitimate soul need for individuation and boundaries. The heart must determine when to be tender and nurturing and when to be tough and unyielding. The heart speaks a language of mysterious paradoxes, a language which Lao Tzu captured eloquently in the ancient Taoist classic, the *Tao Te Ching*. Referring to the virtues of gratitude and acceptance, Lao Tzu says:

> Be content with what you have;
> rejoice in the way things are.
> When you realize there is nothing lacking,
> the whole world belongs to you.[15]

In the "Beatitudes," Jesus stated this same paradoxical truth: "Blessed are the meek: for they shall inherit the earth." (Matthew 5:5) Such intelligence of the heart is meaningless to an ego-based intellect.

Only love can operate simultaneously and effectively at every level of the soul's multidimensional experience, integrating heaven and earth, spirit and will, conscious and unconscious, wisdom and power, energy and form. The personality is hopelessly lost and disoriented without the guidance of love. The purest and most direct experience of the Christ Self in the flesh is the experience of unconditional divine love in the heart center. The heart awakened by the Christ Self extends its love freely, naturally, and gratefully into the world. Love and service are its highest joy and truest pleasure, often guiding the personality to heroic levels of service in its expansive yet practical way. Once the heart, the center of one's personal universe, is healed, there is hope for healing of the farthest fringes of the personality.

While spiritual experience encompasses so many elements in life, it is no surprise that Jesus chose to penetrate to the very core during his short earth ministry—to focus his life in the heart and his teachings on a gospel of love and service. A man once asked Jesus what he should do to inherit eternal life. Jesus affirmed that he need only follow the greatest of the ancient Hebrew laws: "Thou shalt love the Lord thy God with all thy heart, and with all thy soul, and with all thy strength, and with all thy mind; and thy neighbor as thyself." (Luke 10:25-28) Shortly before his death Jesus gave his apostles a new commandment: "That ye love one another; as I have loved you. . . . By this shall all men know that ye are my disciples." (John 13:34-35) Within Buddhism the traditional ideal of the bodhisattva captures and enlivens the spirit of this parting instruction from Jesus. The bodhisattva is an enlightened being who devotes his or her entire existence to the loving service of humanity.

The heart center is the domain of primary focus during the adolescent years, ages 12-17. The onset of adolescence heralds a profound new challenge to that perpetual question, "Who am I." The rapid physical and physiologic changes, including the eruption of libido, are as great as the changes of early childhood. These bodily changes force upon the adolescent the necessity of rapidly and more consciously expanding her idea of self. She must relinquish the continuity of childhood and forge a new sense of adult continuity out of this transitional stage of relative chaos. She must integrate the skills, tools, and self of childhood into a new adult identity and career. She must progress from the morality and values of childhood to the ethics and purposes of adulthood.[16]

Adolescent rebellion against adult authority serves much the same purpose as the negativity of the toddler. Both are a phase in the establishment of a new-found ego identity. Adolescent rebellion is of course more conscious and complex, and therefore more variable. Regardless of the degree of overt rebellion, the teen universally turns to her peers to discover "who I am." Adolescent cliquishness and conformity arises from this urgent need to forge a new identity. She is very concerned with the way she appears in the eyes of her peers, because this is the way she views herself and is the basis of her self-love. Her burgeoning sexuality makes romantic love a possible means to further explore and define her identity as a sexual being.[17]

This care about self-image, reflected in the eyes of peers, leads to the eventual possibility of care for its own sake. This is the care that will come when she can perceive and appreciate her own soul as it is reflected spiritually in the souls of others. As her heart opens, she comes naturally to follow that great commandment of Jesus, "Thou shalt love thy neighbor as thyself." Genuine love of others will always be reflected in love of self, and vice versa.

Separation at the heart chakra results from any cause that disrupts one's ability to nurture and care for oneself. Earlier childhood difficulties often do so, and separation may occur at any time in adult life as well. Adolescence, however, poses a particular threat as well as opportunity in the development of the heart center. Adolescents are so image conscious that a positive image in the eyes of peers can be exhilarating and a negative image crushing. The adolescent who is rejected because of race, economic class, impaired social skills, unappealing looks, or simple inability to gain acceptance by a clique may be literally "heartbroken." The adolescent who is not provided with appropriate limits or boundaries may feel overwhelmed by the challenges of this age. Opposite sex relationships may either strengthen or weaken gender identity. Teen parenthood may disrupt the natural process of self-discovery by forcing premature commitments.

How does the personality respond when its heart center is separated from the Source of love? There are many who respond by pursuing romantic sentiments alone as a substitute for love, sometimes compulsively so in a series of relationships. Everyone has a sense of the most extreme cases of "heartlessness," when the personality becomes self-absorbed in a destructive way and is totally uncaring toward others. In real life, the separation generally takes on a disguise which is less easy to recognize. Such a commonplace blockage is illustrated in the following biblical story:

> Now it came to pass, as they went, that he (Jesus) entered into a certain village: and a certain woman named Martha received him into her house. And she had a sister called Mary, which also sat at Jesus' feet, and heard his word. But Martha was cumbered about much serving, and came to him, and said, "Lord, dost thou not care that my sister hath left me to serve alone? bid her therefore that she help me."
> And Jesus answered and said unto her, "Martha, Martha, thou art careful and troubled about many things: But one thing is needful: and Mary hath chosen that good part, which shall not be taken away from her." (Luke 10:38-42)

Mary sat attentively at Jesus' feet, absorbed in his words and the pleasure of his company. Martha, preoccupied with many household chores, was resentful that Mary did not leave Jesus to help her. Martha is like so many of us, laboring dutifully and joylessly under a sense of heavy obligation, and feeling resentful when others do not feel this same duty to sacrifice their own best interests. When separated from the Christ Self at the heart, just as Martha separated herself literally from Jesus, we create this core negative elemental: "I suffer." Derived from this "unclean spirit" are such associated elementals as:

"I always pay a price for love."
"I'll never regain what I have lost."
"There is always something missing in my life."
"I carry the weight of the world on my shoulders."
"I feel guilty, because I can't do all that I should."
"Love always seems to bring suffering."
"It's my duty to accept the bad."
"I care more than everybody else."

The heart which is separated from love does indeed suffer. It feels a deep sadness and longing at being separated from the greatest and most sublime experience of life. It feels burdened by a load of "shoulds," yet is unable to sacrifice itself enough to meet these assumed responsibilities. Guilt inevitably follows, leeching the energy of the personality by dragging it into preoccupation with perceived failures of the past. Connection with love and the higher Self is nearly impossible in the presence of guilt.

A heart enslaved by the darkness of egotism has one major strategy to survive this pain and salvage a morsel of apparent meaning. It must ennoble its suffering and twist its sense of victimhood into a "spiritual achievement." And so have we as individuals, and certainly as religious institutions, chosen to glorify martyrdom through the millennia. We point to Jesus' death on the cross as the ultimate martyrdom, seemingly justifying our own self-sacrifice forever as "lambs of God." All we are in fact demonstrating is our ignorance of the true nature of love and the simple lesson in love Jesus was trying to teach.

If a mother runs into a burning building to save her child and loses her own life, do we call this martyrdom? Of course not! We call it love. While such a great gift as one's life may appear to be an enormous sacrifice to a detached observer, one who is giving from the depths of genuine love does not experience any sense of sacrifice, martyrdom, or persecution. Full identification with love leads to such a boundless connection with others and such a depth of Beingness that any personal loss on the physical plane is perceived as relatively inconsequential. Whatever the gift may be, a gift of love always enhances and never depletes love.

Jesus once told his disciples, "Greater love hath no man than this, that a man lay down his life for his friends." (John 15:13) Jesus lay down his life and rose from the dead to show once and for all that our true life is of the Spirit, that our reality as Sons and Daughters of God can never be threatened by anything that happens to the physical body. It was a message of peace, comfort, and reassurance. He was revealing a God of unfathomable love, not a god of wrath and terror who demanded appeasement. We do not admire wrath and vengeance in human beings. Dare we project such traits onto God? Can we not at least see our most noble human traits in Jesus and appreciate these as a revelation of God's love? Can we look at the crucifixion without fear?

While the open heart does not suffer from victimhood, it may still be saddened as it empathetically connects with the suffering of others in its human capacity. However, it always responds naturally, spontaneously, and appropriately in such a way as to ease whatever suffering it encounters.

In the "Beatitudes" Jesus addresses this paradox of the spiritually-connected human heart which also mourns: "Blessed are they that mourn: for they shall be comforted." (Matthew 5:4) He was referring to the emotionally sympathetic attitude with which an open heart responds to any suffering. Love is never callused. Jesus goes on to say, "Blessed are the pure in heart: for they shall see God." (Matthew 5:8) This is true because the pure in heart know and care for all Creation as part of their own Self.

The heart chakra is indeed the highest chakra, because it is the command center of the soul's incarnational mission to know itself as love.

The 5th (Throat) Chakra [Self-Expression]

The fifth chakra is located in the general area of the neck and throat and is known as the communication center of the personality. It reflects the ability to recognize one's own truth and needs and communicate these to others. This communication occurs through words, vocal quality of speech, and body language. The fifth chakra influences the mouth, vocal cords, trachea, esophagus, thyroid, and parathyroid glands as well as the vertebrae and associated musculature.

When the fifth chakra is open and healthy, the personality expresses its truth freely, creatively, and effectively. In so doing, the personality needs are met as a natural by-product. The expressed truth may be physical, emotional, intellectual, or spiritual in nature and may arise from the domain of any of the seven chakras. From a spiritual perspective, the physical body has no higher purpose than to communicate one's inner realities to others in the flesh. In Tibetan Buddhism the fifth chakra is also seen as the center which controls the process of dreaming. It is consciously activated to help achieve self-aware, or lucid, dreaming for the expansion of consciousness.

The fifth chakra, like the heart, is a primary focus of development during the years 12-17. The adolescent challenge of ego consolidation is met largely by "bouncing" feelings and thoughts off of peers and by sharing experiences. Erikson's theory explains the close relationship between the heart and communication centers in adolescent experience:

> The danger of this stage is role confusion. . . . To keep themselves together they temporarily overidentify, to the point of apparent complete loss of identity, with the heroes of cliques and crowds. This initiates the stage of "falling in love," which is by no means entirely, or even primarily, a sexual matter—except where the mores demand it. To a considerable extent adolescent love is an attempt to arrive at a definition of one's

identity by projecting one's diffused ego image on another and by seeing it thus reflected and gradually clarified. This is why so much of young love is conversation.[18]

Like heart chakra separation, throat chakra separation may occur at any stage of development and manifest as a failure to communicate the pain of separation in any of the other chakras. In adolescence the previously discussed causes of heart center separation tend to result in a corresponding fifth chakra blockage.

Whenever the separation occurs, the personality is attempting to survive by communicating from a state of cosmic falsehood. Truth is seen as a menace and the real truth of its separation is pain. Therefore, the present-day personality must not express its truth, less its underlying pain reveal the falsehood of its separation from its Christ Self. It must manipulate every situation to its liking by deceit so as keep its illusory self-image intact. It creates this core elemental desire-thought: "I must lie to get what I want." The lies of separation may arise from any of the chakras and include such negative elementals as the following:

"If I express my true feelings and needs, I will be ridiculed."
"If I can figure out what makes people tick, I can con them into
     anything."
"I must be quiet, or I will make a fool out of myself."
"I must tell people what they want to hear, or they will reject me."
"I do not deserve to speak up."
"I must talk constantly to validate myself."
"If I act nice enough, I can get anything I want out of people."
"I must act loving to get sex; I must give sex to get love."
"If I tell how I've been victimized, I can get pity and attention from
     people."
"If I act bossy enough, I can intimidate people into giving me what I
     want."

Jesus encountered a great deal of deceit during his public ministry, and much of it was from religious leaders who feared Jesus' influence over the people. Their usual tactic was to approach Jesus publicly with a facade of sincerity and ask him some question which would entrap him into making a self-incriminating statement. Always did Jesus meet the lie with a truth that served as useful instruction while hurting no one. The following is a notable example of such an encounter:

> And they send unto him certain of the Pharisees and of the Herodians, to catch him in his words. And when they were come, they say unto him, "Master, we know that thou art true, and carest for no man: for thou regardest not the person of men, but teachest the way of God in truth: Is it lawful to give tribute to Caesar, or not? Shall we give, or shall we not give?
>
> But he, knowing their hypocrisy, said unto them, "Why tempt ye me? bring me a penny, that I may see it." And they brought it. And he saith unto them, "Whose is this image and superscription?"
>
> And they said unto him, "Caesar's."
>
> And Jesus answering said unto them, "Render to Caesar the things that are Caesar's, and to God the things that are God's."
>
> And they marvelled at him. (Mark 12:13-17)

If Jesus responds that it is lawful to give tribute to Caesar, he will infuriate and alienate the Jewish masses that detest Caesar's rule over them. If he says the tribute is not lawful, he will be in trouble with the Roman authorities and would likely be arrested on the spot. By responding with a simple truth about the legitimate place of both divine and civil rule, he not only sidestepped this trap but used it as a teaching opportunity.

The Pharisees were a pious elite who served as the lay leaders of the Palestinian Jews. Their lives were devoted single-mindedly to understanding and observing the Hebrew law (the Torah). From the Law they created a complex and oppressive web of rules that covered just about any conceivable social scenario. They held firmly to the ancient belief that the degree of God's favor depended on the degree to which they observed the Law.[19] While many were sincere and well-meaning and did numerous charitable works,[20] they could not fathom Jesus' teaching that God is a merciful Creator-Father who loves men and women unconditionally as his own offspring.

The traditionalism of the Pharisees arose from the earliest era of Judaism, when Yahweh (the Hebrew name for God) was seen as a stern, nationalistic God of judgment, fulminating from Mt. Horeb and delivering the Ten Commandments. It is important to note, however, that Jesus' God-concept had a clear precedent in the writings of several of the later day Hebrew prophets, especially Isaiah. It was no small, vengeful, nationalistic god who spoke the following words through the prophet Isaiah:

> For thus saith the high and lofty One that inhabiteth eternity, whose name is Holy; "I dwell in the high and holy place, with him also that is of a contrite and humble spirit. . . ." (Isaiah 57:15)
>
> Thus saith the Lord, "The heaven is my throne, and the earth is my footstool. . . ." (Isaiah 66:1)

"Bring my sons from far, and my daughters from the ends of the earth; Even every one that is called by my name: for I have created him for my glory, I have formed him; yea, I have made him. . . . This people have I formed for myself; they shall shew forth my praise. . . . I, even I, am he that blotteth out thy transgressions for mine own sake, and will not remember thy sins." (Isaiah 43:6-7, 21, 25)

When we read such lovely and uplifting words as these about God's nature from the great Hebrew prophets, the following quotation from Jesus makes a great deal of sense: "Think not that I am come to destroy the law, or the prophets; I am not come to destroy, but to fulfill." (Matthew 5:17) Jesus' life was a revelation of the loftiest God-concepts ever to grace the planet as well as a demonstration of the universal laws of love and living truth.

Jesus quoted the Hebrew scriptures frequently, always looking for the best of the old to augment and support his own teachings. While he respected the ancient religious traditions of his people, he refused to compromise his portrayal of God as a loving, merciful, and forgiving Creator-Parent. He could not adhere uncritically to a Law which limited his own experience of God's nature. The ongoing tensions between Jesus and the Pharisees had their origins in the clash between their differing God-concepts.

Within religion today can be found parallel differences that arise from contrasting beliefs about God's nature. Much of this controversy still arises from scripture. Can we not see that all written words are only the symbols of spoken words, which themselves can only crudely approximate the truth they seek to express? Should we not follow the example of Jesus and the spiritual masters, living and communicating the truth that flows naturally from the spirit of our own souls? Jesus said, "Neither shall they say, Lo here! or, lo there! for, behold, the kingdom of God is within you." (Luke 17:21) When scripture is read with a spirit-illumined mind to help grasp the truth within, this scripture is serving a holy purpose. The substitution of scripture for living spiritual truth is idolatry.

Truth is truth and lies are lies; love is love and fear is fear. It does not matter what guise these energies take, nor whether the guise is old, traditional, and "respectable," or new, fringe, and "radical." When we are connected to the Source through an open and healthy fifth chakra, we communicate our truth freely, fearlessly, and consistently. Even our pain and human vulnerability we can express without fear, because we know the peace and power of our ultimate reality can never be threatened.

As Jesus once said, "Ye shall know the truth, and the truth shall make you free." (John 8:32)

The 6th (Brow) Chakra [Self-Perception]

The sixth chakra is located between and slightly above the eyebrows. It is sometimes called the "third eye" because it is the seat of spiritual vision and moral discernment. It gives conscious guidance to the lower chakras in much the same way that the eyes guide the physical body. When open and healthy it gives direct, intuitive and conscious insight into one's life that is far more reliable than intellectual analysis. Sensory expansions such as clairvoyance and clairaudience may manifest when it functions in the realms intervening between matter and spirit. The sixth chakra affects the eyes, ears, nose, sinuses, pituitary gland and general endocrine function, as well as some aspects of the central nervous system.

Jesus was surely referring to the open "third eye" in the following passage: "The light of the body is the eye: if therefore thine eye be single, thy whole body shall be full of light." (Matthew 6:22) This singleness of vision is accomplished by the direct perception of the Oneness of all creation. It is the consciousness of Spirit presence beneath and within all physical, emotional, and mental manifestation. Such singleness of vision is equivalent to universal forgiveness. Under the guidance of such clarity and perfect consistency of vision, it naturally follows that, "the whole body shall be full of light." A dualistic perception of "I" and "you" still exists at the brow chakra level, though consciousness is impinging on a mystical state that transcends perception altogether and knows only unity. This is the state of atonement, literally at-one-ment. It is most appropriate that the state of atonement is often called "enlightenment," especially in Eastern circles.

Hindu traditions have long honored the unity consciousness of Jesus' teachings as the greatest expansion of consciousness and the highest form of enlightenment. The Vedas, completed about the sixth century B.C., comprise the basic Hindu scriptures. The Upanishads, or Vedanta, come toward the end of the Vedic literature and contain the fundamentals of Hindu philosophy. The following passages from the Upanishads summarize the concept and basis of the Hindu ideal of enlightenment:

Of a certainty the man who can see all creatures in himself, himself in all creatures, knows no sorrow.

How can a wise man, knowing the unity of life, seeing all creatures in himself, be deluded or sorrowful?

That is perfect. This is perfect. Perfect comes from perfect. Take perfect from perfect, the remainder is perfect.

May peace and peace and peace be everywhere.[21]

Shankara (686-718 A.D.), the great Indian yogi and philosopher, founded the Advaita Vedanta school of Hinduism. Shankara's fundamental principle is that the only reality is God. Such quotations as the following have had a profound influence on Hindu thought and aspirations throughout the centuries:

> This universe is nothing but Brahman (God). See Brahman everywhere, under all circumstances, with the eye of the spirit and a tranquil heart. How can the physical eyes see anything but physical objects? How can the mind of the enlightened man think of anything other than Reality?
>
> He who has learned to see the one Reality everywhere, He is my master—whether he is a Brahmin or an Untouchable.[22]

The enlightened vision of which Jesus and Shankara speak is in truth the vision of angels, who abide themselves in the realms of spirit and can see even confused incarnate humans as fellow spirits of glory.

The sixth chakra domain is a major focus of development during the late adolescent and young adult years, roughly ages 17-21. Having navigated the turbulent seas of adolescence for years in the quest to achieve a solid ego identity, the young adult is finally ready to join his stabilized, mature "I" with others in common and conscious purpose. He is achieving independence from his family of origin and is ready to pursue commitments to intimate relationships, career, and various social and religious affiliations. Higher education is probably helping him learn how to think objectively for himself and structure his beliefs about life. He is opening to the needs and purposes of humanity and exploring his personal values as they relate to society. He is learning to communicate ever more honestly and effectively. He is learning to subordinate his ego to the needs of the group when a common purpose demands it, such as military combat.[23]

Blockage in the sixth chakra indicates a distortion of self-perception with resultant loss of spiritual insight and discrimination capacity. This blockage may result from events and choices throughout one's life. In young adulthood the separation tends to result from any failure to develop intimacy with adult society and commitment to common causes. It is often characterized at this age by isolation, self-absorption, and self-criticism. Whenever the Christ Self is blocked from view, the personality loses its ability to perceive its ultimate reality beneath its many surface flaws. Having no sound basis for moral discrimination, it attempts to compensate by creating, or actually *mis*creating, its own private world of good and bad, right and wrong, black and white, "shoulds and should nots." The personality may become enslaved by a compulsive drive to achieve perfection according to its private definition thereof. Inevitably falling short of its ideal, the personality falls prey to guilt and feels deserving of punishment. Seeing itself in these negative terms, it can only be *more* critical of others, who may well not accept the same standards in the first place. For the self separated at the sixth chakra, its life becomes an exercise in judgment, because it sees only imperfection. From this core elemental are created such elementals as the following:

"I'm wrong; you are wrong."
"I can't do anything right."
"It's all my fault; it's all your fault."
"I can't forgive them."
"I'm defective."
"They're not good enough."
"Mistakes should be punished."
"The worst will happen."
"I'm a miserable sinner and I deserve hell."
"Society is not worth participating in."
"I have nothing to contribute to the world."
"Relationships are a trap."

In "The Sermon on the Mount," Jesus specifically addressed the connection between obstruction of spiritual vision and personal judgment of others:

"Judge not, that ye be not judged. For with what judgment ye judge, ye shall be judged: and with what measure ye mete, it shall be measured to you again. And why beholdest thou the mote that is in thy brother's eye, but considerest not the beam that is in thine own eye? Or how wilt thou say to thy brother, Let me pull out the mote out of thine eye; and, behold, a beam is in thine own eye? Thou hypocrite, first cast out the beam out of thine own eye; and then shalt thou see clearly to cast out the mote out of thy brother's eye." (Matthew 7:1-5)

The "beam in thine own eye" is the blockage of spiritual perception that must be removed before it is possible to see the reality of another person. Otherwise, we see only imperfection, becoming preoccupied with even such tiny flaws as "the mote that is in thy brother's eye." The spiritually perceptive personality is always merciful. Judgment and punishment of wrongdoing is rightly a collective duty of society only.

The following Biblical story gives an example of sixth chakra blockage, once again among religious leaders, and Jesus response to the problem:

> Jesus went unto the mount of Olives. And early in the morning he came again into the temple, and all the people came unto him; and he sat down, and taught them. And the scribes and Pharisees brought unto him a woman taken in adultery; and when they had set her in the midst, they say unto him, "Master, this woman was taken in adultery, in the very act. Now Moses in the law commanded us, that such should be stoned: but what sayest thou?" This they said, tempting him, that they might have to accuse him.
>
> But Jesus stooped down, and with his finger wrote on the ground, as though he heard them not. So when they continued asking him, he lifted up himself, and said unto them, "He that is without sin among you, let him first cast a stone at her." And again he stooped down, and wrote on the ground.
>
> And they which heard it, being convicted by their own conscience, went out one by one, beginning at the eldest, even unto the last: and Jesus was left alone, and the woman standing in the midst. When Jesus had lifted up himself, and saw none but the woman, he said unto her, "Woman, where are those thine accusers? hath no man condemned thee?"
>
> She said, "No man, Lord."
>
> And Jesus said unto her, "Neither do I condemn thee: go, and sin no more." (John 8:1-11)

The scribes and Pharisees, oblivious to all but the woman's alleged sin, judged her guilty of condemnation and death. Jesus, aware of her true inner nature, could see her only as a sister in Spirit. By refusing to condemn her and saving her life in the process, he revealed once again the merciful and loving nature of God.

The story of the woman taken in adultery raises not only the metaphysical problem of spiritual blindness, but also philosophical questions around the issue of morality. Many people would still ask what is wrong with using the Law of Moses as a guide to right and wrong. How often do we hear today some criticism of our secular, pluralistic society for having lost its "moral compass"? Typically this criticism comes from a religious or social conservative who is calling for a return to some idealized code of conduct, a code that lays down definitive standards of right and wrong. In Christian circles such a code is more likely to be derived from the teachings of Paul than the Law of Moses.

While men and women have long debated the proper role of religious laws and behavior codes in the setting of moral standards, Jesus obviously found them inadequate and even dangerous to spiritual well-being. The following is an example of Jesus' teachings to his disciples on this matter:

> Now the disciples had forgotten to take bread, neither had they in the ship with them more than one loaf. And he charged them, saying, "Take heed, beware of the leaven of the Pharisees, and of the leaven of Herod."
>
> And they reasoned among themselves, saying, "It is because we have no bread."
>
> And when Jesus knew it, he saith unto them, "Why reason ye, because ye have no bread? perceive ye not yet, neither understand? have ye your heart yet hardened? Having eyes, see ye not? and having ears, hear ye not? . . ." (Mark 8:14-18)

Jesus chided his disciples because they took him so literally and failed to see his metaphor. The "leaven of the Pharisees" against which he cautioned was the Pharisees' devotion to the forms of religion rather than the substance; the devotion to scripture instead of living spiritual truth, to law instead of love, to judgment instead of mercy, to God's institution rather than God himself. Rather than behavior, Jesus focused on the attitude in one's heart that produced a given behavior. He said, "Blessed are they which do hunger and thirst after righteousness: for they shall be filled." (Matthew 5:6) He said, "Blessed are the peacemakers: for they shall be called the children of God." (Matthew 5:9) Rather than law, Jesus emphasized faith, love, and direct spiritual insight as the true guides to the highest moral discernment.

In the *Tao Te Ching* Lao Tzu says, "Throw away morality and justice, and people will do the right thing."[24] It could easily be argued that the cultures of both East and West are too spiritually backward to turn directly to the Way of the universe (the Tao) or the Father in Heaven for direct and specific moral guidance. Perhaps the "leaven of the Pharisees" is yet necessary to prevent the world from sliding into decadence, hedonism, and disarray.

Yet the "leaven of the Pharisees" is not the "leaven of the spiritual masters." It is not the leaven of the spiritual aspirant seeking to know oneself as the Christ and be whole. For a person of expanding spiritual vision on the path to atonement, we may speak legitimately of a "moral compass" only in reference to the guidance of the Christ Self acting through an open sixth chakra. Any other standard, even scripture itself, is unreliable for the moment-to-moment guidance we need to navigate the intricacies of life. "Having eyes, see ye not? and having ears, hear ye not?" The highest morality, the morality of Jesus, arises from the spiritual insight that comes from the Word of God spoken directly in one's own soul. This Word gives rise naturally to the genuine experience of mercy and forgiveness, because it is the only basis we have for perceiving the spirit essence of each other and ourselves.

The following exchange between the apostle Peter and Jesus shows the radical nature of the true forgiveness that leads to unending mercy:

> Then came Peter to him, and said, "Lord, how oft shall my brother sin against me, and I forgive him? till seven times?"
> Jesus saith unto him, "I say not unto thee, Until seven times: but, Until seventy times seven." (Matthew 18:21-22)

To the egotist, who cannot even conceive of forgiveness in terms other than self-righteousness and martyrdom, this advice is madness. To one whose eye is "single," forgiveness is a natural and joyful way of life. It is joyful because "the whole body is full of light."

The enlightened ones of every religious tradition throughout the ages will affirm the truth of these words of Jesus: "Blessed are the merciful: for they shall obtain mercy." (Matthew 5:7) How could it be otherwise? For they, like Jesus, have heard the last and only judgment of God on his children: "This is my beloved Son, in whom I am well pleased." (Matthew 3:17)

The 7th (Crown) Chakra [Higher Purpose]

A discussion of the seventh chakra cannot even be meaningfully undertaken outside of a spiritual context. Some metaphysical systems recognize the presence of still higher chakras, but these will not be considered for present purposes. The crown chakra is located just above the top of the head and may influence higher cerebral function on a physical level. It may just have well been considered first rather than last, because it is the entry point of spiritual energies into the personality. Therefore it is generally the first point of conscious contact between Spirit and the human mind. It is the realm of those earliest glimmerings of awareness that there might be an unseen reality beyond the physical, emotional and intellectual planes; that one might even have a higher purpose within this unseen reality. The very inner leading to begin a spiritual search is evidence that the Son of God is actually breaking through to the Son of Man in consciousness at the crown chakra level.

The awakening to one's divine inner presence was called salvation by Jesus. Perhaps the personality does not call it salvation or give it any label at all. That does not matter. What does matter is that one is now free from the bondage of matter and the tyranny of time. Healing has not yet been accomplished, to be sure, but salvation has given the seeker the larger soul perspective necessary for genuine and lasting healing to begin. As a conscious child of eternity, one is now in a position to start mastering the flesh and the world by offering them to the higher purposes of the universe. It is finally possible to begin assuming the responsibility God gave man at the dawn of creation: "Be fruitful, and multiply, and replenish the earth, and subdue it: and have dominion over the fish of the sea, and over the fowl of the air, and over every living thing that moveth upon the earth." (Genesis 1:28) Such dominion can only be interpreted as loving stewardship when the "master" is under the guidance of spirit.

It is difficult to discuss the opening of the crown chakra in conventional developmental terms. A conscious spiritual search may begin quite early in youth or never happen in a lifetime. It would be safe to say that the seventh chakra is likely to receive considerable attention in early adulthood as the sixth chakra is opening. The domains of the sixth and seventh chakras are closely related and easily connected in awareness if the person is so inclined. Attention to moral values, intimate relationships, and societal purpose is naturally linked to higher spiritual purpose. Separation at the seventh chakra tends to occur by default whenever the personality becomes entrapped in materialism and egotistical concerns of any sort. Negative experiences with religion in youth drives some people away from spiritual pursuits of all types.

The Gospel of John opens with a grand cosmological description of the problem that exists for man prior to salvation in a state of seventh chakra blockage:

> In the beginning was the Word, and the Word was with God, and the Word was God. The same was in the beginning with God. All things were made by him; and without him was not anything made that was made. In him was life; and the life was the light of men. And the light shineth in darkness; and the darkness comprehended it not. (John 1:1-5)

When the seventh chakra is closed, we fail to comprehend the Christ Self shining within the darkness of our spiritual slumber. That "true Light, which lighteth every man that cometh into the world" (John 1:9) is blocked from our awareness. Being spiritually "lost," we can find no meaning in life apart from the shifting and transient purposes of the world, such as material gain, social status, and physical pleasure. We conclude that life has no higher purpose. From this negative elemental we create many others such as:

"I'm not sure what I really want."

"My life has more meaning than others'."

"My ultimate dream is the dream of my country."

"I just want to have a good time and avoid pain."

"My primary goal is to work hard and be comfortable."

"What matters most to me is a pleasant lifestyle with all the modern conveniences."

"I'll feel fulfilled if people admire me."

"My physical health is the most important thing to me."

In this last story about a Pharisee, commonly told in Christian churches, Jesus addresses the problem of seventh chakra blockage and the essentials of salvation:

> There was a man of the Pharisees, named Nicodemus, a ruler of the Jews: The same came to Jesus by night, and said unto him, "Rabbi, we know that thou art a teacher come from God: for no man can do these miracles that thou doest, except God be with him."
>
> Jesus answered and said unto him, "Verily, verily, I say unto thee, Except a man be born again, he cannot see the kingdom of God."
>
> Nicodemus saith unto him, "How can a man be born when he is old? can he enter the second time into his mother's womb, and be born?"
>
> Jesus answered, "Verily, verily, I say unto thee, Except a man be born of water and of the Spirit, he cannot enter into the kingdom of God. That which is born of the flesh is flesh; and that which is born of the Spirit is spirit. Marvel not that I said unto thee, 'Ye must be born again.' The wind bloweth where it listeth, and thou hearest the sound thereof, but canst not tell whence it cometh, and whither it goeth: so is every one that is born of the Spirit." (John 3:1-8)

We can infer that Nicodemus "had it all" by the standards of his own time and place. As a ruler of the Jews in ancient Palestine, he stood among the religious and social elite and undoubtedly was well off materially. There is no reason to think he had any significant mental, emotional, or physical disorders. Yet a stirring in his soul led him to seek something beyond all that and risk visiting Jesus by night. It is not hard to imagine the surprise of such a mature, upstanding man when Jesus told him he must be "born again." Jesus used the image of rebirth to dramatize the radical change in worldview that results when one is "born of the Spirit" and when the darkness at last "comprehends the light."

Jesus obviously liked the metaphor of the young child's perspective on life to illuminate the nature of spiritual salvation. The following story is very familiar to every Christian school child:

> And they brought young children to him, that he should touch them: and his disciples rebuked those that brought them. But when Jesus saw it, he was much displeased, and said unto them, "Suffer the little children to come unto me, and forbid them not: for of such is the kingdom of God. Verily I say unto you, Whosoever shall not receive the kingdom of God as a little child, he shall not enter therein." And he took them up in his arms, put his hands upon them, and blessed them. (Mark 10:13-16)

The normal young child in a normal family approaches his or her parents with an attitude of complete dependency and a deep, pure, and innocent trust. There is a natural affection between parent and child that does not have to be earned or negotiated. The child receives parental love and mercy freely and confidently. Even in an abusive and unhappy home, no child would question the biologic fact of the parent-son or parent-daughter relationship!

This is the same attitude that Jesus would have us take toward the Father in Heaven. As he once said: "What man is there of you, whom if his son ask bread, will he give him a stone? Or if he ask a fish, will he give him a serpent? If ye then, being evil, know how to give good gifts unto your children, how much more shall your Father which is in heaven give good things to them that ask him?" (Matthew 7:9-11) Whereas man had historically offered sacrifices to appease a god of wrath, Jesus taught that salvation was a free gift to be received by faith—the same faith that an innocent child places in a loving parent. The gift of salvation is nothing more than salvation from ignorance—the ignorance of not knowing that we are eternally the beloved sons and daughters of God. It is received the moment we ask for such reassurance. The Apostle Paul expressed Jesus' teachings on salvation beautifully in the following passage: "By grace are ye saved through faith; and that not of yourselves: it is the gift of God: Not of works, lest any man should boast." (Ephesians 2:8-9)

Faith in a wholly subjective inner experience is a difficult leap for a society which has practically worshipped science and human reason as gods in modern times. While science is perhaps the only legitimate means of understanding the material universe, science runs up against this embarrassing paradox in its exploration of human life: the absolute and final objective reality of our existence, the indwelling spirit or Christ Self, can only be known with assurance subjectively. Any knowledgeable atheist can "disprove" the existence of God by logical argument just as easily as a theologian can "prove" God's existence by reason alone. Belief or disbelief in God as a mental exercise is meaningless. Direct knowledge of God through the exercise of intelligent faith is salvation. Such faith is childlike, but not childish. It is innocent, humble, open-minded, and free from preconception and prejudice. Salvation through faith is the background of all healing and the ultimate hope of human progress.

The story of man's spiritual journey begins and ends in the seventh chakra. It begins with salvation as we, like Nicodemus, allow the crown chakra to open to the possibility of eternal life. God rushes in to assure us that it is so. With continued opening and expansion of this chakra, our life purpose becomes indistinguishable from God's purpose for us. Our perception is transformed by forgiveness. Our own joy is God's joy.

In this or some future lifetime, forgiveness is complete and the story ends with the glory of atonement. It could be said that atonement, or enlightenment, is the beginning of true cosmic citizenship, because the enlightened one has attained a unified, superconscious connection to the cosmos and its purposes. It is the culmination of that long quest to discover "Who am I?" Beyond duality, and yet individually, we work in partnership with God to create beauty and wonder forever. Only eternity will suffice to fully express that "true light which lighteth every man which cometh into the world."

Chakra Connections and the Mind

On the epic adventure to atonement, each chakra domain presents the spiritual seeker with a distinct "level" of mind at which to discover the Self that lies beyond form and definition altogether—the Christ Self or Spirit-ego-self. These levels are known classically as the subconscious, the conscious, and the superconscious minds. Daskalos recognizes the subconscious, the conscious, the Self-conscious, and the Self-Superconscious levels of mind.

The subconscious mind, first envisioned by Freud, may be considered the repository of life's early experiences and the center of instinctual awareness. By definition these early memories are most often below the level of conscious awareness. Nevertheless they dominate the present-day personality, which has not brought the energy carried by these memories into conscious awareness for healing. In the context of healing, it therefore becomes most important to study and work with the contents of the subconscious. The subconscious mind as it relates to the 7 chakras will now be considered briefly. A more intensive analysis of the subconscious, as well as the higher levels of mind, will be done in later chapters.

Chakra domains 1, 2, and 3, the biological, the interpersonal, and the social, hold three levels of memory that are predominantly unconscious.

These are the domains, therefore, that primarily hold the elementals of the subconscious mind. The nature of separation at these three domains has been previously discussed. The present-day personality is dominated so heavily by subconscious elementals of separation that it can be said to reside in the subconscious mind at chakras 1-2-3.

While presented individually and systematically, the chakras do not of course function in isolation from each other. Every domain of experience has an impact on every other one. When egotism dominates the personality, the ego's conscious view of self becomes enslaved by the negative elementals of the subconscious mind. The ego sees and identifies with a false self; it becomes a manipulative strategist with a conscious control plan to carry out the agenda of separation that now rules it. It cannot see a reflection of higher values and virtues, nor serve a higher soul purpose. The ego carries out this agenda through chakras 4-5-6, which essentially express on a more conscious level the pre-existent and dominant subconscious elementals of separation within chakras 1-2-3. The higher, more conscious, centers are actually closer to the reality of the subconscious mind in this unhealed state.

There is a natural connection between the lower and upper chakras. The image of breast-feeding, for instance, illustrates the natural connection between the first (root) chakra and fourth (heart) chakra. When the heart is dominated by the subconscious elemental, "I am unworthy to exist" (#1), it can hardly care for itself. It experiences suffering and despair. A connection between the second (sacral) and fifth (throat) chakra is seen in the realm of romance and love-making. If the elemental "I am vulnerable to others" (#2) is dominant, the fifth chakra will try to protect the self by manipulation and deceit, hiding its fear. Relationships will be sabotaged. The link between the third (solar plexus) and sixth (brow) chakras is shown by the relationship between achievement and vision in society. If the elemental "I am helpless" (#3) dominates, then "I see only imperfection in myself" (#6) to block my success. The enslavement of the lower six chakras is accompanied by a blockage in the seventh (crown) chakra that manifests itself as a feeling of aimlessness and purposelessness, previously discussed.

V

HOME OF THE PRESENT-DAY PERSONALITY
The Subconscious Mind

The Enneagram personality types are defined according to energetic trends caused by separation from Spirit. From a higher perspective, it would therefore be more accurate to say that the types are the nine major ways personality appears to be what it is *not*. In this respect it is an exercise in absurdity. Separation itself is a cosmic absurdity. To investigate what anything, including personality, actually *is* in a final sense is to enter a realm of deep mystery. Yet certain aspects of this entity called personality can be described, even if not understood.

Personality is always uniquely and unchangeably recognizable as *me*, even though the soul of its association is constantly growing and changing. Through ego self-awareness it always recognizes itself as individuated, whether it identifies with the body of a mammal or a formless spirit of divine light. Personality possesses free will and capacity for self-determination. It is able to alter the course of its destiny by choice at any given moment and at any conceivable level of consciousness. Daskalos calls the genuine personality the permanent personality, as noted in Chapter 2, and describes it as a direct projection of form into the soul by the Spirit-ego-self, which is itself formless.[1] Could the bestowal of individual personality be other than a gift of God, the same God who has established us as sons and daughters through the gift of the Christ Self and given us the supersubstance of mind for unrestricted use? For "every good gift and every perfect gift is from above, and cometh down from the Father of lights, with whom is no variableness, neither shadow of turning." (James 1:17)

At this beginning stage of our soul journey and for present purposes, it is necessary to focus on the present-day personality, which Daskalos defines as the sum total of one's elemental creations of mind. It is also practical for healing purposes to view one's Enneagram personality type as if it were really oneself. While the reason for a particular trend of separation, the personality type, is sometimes a mystery, the Enneagram assumes there is a soul purpose in the process. It exposes the blind spots in one's awareness in such a way that he or she can discover a particular path to transformation and self-realization, awakening the Christ in one's heart. This is one's primary soul task, or life purpose. Emotional healing and life purpose are intimately connected in the life of the soul. The soul will not therefore allow us to ignore the shadows of the present-day personality, which are based in the subconscious mind. The soul must bring light into the dark places where love has been forgotten. These will now be further explored.

The Houses of Illusion

Each personality type of Enneagram theory resides within the psycho-spiritual domains of the seven chakras. As in the "Parable of the Unclean Spirits" previously discussed, these seven chakras may be likened to seven rooms of a house. The first three chakras, or "rooms," are located below the surface in the basement or cellar of the house. This underground level represents the subconscious mind, which is hidden from view. The other four rooms of the house are above ground and represent chakras 4-5-6-7.

The house of the present-day personality is enslaved by the darkness of egotism and ruled by that master demon, the "Prince of Devils," who says, "I am separate from God." Though his nefarious and grandiose presence haunts the entire house, he has recruited seven lords of illusion "more evil than himself" to do the actual "dirty work" of running the household. Each is a specialist in the domination of a particular chakra domain. The three most powerful of these lords, the "lords of the subconscious," serve their master from the cherished positions underground. The "lord of unworthiness" occupies room #1, the root chakra, where he can most effectively debase the personality's very existence with shame. The "lord of interpersonal vulnerability" rules from room #2, the sacral chakra, where he can most favorably intimidate the personality with fear and guilt. The "lord of helplessness" reigns from room #3, the solar plexus chakra, where he can best bully the personality into childlike dependence and feelings of incompetence in the world.

The three lords of the subconscious, a ruthless oligarchy, lay down the law to the "lords of consciousness" in the four rooms above. These are the ones who say, "I suffer" (#4—the heart chakra), "I must lie to get what I want" (#5—the throat chakra), "I perceive only imperfection" (#6—the brow chakra), "Life has no higher purpose" (#7—the crown chakra). These four lords are given one final and overarching order, which says, "Serve us as you will and recruit as many assistants as you like, but above all else, do not allow the light to enter this house!"

Even with the most valiant of egotistical efforts, the confederation of lords cannot completely block the brilliance of the Light that constantly seeks to shine into the darkness of the present-day personality. The result is a configuration of dark shadows within the house. The seven lords of illusion with their shadowy miscreations comprise what was previously called the "inner Judas" of the personality. The nine personality types of the Enneagram are distinguished only by the particular configuration of shadows in each of their seven-room houses. One house is not inherently better or worse than the other. By analyzing the particular influences of the three subconscious lords on each house, the distinctive "face of Judas" for each personality type can be more clearly discerned and brought consciously to the light.

The Faces of the "Inner Judas"

When separated from its Source, the personality seeks validation outside its Self and attempts to manipulate or control external factors to compensate for what it believes it's lacking. Each of the nine personality types attempts this impossible task in its own characteristic way. Potential causes of separation during the process of personality development are detailed in Chapter 4. Root chakra separation commonly occurs at ages 0-3, sacral chakra separation at ages 3-7, and solar plexus chakra separation at ages 7-12, because these are the ages of developmental focus as the personality matures through chakra domains 1-2-3. The specific manifestations the separation takes in all three chakra domains of the subconscious will now be considered for each personality type. These were derived from clinical application of Enneagram and chakra theory. By exposing the multiple faces of the inner Judas which betrays the inner Christ, a deeper understanding of our subconscious motivations can perhaps be gained and the healing process facilitated.

Separation at the 1st (Root) Chakra

> Domain: Self-Image—biological, physical safety and security, libido, procreational urges.
> Age of Separation: 0-3 years
> Core Elemental: "I am unworthy to exist."
> Passion: Shame

Type One [The Critical Self]—"I feel I don't deserve to have my basic desires fulfilled. I worry about what I should do as opposed to what I want to do. This constant worry makes me nervous and irritable."

Type Two [The Sacrificing Self]—"I don't feel secure in my life, so I must be seen as first in order to see my own value. The best way to be seen as first is to fulfill others' needs and make myself indispensable to them. This is my best chance to get security and safety and be treated as special."

Type Three [The Success-Driven Self]—"I don't feel worthy to exist, so I worry constantly about safety, security, and money. To compensate for these feelings, I need to project an image of physical comfort and confidence in my ability to provide for myself. I drive myself mercilessly to achieve this image and get no real pleasure in doing so."

Type Four [The Melodramatic Self]—"I feel worthless, like some sort of defect of nature. I just don't have what it takes to get on in life. It all makes me very depressed. The only way I can fill this huge gap inside is to do more and more and more, overextend myself, live on the edge."

Type Five [The Isolated Self]—"Since I don't deserve to exist, I'm always in danger of losing even the little I have. My best chance for survival is to hoard all the time, space, energy, knowledge, and possessions I can muster."

Type Six [The Doubtful Self]—"Since I'm unworthy to exist, I must be on constant guard against being destroyed. Danger lurks everywhere."

Type Seven [The Pleasure-Seeking Self]—"I feel unworthy, so I must inflate my feeling of self-worth with lots of cool experiences and reinforce my self-image by associating with people that find me lots of fun. I just can't make it on my own."

Type Eight [The Controlling Self]—"Feeling unworthy to exist, I must fight and control everything around me to preserve my safety. The best defense is always a good offense."

Type Nine [The Neglected Self]—"I suppose I just have to accept the fact that I'm unworthy and insignificant. If I can fill up my days with enough little pleasures and trivial pursuits, maybe I can ignore the fact that I'm not receiving any nurturing in my life."

Separation at the 2nd (Sacral) Chakra

Domain: Inner Feelings-Interpersonal, Sexual, Emotional love.
Age of Separation: 3-7 years
Core Elemental: "I feel emotionally vulnerable in relationships."
Passion: Fear

Type One [The Critical Self]—"I fear that I will lose my own sense of perfection and internal control when in a relationship. I avoid this feeling of vulnerability by blaming the other person for what he/she is not doing correctly and feeling justified in this anger.

Type Two [The Sacrificing Self]—"I fear you will have power over me if you know me or pursue me." Male—"I avoid this fear by pursuing and wooing you, giving of everything but my real feelings." Female—"I avoid feeling overpowered by aggressive seduction and by becoming indispensable, and therefore needed."

Type Three [The Success-Driven Self]—"I fear you will reject me if the truth about me is revealed. Therefore I will conform to an acceptable image of male or female in order to be accepted."

Type Four [The Melodramatic Self]—"I fear that if I surrender to love, the other person will abandon me because of my inferiority. I must compete with the other person to feel good enough so as not to be abandoned."

Type Five [The Isolated Self]—"I fear being swallowed up by a relationship. I try to compensate by placing the relationship in an isolated compartment of my life, thus preserving time, space, and energy for myself."

Type Six [The Doubtful Self]—"I fear that I will be hurt and taken advantage of in a relationship, because I feel cut off from the Source of strength and courage. I try to compensate for this feeling of vulnerability by substituting an outer figure of strength and authority. Either person may play this role, but someone must be in charge."

Type Seven [The Pleasure-Seeking Self]—"I fear I will be exposed as a fraud. I can compensate for this fear by seducing people into accepting me through excitement, fun, opportunity, and grandiose plans."

Type Eight [The Controlling Self]—"I fear being hurt and taken advantage of in a relationship. I attempt to avoid this pain by possessing and controlling the object of my love."

Type Nine [The Neglected Self]—"I fear I will be unseen and unheard in a relationship because of my feeling of insignificance. I can compensate for this feeling of vulnerability by merging with the other person."

Separation at the 3rd (Solar Plexus) Chakra

Domain: Self-concept - Social, Career.
Age of Separation: 7-12 years
Core Elemental: "I am helpless."
Passion: Anger

Type One [The Critical Self]—"I feel helpless in the world, because whatever I want seems to clash with society's expectations of me. There's not much to do but go along dutifully with what society wants, because that's what a good person does. I could never be a selfish person. I do feel resentful about always having to put myself last, but if everyone else would think about other people for a change, the world would be a much better place."

Type Two [The Sacrificing Self]—"I feel helpless in the world because I have no innate value to society. I overcome this feeling by taking on an important caretaking role. I need to be needed. What makes me feel good about myself is to align myself with powerful people and make myself indispensable to them. If they don't recognize how much they need me and show some appreciation, watch out! I can get really bossy and lash out in anger at them."

Type Three [The Success-Driven Self]—"I'm a team player from the word 'Go!' and I need everyone else on the team to do their part. If they don't, I can push them pretty hard. Team success is very important to me, because that's the way I feel my own success as a person. If the team lets me down, I feel totally helpless and angry, but of course I can't show these nasty feelings. It would ruin my successful reputation and upbeat image. There's nothing to do but numb my feelings and charge on. Sure, work's a grind, but things will get better if I just hang in there!"

Type Four [The Melodramatic Self]—"I believe in individuality, in being my own unique, special self. I see no value in losing myself in a crowd. Still, I must admit it really upsets me when other people don't see how special I am and don't approve of my independent ways. When this happens (and it usually does), I feel so abandoned and helpless. I'm envious of the way such ordinary people can do so well out there, but usually I just feel ashamed at being such a misfit. Well, if people don't approve of me, they'll just have to take care of me. That's good enough for them, because I'm worth a lot more to them than they'll ever know!"

Type Five [The Isolated Self]—"It amuses me to watch the world go by with all its petty concerns, but I prefer not to get involved. I'm always trying instead to find a place in the world and get control of my life by accumulating lots of knowledge. Unfortunately, society just doesn't appreciate the life of the mind. Even if it did, society wouldn't seek me out for advice, and I'm not about to go out pushing my ideas on people. I feel helpless because of my inability to have any real impact on society, and respond out of anger and frustration by withdrawing to myself and the inner life. In this isolation, I sometimes feel weird and out of contact with reality. I find myself compulsively doing self-destructive and unpredictable things."

Type Six [The Doubtful Self]—"I seek approval in work or group situations to avoid the sanctions of the social authority that I fear. I play the game well by coming across as dutiful, loyal, warm, and I am generally well-liked. I never feel I can trust the authority I'm yielding to, however, regardless of what I do. I must be hypervigilant against being hurt. I feel helpless and frustrated by this pressure and doubt I feel in the presence of social authority. I feel inferior and vulnerable and can never relax. Should some big shot threaten me or a fellow underdog, I may turn aggressive in our defense to keep the situation from getting out of hand.

Type Seven [The Pleasure-Seeking Self]—"I'm a dreamer by nature, full of plans, options, and big ideas. I'm a great entertainer and I love to be center of attention at a party. I must admit, however, that it gets on my nerves to have to *work* with a group of people. I really like to do my own thing, and a group cramps my style and limits my options terribly. Unfortunately, I have no choice but to pretend to go along with the group, and that makes me feel helpless. I compensate by imposing an arbitrary order in my life, even becoming obsessive-compulsive. It's not pleasant, but at least its my own doing."

Type Eight [The Controlling Self]—"Being in charge of a group and taking control makes me feel good about myself, and the larger the group the better. I tune in to every member of the group and find out quickly who is likely to challenge my authority and who will accept it. I try to put an end to any challenges quickly. Should I lose the support of the group and have to give up my position as boss, I withdraw into a hurt, mistrustful, defensive posture."

Type Nine [The Neglected Self]—"Feeling unimportant, I try to gain social approval by merging with whatever group I happen to be associated with and creating no conflicts. Since I have trouble asserting myself and saying 'No,' I tend to be used and dominated by the group. This makes me feel helpless. My helplessness manifests as passive-aggressive behavior which paralyzes me."

The "faces of Judas" that arise from the subconscious home of the present-day personality may be caricatures of real life personalities as they are presented above. Nevertheless they do show trends of separation that most of us can identify with to at least some extent. All of these states imply a collaboration of the "lords of consciousness" in the higher chakra centers and reveal a posture that is fundamentally defensive. The personality is trying to protect itself from the feelings and consequences of the shame, fear, and helplessness which rules it while leaving intact the separated state that caused these feelings. In the end, these are all exercises in futility.

In whatever way the present-day personality attempts to defend a state of separation, it is trying to defend a lie against the truth. It is suffering and dying to hold a pattern of shadows together, believing itself to be that. Who knows what treasures would be revealed if we allowed the light within to shine into our "houses of darkness." Is it possible we would find peace in place of anger, joy in place of suffering, love in place of fear? Is it not worth taking the chance to find out? The "Parable of the Prodigal Son," discussed in the next chapter, reveals the universal journey of transformation from darkness and despair into love and light.

VI

THE UNIVERSAL JOURNEY
OF TRANSFORMATION
The Parable of the Prodigal Son

A certain man had two sons: and the younger of them said to his father, "Father, give me the portion of goods that falleth to me." And he divided unto them his living.

And not many days after the younger son gathered all together, and took his journey into a far country, and there wasted his substance with riotous living.

And when he had spent all, there arose a mighty famine in that land; and he began to be in want. And he went and joined himself to a citizen of that country; and he sent him into his fields to feed swine. And he would fain have filled his belly with the husks that the swine did eat: and no man gave unto him.

And when he came to himself, he said, "How many hired servants of my father's have bread enough and to spare, and I perish with hunger! I will arise and go to my father, and will say unto him, 'Father, I have sinned against heaven, and before thee, and am no more worthy to be called thy son: make me as one of thy hired servants."

And he arose, and came to his father. But when he was yet a great way off, his father saw him, and had compassion, and ran, and fell on his neck, and kissed him. And the son said unto him, "Father, I have sinned against heaven, and in thy sight, and am no more worthy to be called thy son."

But the father said to his servants, "Bring forth the best robe, and put it on him; and put a ring on his hand, and shoes on his feet: and bring hither the fatted calf, and kill it; and let us eat, and be merry: For this my son was dead, and is alive again; he was lost, and is found." And they began to be merry. (Luke 15:11-24)

The value of the parable as a teaching tool lay in the fact that Jesus could plant seeds of truth in the minds of his listeners while giving them the leeway to interpret his stories in accordance with their own intellectual capacity and spiritual insight. It was also a way to sidestep premature controversy with the religious authorities that monitored him. They constantly sought ways to make trouble for him and force him to abort his mission. Therefore, ". . . without a parable spake he not unto them: and when they were alone, he expounded all things to his disciples." (Mark 4:34)

The Parable of the Prodigal Son is one of the most frequently told parables of Jesus, because it reveals so much about the forgiving and merciful nature of God. It can also serve as an allegory of the universal journey of transformation from the depths of separation to the heights of atonement via the various stages of consciousness. The process of separation and the return to love will be presented step by step according to the parable.

> *A certain man had two sons: And the younger of them said to his father, "Father, give me the portion of goods that falleth to me." And he divided unto them his living.*

These opening lines illustrate the state of grace that exists in the awareness of the presence of God. This is the same state that existed for Adam and Eve prior to the "Fall" and was symbolized by the star within the circle. God shares everything freely with us, even "his living," that fragment of his own Self that we call "the Christ Self," the "Spirit-ego-self," or "the true light which lighteth every man that cometh into the world." (John 1:9) What we do with our gifts is our own decision, for "he (God) maketh his sun to rise on the evil and on the good, and sendeth rain on the just and on the unjust." (Matt. 5:45)

> *And not many days after the younger son gathered all together, and took his journey into a far country, and there wasted his substance with riotous living.*

These lines illustrate that entrance into the illusory state of ego separation, the "Fall," where the awareness of the presence of God is lost. It was symbolized previously by the placement of the lower triangle of the six-pointed star outside the circle of atonement. This part of the story also illustrates why so many spiritual seekers find the word "ego" practically synonymous with "devil." The goal of some Eastern paths is to annihilate ego altogether and merge into the Absolute without the encumbrance of individual identity.

Western religious traditions, however, tend to preserve philosophically the worth of individuality. There is no record that Jesus ever devalued the mere fact of individual personality identity in any way. In fact he ministered so attentively to individual men, women, and children that he affirmed by his acts as well as his words their worth as children of God. Ego, in the most abstract sense, is that mysterious aspect of the human personality which allows one to be aware of his or her individual self at any state of consciousness. Ego is an essential factor which distinguishes humanity from the animal kingdom and is a gift which forms a core element of our progressing soul nature.

The problem for our personalities at early stages of growth is not the existence of ego, but rather what it identifies with and thus believes itself to be. What ego sees are the creations of one's own mind, i.e., a collection of elementals. This network of elementals forms the basis of one's self-image; so what we see as we observe ourselves through ego function is quite literally imaginary. For most of us this self-image is a "devil," because we become satisfied that "this is myself" and allow this illusionary self to block our view of our true Spirit Self. This identification with one's elemental creations is called egotism, as previously discussed. Egotism is the origin of the present-day personality and produces the experience of hell. The ego tends to be equated with egotism, and not unreasonably so for practical spiritual instruction. This is where it gets its bad reputation.

The Parable of the Prodigal Son reminds us, and Daskalos teaches, that we most commonly create elementals subconsciously in response to material cravings. These desire-thoughts, or "unclean spirits," serve our desires by creating the conditions for satisfaction at the expense of happiness. In so doing, these negative elementals bind the present-day personality to the material plane as its slave, creating the conditions for suffering. The Parable illustrates the primal material enslavement of addiction consciousness and how this enslavement dissipates our life "substance"—what Daskalos calls our "etheric vitality."

While every form of egotism is rooted in some form of enslavement to the material plane, egotism often takes subtler and more clever forms than that of simple material substance or pleasure addiction. The ego enslaved by egotism is such a trickster that it can successfully manipulate situations where it technically should have no business at all. In fact, the enslaved ego often prefers those realms where it can enter incognito, because it can most reliably preserve itself when it can't be seen for the "devil" it is. Prime examples of such ego subterfuge are found in religion and psychotherapy.

Personalities caught up in religious egotism, or religiosity, typically view themselves in moralistic terms that may assume either the inflated or deflated aspect of a given negative elemental. On one hand, religious egotism likes to clothe itself in strengths and see itself as good, very good. This is that quality of self-righteousness which Jesus encountered so often among the Pharisees and other religious leaders of his day. As Jesus himself was the object of so much adoration as a spiritual teacher, he understood that he likewise had to stay vigilant against the snare of this inflated elemental called self-righteousness. The following story illustrates his concern:

> And a certain ruler asked him (Jesus), saying, "Good Master, what shall I do to inherit eternal life?"
> And Jesus said unto him, "Why callest thou me good? none is good, save one, that is, God." (Luke 18:18-19)

While it might appear that Jesus was rebuking this ruler, on closer consideration it is evident that this statement was meant as much for himself as it was meant to steer the ruler away from the snare of religiosity. Jesus went on to answer the man's question.

The authors once asked Daskalos what form of egotism he considered to be the most dangerous. He immediately responded, "a demon disguised as an angel of light." Pride is the most noteworthy of these demons and was the downfall of the mighty angel Lucifer, according to semitic traditions. Self-righteous pride could not exist without a "deflated" twin, an inverted form of pride called guilt. Guilt, as used in this context, is not that healthy, transient sense of remorse that's needed to change an attitude or behavior. Guilt is that deflated elemental of religiosity which says, "I am a miserable sinner and I deserve hell." Jesus was equally free from the influences of guilt and self-righteousness. One of his closest associates, Mary Magdalene, was an ex-prostitute. Prostitutes were considered among the worst of "miserable sinners" in that day. Jesus was constantly under attack from the religious leaders for keeping company with "publicans and sinners." His manner of relating to even the overt "sinners" as a brother in spirit did much to dispel guilt as he went about the work of healing.

Guilt keeps a person locked into the mistakes and attitudes of the past, making effective change *now* all but impossible. While religious egotism puffs itself up and shrinks itself incessantly like the puffer fish, it remains oblivious to the true grandeur and genuine holiness of the Christ Self within. Religion must help de-energize the tenacious twin elementals of self-righteousness and guilt if it is to inspire genuine change in the personality.

Egotism infiltrates psychotherapy in much the same manner as it does religion. Egotism's goal is always to validate the existence of the false, separated self and its unfulfilled desires, even at the expense of suffering and hardship of the personality. It does so in psychotherapy by substituting one self-image for another, puffing up one elemental and deflating another. It takes seeming strengths and congratulates itself for being "good," then wrings its hands about the deflated elementals that make it "bad." All the while the enslaved ego is thoroughly satisfied with itself, because it has kept these elementals vitalized by all the attention to them and thus preserved itself. The enslaved ego may keep "puffing" in psychotherapy for years, fascinated by endless self-analysis and satisfied that it's preventing any genuine change, if this is what the personality wants. The present-day personality can be very clever indeed as it clings to its illusions and distances itself from healing!

Psychotherapy faces a common and difficult challenge from the wiles of egotism when it deals with the emotional consequences of early childhood trauma. Therapy attempts to bring these traumatic memories into conscious awareness for healing. If the therapy is strictly ego-based, it may unwittingly perpetuate a sense of victimization and powerlessness that arises from the immature world view of the wounded "inner child." According to the eminent Jungian psychologist James Hillman, this is the error that frequently sabotages inner child work.[1]

Hillman espouses the idea that each child has an "acorn" within, the seed of a soul mission which is fostered by the child's particular circumstances and in turn influences the child's life deeply. From this perspective, trauma and difficulty may have a much deeper meaning than an ego-based or developmental psychologist can appreciate. Hillman cites several examples of adult greatness that were preceded by corresponding childhood difficulty or trauma, such as the life of Winston Churchill. Churchill as a boy had a lot of trouble with language—reading, writing, speech, spelling. Hillman postulates that these childhood difficulties arose from his soul knowledge that he would one day have to save the Western world through his communication abilities, and that it was simply too much for a child to handle.[2]

Hillman goes so far as to assert, "In your pathology is your salvation."[3] This same theme has been expressed in different ways throughout this book. Each form of psychopathology casts a particular shadow of separation in particular domains of the psyche. These shadows, while experienced as suffering, give the soul its unique mission of incarnation to bring love and light to fear and darkness. The soul, under the unfathomable guidance of the Spirit-ego-self, finds a way to encounter the challenges it needs in order to achieve its particular mission of greatness. Many of our soul challenges arise from the physical, emotional, mental, and social traumas of childhood. Hillman says, "Wounds and scars are the stuff of character. The word character means, at root, 'marked or etched with sharp lines,' like initiation cuts."[4] It is through the encounter with hardship and trauma that the soul has the opportunity to gain strength and resilience.

As adults we do far better to accept our soul challenges gracefully than to forever feel sorry for ourselves. This is not to justify any harm done consciously to a child or to an adult. As Paul said, "Be not deceived; God is not mocked: for whatsoever a man soweth, that shall he also reap." (Galatians 6:7) Spirit can, however, take our best efforts, even the abysmal failures of ignorance and separation, and turn it all to the good. There is no greater joy for the soul than to participate in such a divine adventure. The Prodigal Son is now about to experience the consequences of his ignorant choice for separation and begin the journey back to love.

> And when he had spent all, there arose a mighty famine in that land; and he began to be in want.

The Prodigal Son, having wasted the "substance" he was so freely given through addiction consciousness, has cut himself off from the Source of all vitality and has no way to replenish it. In this "land of famine," the state of separation, he is now in want. He is separated at the first chakra domain, which governs those issues around self-preservation, physical survival and security. His life is ruled by that subconscious elemental which says, "I am not worthy to exist." He will look outside himself to this barren land for help and devise one of nine "control plans" to survive first chakra separation, as discussed in the previous chapter.

> And he went and joined himself to a citizen of that country; and he sent him into his fields to feed swine.

In the land of separation and scarcity, the Prodigal Son now enters the second chakra domain of the subconscious mind, that of personal relationships. He is looking for validation of himself as a personal entity, but again does so outside of himself and out of a sense of lack. He and the citizen of that country join in a mutual state of fear and a sense of vulnerability. Neither really trusts the other, but they use each other in such a way as to maintain mutually the state of egotism. They each do so in one of the nine ways discussed previously under second chakra separation. The core elemental, "I am vulnerable to others," and its associated elementals are the "swine" that the Prodigal Son feeds and his associate maintains. In a relationship driven by subconscious forces, both partners feel dissatisfied and sold short, because neither can ever fill the other's inner void.

> *And he would fain have filled his belly with the husks that the swine did eat: and no man gave unto him.*

The Prodigal Son is now feeling the utter helplessness in the world that results from third chakra separation. His life is a struggle. He's achieved nothing of worth in the world and has no recognition or respect. Meanwhile the subconscious "swine," which maintain his powerless relationship to the world, feed fat off his life force. They accomplish nothing other than the preservation of their own existence. They manage to keep the Prodigal Son convinced that little as he is, he is nothing at all in the world without them. They know that their own power would be lost should his personality gain any true power. The Prodigal Son seizes upon one of the nine control plans of third chakra separation in a desperate attempt at social validation, yet "no man gave unto him" any respect or acknowledgment. His control plan is a failure. All the while, he continues to submissively feed his "inner swine."

The present-day personality of the Prodigal Son has made its home among the veil of negative elementals in the first three chakra domains that comprise the subconscious mind. The higher faculties of the mind do nothing but serve the swine that now dominate the subconscious. These "unclean spirits," created to serve the material cravings of the personality, now betray the Prodigal Son by binding and nailing his hands and feet to the material world. He bleeds and suffers as on a crucifix, unable to see the light of his own Christ Self that would so readily save him in this, his dark night of the soul. This state of crucifixion prior to salvation and healing was symbolized in Chapter 3 as the cross in a veil of negative elementals outside the circle of atonement.

> *And when he came to himself, he said, "How many hired servants of my father's have bread enough and to spare, and I perish with hunger! I will arise and go to my father, and will say unto him, 'Father, I have sinned against heaven, and before thee, and am no more worthy to be called thy son: make me as one of thy hired servants.'"*

Eventually, the Prodigal Son suffers enough to recognize the original wound of separation. He admits that he has been starved nearly to death by the subconscious elementals of addiction consciousness that he feeds. He has decided that he would prefer to serve his father humbly as a hired hand, if it comes to that, than to continue feeding these swine; he will accept his Father's free gift of salvation and take charge of his destiny. The Prodigal Son is now in the fourth chakra domain, the first level of conscious awareness, and the way is open for healing and transformation. The "unclean spirits" of the subconscious, which make his heart suffer, are losing their grip on his conscious mind. In time, these swine will weaken into a dormant state from his conscious neglect of them. He will replace them with virtues on the journey home.

It appears necessary for virtually all of us, like the Prodigal Son, to discover through our own unique experiences that the illusions of egotism simply do not work. While theoretically possible, it is exceedingly rare for any person to "come to himself" without the stimulus of a certain amount of pain and suffering. The time this process takes and the intensity of the associated suffering vary greatly from one soul to another. Buddhist philosophy actually rests on the premise that suffering exists as a universal fact of human experience. This is the "First Noble Truth" of Buddhism.

This suffering need not go on forever, regardless of what the external circumstances of one's life may be. At some point we gain the capacity to choose how we want to live. As Daskalos says, we may live consciously in love, light, and joy or we may continue to live subconsciously in darkness, driven by the "whips of destiny." With the acceptance of salvation, there is created in the heart an immediate expansion of consciousness and a longing to return to the Source of life. The awakening personality finds ways to look consciously at the elementals of separation it has created in the lower centers. It then dis-identifies with them through a process that says, "I created you, but I am not you. I don't need you any more." It creates virtue, or positive elementals, in their place. However we go about the process, it is the intention to "arise and go to my Father" that is key.

> And he arose, and came to his father. But when he was yet a great way off, his father saw him, and had compassion, and ran, and fell on his neck, and kissed him. And the son said unto him, "Father, I have sinned against heaven, and in thy sight, and am no more worthy to be called thy son."

The Prodigal Son has now ascended to the fifth chakra domain, that realm of consciousness where devotional love extends itself to others and the personality expresses its truth fearlessly. It might be considered the realm of conscious relationship, where communication flows freely and truthfully out of a conscious heart connection. The father runs a great distance to meet the son and embraces him, expressing that "joy in heaven over one sinner that repenteth, more than over ninety and nine just persons, which need no repentance." (Luke 15:7) The son, feeling unworthy of this compassion, expresses the remorse he feels for having been such a foolish ingrate. He is really asking for forgiveness.

These few lines from the parable reveal the essential ingredients in psychotherapy, and in any successful relationship, for that matter. Progress will flow from even the most ego-based systems of therapy if the therapist genuinely cares about the client and the client is genuinely motivated to express his or her truth and change his or her mind about "Who I am." Effective psychotherapy, or repentance, brings "unclean spirits" and the "sins" they provoke into the conscious and compassionate embrace of the therapist. Each of these "demons," if examined closely, will reveal in hiding some angelic virtue that is waiting for an opportunity to emerge and find expression in the personality. Within the father's embrace, a son of rebellious disloyalty and ingratitude is transformed into a son of unsurpassed devotion and loving appreciation.

> But the father said to his servants, "Bring forth the best robe, and put it on him; and put a ring on his hand, and shoes on his feet: and bring hither the fatted calf, and kill it; and let us eat, and be merry: For this my son was dead, and is alive again; he was lost, and is found.

With continued devotion to love and truth, and their extension in service, consciousness expands into that state which Daskalos calls Self-consciousness. This is that perception of the self as Spirit-ego-self, or Christ Self. With the perception of self as Spirit comes the perception of others as Spirit; this is that sixth chakra realm of expansion called forgiveness of which Jesus and Shankara spoke so passionately. It is the domain of final resignation to the truth, which the Prodigal Son now enters. Self-consciousness still holds onto a dualistic me-you perception, but marks the early stages of true personality transformation.

How can the personality, which has only seen itself through ego function as a network of elementals, come to see itself as that which is beyond mind and its creations altogether? According to Daskalos we can only see the higher spirit Self by a process of reflection. As noted in Chapter 2, the higher mind, or "mind of Christ," serves as a mirror to reflect the Christ Self into our awareness. How clearly we can see and know the Christ Self as our true Self depends on the quality of the "mental mirror." The quality is refined by an ongoing process of purification, i.e., the creation of virtuous thought forms within each chakra domain to replace the "unclean spirits" which mar the purity of the mind at that level. The greater the purity of mind within any domain, the easier and more natural it is for the Christ light to reflect itself into our awareness and the less likely we will identify with elementals at this level. This is the real goal of virtue so far as the soul is concerned. A virtue is not a virtue if the ego looks at it directly and identifies with it. In this case the elemental is a "strength" of the personality, or inflated negative elemental.

Forgiveness' great challenge lies in the necessity of eventually extending it to everyone without exception and in every conceivable situation. If forgiveness is not radical and all-encompassing, we find ourselves in the impossible predicament of singling out people in whom Spirit is *not* present. This is the reason that Jesus gave his disciples such unprecedented instructions as the following:

> "Ye have heard that it hath been said, 'Thou shalt love thy neighbor, and hate thine enemy.' But I say unto you, 'Love your enemies, bless them that curse you, do good to them that hate you, and pray for them which despitefully use you, and persecute you; that ye may be the children of your Father which is in heaven."
> (Matt. 5:43-45)

The Prodigal Son has achieved the forgiveness he seeks. The father sees beneath his son's surface human flaws to the reality of his true nature. He honors his son as he would a divine being, as he pours forth the spirit of that beautiful Indian greeting, "Namaste!" ("to the divine in you"). The Prodigal Son is safely on the path to enlightenment.

> *And they began to be merry.*

With wholehearted devotion to love and truth and the achievement of consistent forgiveness toward all beings, the personality finally breaks into the state which Daskalos calls Self-superconsciousness. This is the realm of unified consciousness, or atonement, in which the personality *knows* itself to be in a state of *at-one-ment* with All-That-Is, yet maintains an individual identity. At first this state of enlightenment may be achieved in fleeting glimpses only. When enlightenment does become stabilized, still higher and higher levels of unified awareness and truth comprehension are left to be achieved. These enigmatic realms of divine potential lie within the seventh chakra domain and above. Daskalos also refers to this final God-knowing experience as *theosis.*[5]

This is the realm the Prodigal Son has now entered, a mystical state of oneness and merriment in the light of Christ. Atonement marks the beginning of true universe citizenship and an eternal "cosmic career" of co-creation with God. It is the crowning achievement of the soul. Unconditional love reigns supreme in the personality and nothing is unforgiven. Eternity itself cannot exhaust the limitless potential of the Christ Self.

The Symbolic Journey of Transformation

The levels of consciousness may be summarized on this diagram of the present-day personality, still "crucified" and awaiting healing of its separation from God in awareness:

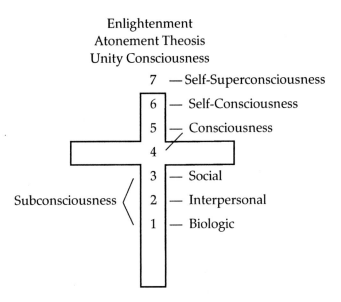

The "Fall" of Adam and Eve was presented allegorically in Chapter 3 as our own fall in awareness. This fall was depicted symbolically as ego separation followed by personality crucifixion. As noted earlier, these symbols could be used in the same manner to depict the departure of the Prodigal Son into the "land of famine" and his suffering there. Now that the Prodigal Son has returned to the Father, the healing of the separation and journey of transformation as it applies to all of us will be symbolized as well.

The process of healing begins the moment we "come to ourselves" and invite the presence of the Christ Self into awareness through faith. This is salvation, the entrance into the state of conscious self-determination by an act of will. As we "arise and go to the father," we make our own decisions intelligently under the inspiration of the Christ Self rather than subconsciously, under the domination of negative elementals of the lower chakra domains. As we dis-identify with these "unclean spirits," they begin to weaken and lose their grasp on our minds. In their place we create virtues at every chakra domain to purify the mind, as below:

Negative Elementals of Separation	Corresponding Virtues of Healing
Root Chakra (#1)—"I'm unworthy to exist."	"I have infinite worth as a Child of God."
Sacral Chakra (#2)—"I'm vulnerable in relationships."	"I trust every other Child of God."
Solar Plexus Chakra (#3)—"I'm helpless."	"I can do all things through Christ which strengtheneth me." (Philippians 4:13)
Heart Chakra (#4)—"I suffer."	"As love incarnate, I care for my neighbor and all creation as my Self."
Throat Chakra (#5)—"I must lie to get what I want."	"I express my truth freely and fearlessly."
Brow Chakra (#6)—"I perceive only imperfection."	"I perceive the perfection of Spirit within all beings."
Crown Chakra (#7)—"Life has no higher purpose."	"I am an eternal co-creator with God."

The mind becomes progressively clearer and more refined, serving as a mirror to reflect one's own Spirit Self and that of others into our awareness. Forgiveness naturally unfolds as we identify more and more with Spirit and less with our elemental creations of mind. Consciousness expands.

This process of healing and transformation is symbolized below by the cross (the present-day personality) within the star (the soul—the divine and human natures reunited), and both within the circle of atonement (the unlimited possibilities of ever-expanding unity consciousness, or enlightenment):

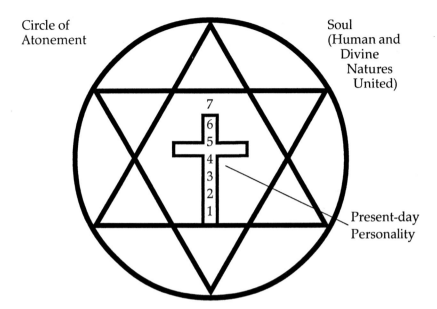

Circle of Atonement

Soul (Human and Divine Natures United)

Present-day Personality

Once all things have been forgiven and the personality breaks into the realm of atonement, the conditions of mind that created the suffering of the present-day personality no longer exist. The cross may now return "to the dust from which it came." (Genesis 3:19) The permanent personality, one with its own soul, resurrects from the dust of the present-day personality and knows itself to be at one with all creation in the light of Christ. The soul has reunited consciously in the Garden which it never really left, but with the experiential knowledge of itself as the incarnation of love, symbolized below:

Enlightened Permanent Personality

Understanding Zorba

I dance the pain until it stands
in acrid drops like olive brine
upon my face

I dance the crystalline tears
that long ago turned
my shoulders into stone

I dance the sorrow
of love turned to hatred
and hatred to indifference

I dance the fear of
loneliness and the anguish
of abandonment

I dance the anger
until it rages free
and runs down my arms
like rivers

I dance the disappointment
of expectations unfulfilled
and dreams too long
deferred

I dance all my demons
into dust beneath my feet
sweeping them away
in spiraling centrifuge

Only then can I dance
that which sings
the heart and blood

In the space
between the spaces
that lie between the words

Where words have no meaning
I dance and joy IS . . .

                                        Donna Overall

VII

AWAKENING LOVE
CONSCIOUSLY
Nine Directions Home

The Decision to Return

Separation takes as many illusory forms as there are human beings, though it tends to occur along the general lines discussed previously. At whatever time and circumstances the light dims in awareness and the "inner Judas" assumes control of the personality, the experience of love diminishes and suffering ensues. This "Fall" in awareness from grace and the egotism which maintains the ignorance are subconscious processes. The return home, however, must be undertaken consciously. As in the "Parable of the Prodigal Son," this decision for salvation is typically made under the pressure and disillusionment of a certain amount of suffering—the suffering that invariably arises from ignorance. The grace of the inner Christ light awaits only our decision to accept it back into consciousness by faith.

The saving awareness of the inner light leads to a profound change of mind about "who I am" and "what I want to create in my life." The Greek word *metanoia* signifies primarily a "change of mind" and translates into the English "repentance." The concept of repentance has fallen into some disrepute in modern times because of its undertones of religiosity. Genuine repentance, however, does not mean that one sees oneself as "bad" and decides to be "good." Rather it is to drop all notions of "good" and "bad" completely and accept one's true holiness as a son or daughter of God. Repentance is not just contrition or remorse, but more fundamentally the alignment of one's whole being with God. Repentance meets grace in the heart and the journey of healing and transformation is underway.

Salvation and healing are ultimately consequences of free will choice, as has been emphasized. The two most distinguishing characteristics of human beings are ego self-awareness and free will. No power or personality in heaven or on earth can interfere with our God-given right to see ourselves and construct our personal realities as we choose. So powerful and fundamental to reality is the human will that one might merely say with finality, "I choose to awaken love in my heart," and it would immediately be so. Buddha's enlightenment under the Bodhi tree occurred as a result of such a supreme and final intention. Yet even Buddha did not reach this point of readiness until he had struggled for years on paths that seemed futile.[1]

Finding the Way

Readiness for the final leap into atonement, or "Buddhahood," is fostered by gaining awareness of the blind spots in one's personality, then acting consciously to forgive, or bring light to these hidden places. The personality finds them very comfortable to ignore, however. Without conscious focus on one's "inner Judas," the spiritual seeker may simply intensify the awareness of light where it is already present. Thus may he or she avoid any real challenges to the present-day personality and actually use spirituality as an escape from genuine healing. Illumination of one's shadow is always disconcerting and is accompanied by a certain amount of turmoil and confusion. The "unlearning" involved in growth toward the light should therefore be undertaken as consciously as possible.

Enneagram theory is helpful because it can lead one to identify the core vice, often unrecognized, around which the present-day personality is organized. It is a metaphysical law that energy follows thought; so the more attention is focused on the core elemental, the more it is vitalized. The only effective route to freedom from this vice's control is to replace it actively with its corresponding virtue. As Paul said, "Be not overcome of evil, but overcome evil with good." (Romans 12:21)

Virtue is created in accordance with spiritual principle, and one or more spiritual principles can be identified which direct the creation of any given virtue. By extension, the same principle governs the direction of the personality type whose mission it is to create that virtue. The virtue is experienced

as a bodily-felt sensation of truth and expressed as spontaneous, unpre-
meditated acts of goodness. These expressions are the direct reflections of
the Spirit-ego-self into one's daily life. They are the highest and most natural
expressions of ethical behavior, because they arise not so much out of a
sense of duty as the intention to love. Virtuous expression is not concerned
about proving the self; this is the domain of the separated ego.

Humanity's highest spiritual longings lie in the quest to align ourselves
with the high spiritual principles that govern our lives and all creation. The
prayer that Jesus taught his disciples, known as "The Lord's Prayer," expresses these longings:

> *Our Father which art in heaven, Hallowed be thy name. Thy kingdom come.
> Thy will be done in earth, as it is in heaven. Give us this day our daily bread. And
> forgive us our debts, as we forgive our debtors. And lead us not into temptation, but
> deliver us from evil: For thine is the kingdom, and the power, and the glory, for
> ever. Amen.* (Matthew 6:9-13)

Bennett has shown a correlation between the Lord's prayer and the
nine points of the Enneagram.[2] Nine specific instructions, each applicable to
one of the nine points, can be identified within The Lord's Prayer to help
each personality type understand the spiritual principle(s) which govern its
existence. This instruction can direct the personality toward the creation of
its core virtue out of the wound of its core vice. "In our pathology is our
salvation."

The ascension from subconscious enslavement toward the freedom of
atonement, as discussed in "The Parable of the Prodigal Son," is the vertical
element of transformation that is symbolized by the upright beam of the
cross. At each chakra domain the personality is focused on a particular area
of learning and mastery. At the same time a horizontal development is
taking place at each chakra based on the duality of the male and female
experience of life. Chinese theory refers to the archetypal male principle as
yang and the archetypal female as yin; Carl Jung refers to the male arche-
type as the animus and the female the anima. This horizontal range of
experience is symbolized by the horizontal beam of the cross, the right half
representing the male, or yang, direction and the left half the female, or yin.
The yang, or male, domain includes left-brained experiences, outer realities,
abstract reasoning, intellect, objectivity, activity, duty, work, science, and
the like. The yin includes right-brained experiences, inner realities, intuition, emotion, subjectivity, receptivity, art, play, sensuality, music.

The Healing Mandala

The symbol of healing may be adapted specifically to each of the nine personality types so as to depict the ideal flow of healing currents for each type. In this manner the symbol may function as a mandala for its associated personality. A mandala is a symbolic visual representation of the flow of spiritual energies. It is typically circular with balanced geometric patterns and is used to facilitate contemplation on given themes. Traditionally the use of mandalas has been associated mainly with Tibetan Buddhism.

The healing mandala, as it will be used in the context of this book, displays at the top of the cross the instruction from the Lord's Prayer and the spiritual principle(s) connected to this instruction. The core vice is shown at the foot of the cross and the ideal yin and yang qualities to be developed on the crossbeam. To a large extent it is the particular quality of the male-female expansion that gives direction to the transformational process. The core virtue, or "soul task for self-realization," is shown at the heart chakra where the beams intersect. Visually it is evident why love in the heart is central to the transformation process and why personality unification most effectively and reliably occurs at this level. The heart is the meeting point of the personality's ascent through repentance and Spirit's descent into the personality through grace. It is also the point of "divine marriage" between the archetypal male and female aspects of the personality. The heart is the "command center" of the soul, because it is the point where the Son of Man unites with the Son of God and the animus joins the anima.

The personality, once unified and expanding at the heart, can continue moving upward in consciousness toward atonement, still expanding, without sacrificing any of its gains. Premature vertical ascension, without concomitant emotional, physical, interpersonal, and social development, may produce a state of mind that is blissful and enchanting, yet disconnected from the human nature and destabilizing. Like the mythical Icarus, there is the likelihood that the personality will fly too close to the sun with "wings of wax" and come crashing back to earth when the wings melt. Integrated development at the heart will fortify the "wings" of mortal experience, allowing a safe and confident ascent to the higher realms of God-consciousness. The awakened heart will not leave any part of oneself behind on the journey, because it is joined to all. It demands that one bring the body, emotions, and mind along, even as it extends a hand to others along the way.

When the personality is moving toward its qualities of resilience, according to Enneagram theory, it is moving generally in the direction of its core integrating virtue at the heart. It does so in terms of both its ascent and its horizontal expansion. When it regresses toward its shadow side, it tends to entrench more deeply into the separation of its core vice, postponing its enlightenment and prolonging its suffering. The direction of transformation and regression for each personality type are given in the Enneagram summary charts in the Appendix.

The general structure of the healing mandala is pictured. A specific discussion of each of the nine personality types will follow. For the purpose of these presentations, the cross alone will be extracted from the healing mandala and used to present the particulars of the energetic flow toward healing for each type. Each discussion will include a particular instruction from the Lord's Prayer and a parable or example from the life of Jesus which aids practical understanding of this instruction. From these instructions and their examples will be derived guiding spiritual principle(s) for the personality type. Quotations or lessons from some spiritual tradition and relevant brief discussion will follow for each. The direction of transformation and regression will be noted as well as the soul type and transformed self for each personality type.

Each discussion will end with a practical exercise specific for the healing of that particular pattern of wounding. All of these exercises may be done regardless of one's personality type and at any time, perhaps as part of a nine step program. Each of us has experienced, to a greater or lesser degree, the patterns of separation for every other type.

THE HEALING MANDALA

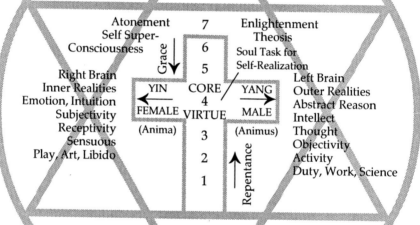

GUIDING
SPIRITUAL PRINCIPLES

Atonement   7   Enlightenment
Self Super-   Theosis
Consciousness   6   Soul Task for
     Grace   5   Self-Realization

Right Brain   Left Brain
Inner Realities   YIN   CORE   YANG   Outer Realities
Emotion, Intuition   4   Abstract Reason
Subjectivity   FEMALE   VIRTUE   MALE   Intellect
Receptivity   (Anima)   3   (Animus)   Thought
Sensuous   Objectivity
Play, Art, Libido   2   Activity
         1   Repentance   Duty, Work, Science

CORE
VICE

CORE VICE - LAZINESS
PERSONALITY EXPRESSION OF THE PRODIGAL SON:
THE NEGLECTED SELF

Instruction: "Our Father"

Examples: The Vine and the Branches, The Parable of the Lost Sheep

"I am the vine, ye are the branches: He that abideth in me, and I in him, the same bringeth forth much fruit: for without me ye can do nothing. If a man abide not in me, he is cast forth as a branch, and is withered; and men gather them, and cast them into the fire, and they are burned. If ye abide in me, and my words abide in you, ye shall ask what ye will, and it shall be done unto you. Herein is my Father glorified, that ye bear much fruit; so shall ye be my disciples." (John 15:5-8))

"If a man have an hundred sheep, and one of them be gone astray, doth he not leave the ninety and nine, and goeth into the mountains, and seeketh that which is gone astray? And if so be that he find it, verily I say unto you, he rejoiceth more of that sheep, than of the ninety and nine which went not astray. Even so it is not the will of your Father which is in heaven, that one of these little ones should perish." (Matthew 18:12-14)

Lesson: The Principle of Oneness

The Principle of Oneness is a spiritual principle that arises directly from the very fact of our Father's existence. The reality of a Creator mandates that all creation arises from him and is therefore one forever. As souls endowed with the spirit of this same Creator-Father, our life itself flows from this Vine of which we are branches. The fruit we each are asked to bear in partnership with God is sacred fruit; one branch is not more or less important than another. Our Father will seek out the lowliest of his children gone astray, because each is essential to complete the whole, even his own Self.

Discussion

The soul task for the Neglected Self is to resolve the dichotomy between merging as one and expressing oneself uniquely within the divine unity. It is to stay connected in awareness to the vine while simultaneously appreciating oneself as a unique branch that is called to bear its own fruit purposefully. Only love in the heart can solve this divine dilemma. Once the "lost" personality feels the focused love of the Good Shepherd, it will naturally see the folly in neglecting its own self. Only through deep appreciation of its own Self can it merge meaningfully in love with God and the rest of creation.

This consciousness is expressed by the Sufi (mystical Islamic) writer Shaykh Bahauddin Ibrahim Ata-ullah Ansari, who says:

> When the sufi is cleansed from the rust of lust and of nature, his heart is purified and his spirit emerges out of all mundane relations, in the love of God, his affair rests at the disposal of the Almighty. The sufi can do anything he likes by the command of God.
>
> In this state whatever the sufi does he does it by the Command of God; whatever he says, he says it by God's Command; and whatever he sees he sees by His Command. This state has been termed "Ittisaf," (viz., the state of being adorned with the attributes of God). . . .
>
> When iron is put into fire it assumes the attribute of fire; it is even called fire; it comes to have the same properties as fire has. It can burn other things. [3]

Shah Isma'il Shahid comments further on the above statement:

> This piece of iron is in reality iron only, but, due to the great numbers of the flames of fire, its nature concealed itself along with its properties and effects; the same effects and properties began to emanate from it which flow from fire. Even this, strictly speaking, will not be right; what should be said is that these effects are now emanating from the fire alone, which is surrounding the iron-piece. But since the fire has made this iron-piece its mount and has regarded it as its throne of kingdom, its effects and properties can be related with the iron-piece. Consequently the verses: "I did it not of my own accord. . . So thy Lord desired" point to the same state.
>
> In brief, had this iron-piece been gifted with the power of speech, it would have with a hundred tongues vociferously announced its identification with the very essence of fire, forgetting its reality for a while, while it might have cried out, "I am a ember of the blazing fire; I am that alone on which depend the works of blacksmiths, cooks and all artisans and all technicians." Similarly, when the billows of Divine attraction drive the perfect self of the devotee into the unfathomable depth of the ocean of Unity, he cries out involuntarily:
> "I am God' (Ana'l Haqq)
> "Within my vesture is naught but God
> "Glory to me, how sublime is my majesty
> "I am the Sole Actor in the world." [4]

Transformation, Expansion, and Regression

When the Neglected Self is transformed into the Minister of Purpose it expresses purposeful action and it shows self-initiative and right action in life situations. It is present and self-motivated for self-development. It expresses its strengths, talents and abilities and individuality grows. The "male," or yang, expansion is self-motivation and self-direction. The "female," or yin, expansion involves self-recognition and self-sufficiency.

When the Neglected Self resists transformation it entrenches more deeply into its vice, laziness or self-forgetting. It shows confusion, paralysis, and self-sabotage, becoming ambivalent about taking right action. It becomes afraid of worst-case scenarios, amplifying fear and external conditions to overwhelming proportions.

These energetic trends are consistent with Enneagram personality type nine.

Soul Type: Angelic

Separated Self	**Transforming Principle**	**Transformed Self**
The Neglected Self	The Principle of Oneness	Minister of Purpose

---

Exercise for The Neglected Self: "Our Father"

Take a deep breath and relax.

Look at a person that you feel you have neglected or left unrecognized for their contribution to you. Allow yourself to feel the situation and circumstance clearly. As you look at this person, look deeply into their eyes and imagine that you come out of your body and step into their body.

Look back through their eyes at yourself. As you look back at yourself, how does it feel to be ignored and unseen?

Now, step back into your body and look through your own eyes again, back at the person you were excluding. Now become your loving self, feel the Christ love with you, and send out your love to that person you neglected and touch their heart. See their love. Recognize your oneness with them.

MINISTER OF PURPOSE
"Our Father"

PRINCIPLE OF
ONENESS

Grace ↓

Self-Sufficiency
Self-
Recognition

Yin ← LOVE AS PURPOSEFUL ACTION → Yang

Self-Motivation
Self-Direction

Repentance ↑

LAZINESS
The Neglected Self

CORE VICE – SELF-RIGHTEOUS ANGER
PERSONALITY EXPRESSION OF THE PRODIGAL SON:
THE CRITICAL SELF

Instruction: "Which art in heaven"

Example: Parable—Treasure in a Field

> The kingdom of heaven is like unto treasure hid in a field; the which when a man hath found, he hideth, and for joy thereof goeth and selleth all that he hath, and buyeth that field. (Matthew 13:44)

Lesson: The Principle of Self-Sufficiency, The Principle of the Growth of Love

Daskalos teaches that Absolute Infinite Beingness, or God, exists in a state of Absolute Self-sufficiency. Everything needed for existence or self-expression can be found within Absolute Beingness. Final authority over all creation comes from Absolute Beingness as well. That individualized bestowal of Absolute Beingness, the Spirit-ego-self, is eternally present within each human soul to guide us with the same divine authority while attending at the same time to our every need. The Spirit-ego-self is that "treasure in the field" for which the man sells all that he has and buys the field itself. The treasure assures him of absolute self-sufficiency forever. Jesus said, "Neither shall they say, 'Lo here!' or 'lo there!' for, behold, the kingdom of God is within you." (Luke 17:21)

Jesus also said, "Be ye perfect, even as your Father which is in heaven is perfect." (Matthew 5:48) It is notable that he said "Be perfect" rather than "Do perfect." To be perfect is to claim the perfection of the "treasure in the field," the kingdom of heaven within and accept its guidance. Paradoxically, to be perfect in this sense is to acknowledge our human limitations and recognize that no matter what we do, or how much we grow toward love, we can never achieve the final perfection of the Christ Self outside of eternity. Perfection of our divine nature implies imperfection of the human nature. Recognition of the treasure in the field will lead us naturally to honor it by cultivating the field itself, our human nature, as beautifully as possible. Step by step, lifetime after lifetime, we grow toward the finality of love that is held in the depths of the divine and perfect Christ Self.

Discussion

These spiritual principles governing divine perfection in creation give very useful direction to the journey of The Critical Self. The Critical Self fails to abide by these principles when it seeks authority and standards of perfection outside itself rather than within. It seeks to achieve love by doing perfectly according to these arbitrary external standards rather than simply accepting the love that is already there. A person in this trap loses touch with his or her true Self, leading to dissatisfaction with life, emptiness, frustration, irritability, and compulsive behavior.

The soul task of the Critical Self is to achieve peace of mind by turning to the perfection of absolute beingness within. Knowing that he or she is evolving toward this inner perfection, but will never actually reach it fully in experience, he/she can take time to relax, enjoy life, and find pleasure in simply being. Wholeness becomes more important than perfection. Out of such serenity will flow a quality of action and achievement that the transforming personality would have hardly believed possible. Lao Tzu well understood the paradoxical relationship between being and doing, between divine perfection and human imperfection, as illustrated in these passages from the Taoist classic, the *Tao Te Ching:*

> True perfection seems imperfect,
> yet it is perfectly itself.
> True fullness seems empty,
> yet it is fully present.
>
> True straightness seems crooked.
> True wisdom seems foolish.
> True art seems artless.
>
> The Master allows things to happen.
> She shapes events as they come.
> She steps out of the way
> and lets the Tao (the Way) speak for itself...
>
> The Master acts without doing anything
> and teaches without saying anything.
> Things arise and she lets them come;
> things disappear and she lets them go.
> She has but doesn't possess,
> acts but doesn't expect.
> When her work is done, she forgets it.
> That is why it lasts forever. [5]

Transformation, Expansion, and Regression

When the Critical Self is transformed into the Compassionate Comforter it achieves tranquility and in so doing it becomes more playful, optimistic, inventive, creative, and productive. He or she begins to accept the necessary limitations of reality and starts to enjoy life. Expansion in the yang direction produces manifestation of ideals, compassionate support, and decisive action. Yin expansion results in play, spontaneity, inner harmony, surrender of effort, and adaptive behavior.

When the Critical Self resists transformation it becomes more embroiled in its vice of self-righteous anger and it becomes disillusioned with ideals, depressed, self-destructive, and angry with life as it is. He/she feels like a misfit and is envious of those who appear to be fulfilled.

These energetic trends are consistent with Enneagram personality type one.

Soul Type: Angelic

Separated Self	Transforming Principle	Transformed Self
The Critical Self	Principle of Self-sufficiency	The Compassionate
	Principle of the Growth of Love	Comforter

Exercise for The Critical Self: "Which art in heaven"

Close your eyes. Breathe deeply.

Allow yourself to look in front of you into a full length mirror. Feel your desire to realize true perfection and autonomy in your life. Imagine the doors of the mirror opening, leading you onto a path into a beautiful garden temple of light.

As you look within the temple, call on the Christ Self to appear to you. Allow him to place his hand onto your heart. Feel his love as your own love. He says to you, "Somewhere in this temple garden is buried the treasure of your Selfhood, the priceless pearl that you are. Would you like to find it?"

Allow him to take you by the hand and let him show you where it is. Once you have found it, take it into your heart and ask a question about your life. Receive an answer. If the answer does not come immediately, ask to be shown in time or given an outer sign that allows your understanding to unfold.

THE COMPASSIONATE COMFORTER
"Which art in heaven""

PRINCIPLE OF SELF-SUFFICIENCY
PRINCIPLE OF THE GROWTH OF LOVE

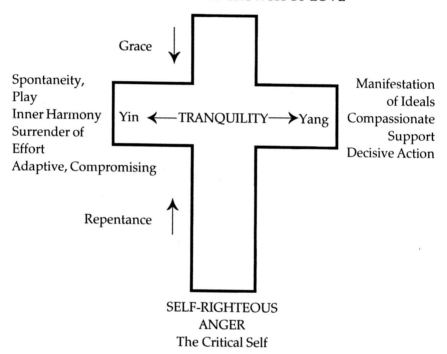

Grace

Spontaneity,
Play
Inner Harmony   Yin ←——TRANQUILITY——→Yang
Surrender of
Effort
Adaptive, Compromising

Manifestation
of Ideals
Compassionate
Support
Decisive Action

Repentance

SELF-RIGHTEOUS
ANGER
The Critical Self

CORE VICE – PRIDE
PERSONALITY EXPRESSION OF THE PRODIGAL SON:
THE SACRIFICING SELF

Instruction: "Hallowed be thy name"

Examples: Parable of the Talents, The Great Commandment

For the kingdom of heaven is as a man traveling into a far country, who called his own servants, and delivered unto them his goods. And unto one he gave five talents, to another two, and to another one; to every man according to his several ability; and straightway took his journey.

Then he that had received the five talents went and traded with the same, and made them other five talents. And likewise he that had received two, he also gained other two. But he that had received one went and digged in the earth, and hid his lord's money.

After a long time the lord of those servants cometh, and reckoneth with them. And so he that had received five talents came and brought other five talents, saying, "Lord, thou deliveredst unto me five talents: behold, I have gained beside them five talents more." His lord said unto him, "Well done, thou good and faithful servant: thou hast been faithful over a few things, I will make thee ruler over many things: enter thou into the joy of thy lord."

He also that had received two talents came and said, "Lord, thou deliveredst unto me two talents: behold, I have gained two other talents beside them." His lord said unto him, "Well done, good and faithful servant; thou hast been faithful over a few things, I will make thee ruler over many things: enter thou into the joy of thy lord."

Then he which had received the one talent came and said, "Lord, I knew thee that thou art an hard man, reaping where thou hast not sown, and gathering where thou hast not strawed: And I was afraid, and went and hid thy talent in the earth: lo, there thou hast that is thine."

His lord answered and said unto him, "'Thou wicked and slothful servant, thou knewest that I reap where I sowed not, and gather where I have not strawed: Thou oughtest therefore to have put my money to the exchangers, and then at my coming I should have received mine own with usury. Take therefore the talent from him, and give it unto him which hath ten talents. For unto every one that hath shall be given, and he shall have abundance: but from him that hath not shall be taken away even that which he hath." (Matthew 25:14-29)

A lawyer once asked Jesus, "Master, which is the great commandment in the law?"

Jesus said unto him, "Thou shalt love the Lord thy God with all thy heart, and with all thy soul, and with all thy mind. This is the first and great commandment. And the second is like unto it, Thou shalt love thy neighbor as thyself. On these two commandments hang all the law and the prophets." (Matthew 22:36-40)

Lesson: The Principle of the Grace of God, The Principle of Love

Grace and love are too close to the Heart of God to be meaningfully defined in words. It can be safely said, however, that The Principle of the Grace of God and The principle of Love operate in complete reversal to the laws of the world. This is the reason that The Parable of the Talents, a parable about grace, makes no sense when interpreted from a material point of view. The talents, or grace, are given to each servant according to his "ability," which may be interpreted as his ability to receive. The ability to receive is actually a measure of gratitude. The two servants who doubled their talents did so by sharing according to the Principle of Love: The love in one's heart grows to the extent it is freely given away. They followed the "great commandment" in their love of the Lord and the second, "to love thy neighbor as thyself." The servant who buried his talent never really received it; otherwise he would have shared it and it would have grown according to the true nature of love. His flaw was ingratitude and the pride that it implies.

In a sense grace and love define one another. Grace is the free, unlimited, and spontaneous sharing of love. Grace gives freely because of love's unconditional nature—it expects nothing in return. Love naturally extends itself through grace, because it grows by so doing. Gratitude is the most natural response to the love of God, and it is the means by which the heart opens to receive even more love. "For unto every one that hath shall be given, and he shall have abundance."

Humility is the knowledge of being sustained by grace. True humility knows one's own needs at every moment in life while giving thanks at the same time for the grace which is present to meet these needs. As Jesus said, "Your Father knoweth what things ye have need of, before ye ask him." (Matthew 6:8) Grace, however, cannot be contained to the meeting of one's own needs. It overflows naturally to others in loving service, making no demands on anyone. The flow of love returns from the world in ever greater abundance and gratitude abounds, continuing the cycle. Contained in "Hallowed be thy name" is the highest prayer, because it is a prayer of gratitude and humility. Grace sustains us, grace awakens us, and grace guides us to ourselves—effortlessly.

Discussion

Grace and love represent the single greatest challenge to egotism's clever ways, so the ego often likes to rise to the challenge via that "demon disguised as an angel of light" called pride. By appearing selfless and noble, The Sacrificing Self has discovered a particularly insidious way to cut itself off from awareness of the grace of God. While giving freely with one hand, the other hand is maneuvering to take back love it believes it doesn't have. This kind of giving is sometimes called egocentric generosity, because it is giving to get. The Sacrificing Self represses awareness of its real needs, avoiding the grace that would meet these needs. It tries to push the separated self to the forefront, yet covers up its intentions through the appearance of noble self-sacrifice. It is no wonder that martyrdom has taken such a hold on us collectively, through religious egotism, as well as individually in our daily lives!

Martyrdom rapidly loses its appeal to the Sacrificing Self in transformation, whose well-nurtured heart is becoming an engine of holiness. In harmony with the Principles of Grace and Love, this heart generates love perpetually and bountifully through gratitude, humility, unrestrained generosity, and service. This transformed personality, now the Humble Servant, understands the true meaning of this advice from Jesus: "Whosoever will be chief among you, let him be your servant." (Matthew 20:27)

The Apostle John said, "We love him, because he first loved us." (1 John 4:19) The love and grace of God are lauded in this tribute by the eleventh century Persian mystic Abu Hamid Al-Ghazali:

> Man loves God because of the affinity between the human soul and its source, for it shares in the divine nature and attributes, because through knowledge and love it can attain to eternal life and itself become Godlike. Such love, when it has grown strong and overwhelming, is called passion, which is love firmly established and limitless. It is reasonable to give this passionate love to that One from whom all good things are seen to come. In truth, there is nothing good or beautiful or beloved in this world that does not come from his lovingkindness and is not the gift of his grace, a draught from the sea of his bounty. For all that is good and just and lovely in the world, perceived by the intellect and the sight and the hearing and the rest of the senses, from the creation of the world until it shall pass away, from the summit of the Pleiades to the ends of the earth, is just a particle from the treasure of his riches and a ray from the splendor of his glory. Is it not reasonable to love him who is thus described, and is it not comprehensible that those who have mystic knowledge of his attributes should love him more and more until their love passes all bounds? To use the term

"passion" for it is indeed wrong, for it fails to express the greatness of their love for him.

Glory be to him, who is concealed from sight by the brightness of his light. If he had not veiled himself with seventy veils of light, the splendors of his countenance would surely consume the eyes of those who contemplate the beauty which is his. [6]

John goes on to say, "If a man say, 'I love God,' and hateth his brother, he is a liar: for he that loveth not his brother whom he hath seen, how can he love God whom he hath not seen? And this commandment have we from him, 'That he who loveth God love his brother also.'" (1 John 4:20-21) Love and service are the cornerstones of the gospel of Jesus.

Transformation, Expansion, and Regression

When the Sacrificing Self transforms into the Humble Servant it begins to accept real needs as valid and feels worthy to receive love. It becomes more autonomous, creative, and unique in its expression. The drive to constantly self-sacrifice weakens.

Expanding in the yang direction, it becomes independent, creatively motivated for self-fulfillment, and learns to give love authentically. Yin expansion brings true empathy and genuine appreciation of others' needs, self-appreciation, and the ability to receive love authentically.

When the Sacrificing Self resists transformation it moves deeper into its vice of noble egotism and it will erupt angrily over unfulfilled needs, becoming vengeful and vindictive. It sabotages opportunities to receive from others. It feels dominated and struggles over issues of dependency vs. freedom. It tends to develop psychosomatic disorders as indirect expressions of stress and lack of fulfillment. It develops aggressive responses to underlying feelings of helplessness and fear, demanding attention and a sense of being valued, secure, and cared for.

The energetic trends above are consistent with Enneagram personality type two.

Soul Type: Heroic

Separated Self	Transforming Principle	Transformed Self
The Sacrificing Self	Principle of the Grace of God	The Humble Servant
	Principle of Love	

Exercise for The Sacrificing Self: "Hallowed be thy name"

One of the exercises you can do to get back into attunement with humility is to go out into nature, into the woods. Go to a quiet place where there is just nature and silence. There you have nothing to reach out or grasp for, no words. Just ask yourself one question in the silence.

Who am I?

Second exercise.

Close your eyes and breathe deeply.

Visualize yourself at home in your daily life, in your daily thoughts, feelings, actions, your desires and passions. Imagine at the border of your property a deep cliff or chasm. Across this cliff is a sturdy bridge. Walk to the center of the bridge and ask yourself, "If I were to cross the bridge into an entirely new life-space (i.e., an undeveloped property), what would I desire to take with me?"

Thereafter see yourself stepping to the end of the bridge. There stands your guardian angel. Now once again ask him/her as you look into his/her eyes, "What do I really need to take with me into my new cycle of life (new beginnings)? What can I let go of?"

THE HUMBLE SERVANT
"Hallowed be thy name""

PRINCIPLE OF THE GRACE OF GOD
PRINCIPLE OF LOVE

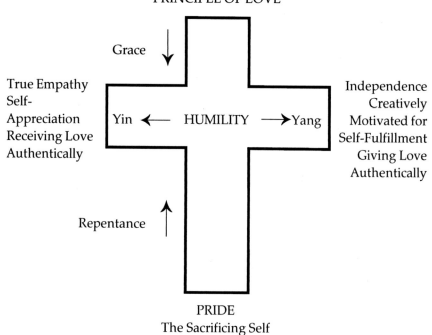

Grace

True Empathy
Self-
Appreciation   Yin ← HUMILITY → Yang
Receiving Love
Authentically

Independence
Creatively
Motivated for
Self-Fulfillment
Giving Love
Authentically

Repentance

PRIDE
The Sacrificing Self

CORE VICE – DISHONESTY
PERSONALITY EXPRESSION OF THE PRODIGAL SON:
THE SUCCESS-DRIVEN SELF

Instruction: "Thy kingdom come"

Example: Parable of the Sower

> Behold, a sower went forth to sow; and when he sowed, some seeds fell by the way side, and the fowls came and devoured them up: some fell upon stony places, where they had not much earth: and forthwith they sprung up, because they had no deepness of earth: and when the sun was up, they were scorched; and because they had no root, they withered away. And some fell among thorns; and the thorns sprung up, and choked them: but other fell into good ground, and brought forth fruit, some an hundredfold, some sixtyfold, some thirtyfold. Who hath ears to hear, let him hear.
>
> Hear ye therefore the parable of the sower. When any one heareth the word of the kingdom, and understandeth it not, then cometh the wicked one, and catcheth away that which was sown in his heart. This is he which received seed by the way side. But he that received the seed into stony places, the same is he that heareth the word, and anon with joy receiveth it; yet hath he not root in himself, but dureth for a while: for when tribulation or persecution ariseth because of the word, by and by he is offended. He also that received seed among the thorns is he that heareth the word; and the care of this world, and the deceitfulness of riches, choke the word, and he becometh unfruitful. But he that received seed into the good ground is he that heareth the word, and understandeth it; which also beareth fruit, and bringeth forth, some an hundredfold, some sixty, some thirty. (Matthew 13:3-9,18-23)

Lesson: The Principle of Cause and Effect, The Principle of Belief

The Principle of Cause and Effect, known as the Law of Karma in Eastern metaphysics, is that spiritual Principle which says that for every action there is a reaction, or that we "reap what we sow." It is often interpreted to mean that we get the punishment we deserve. While we do indeed "get what we deserve," The Principle of Cause and Effect is actually an impersonal spiritual principle that is built into the structure of creation and acts automatically in our lives. According to Eastern thought, karma may operate over numerous lifetimes. Destructive actions bring about "bad karma"—an account to be settled.

The Principle of Cause and Effect may be tempered by the Principle of the Grace of God or the Principle of the Mercy of God. According to Daskalos it is repentance, or metanoia, that triggers the intervention of these other divine Laws and allows the Principle of Cause and Effect to be transcended. The relationship between the Principles of Cause and Effect, Grace, and Mercy are mysterious. They interrelate in our lives according to the transcendental insight of God into our hearts. Similarly, when "bad things happen to good people," it is presumptuous to attribute all of this to the Principle of Cause and Effect. What we call "bad" from our limited human perspective may be anything but bad from the vast perspective of the Christ Self, which seeks to prepare our souls for the grand achievements and high adventures of eternity.

In addition to illustrating that "we reap what we sow," the "Parable of the Sower" shows that "we reap according to how and where we sow." Jesus stated this principle more bluntly when he said, "Give not that which is holy unto the dogs, neither cast ye your pearls before swine, lest they trample them under their feet, and turn again and rend you." (Matthew 7:6) Positive actions bring about the most positive results if performed consciously, with care and discernment, so as to bring about the greatest possible good with any given expenditure of effort. This is a challenge in the art of living that intrigues and stimulates anyone involved in the ministry of love.

Finally, the "Parable of the Sower" illustrates what might be called "The Principle of Belief," which says we create our personal realities through belief, thought, and attitude. As discussed in Appendix III, we do so through the creation of a network of elementals, analogous to the manner that the master universe is created from the supersubstance of Mind, according to the Will-Pleasure of Absolute Infinite Beingness. Imagination and belief shape our future. Every thought, such as the thought of freedom or love, solidifies into a future condition. We are all showered daily with "seeds" of truth and grace. Whether we disregard, abandon, choke off, or nurture these seeds as they take root will determine when "the kingdom comes" in our hearts. Jesus said, "Take no thought, saying, 'What shall we eat?' or, 'What shall we drink?' or, 'Wherewithal shall we be clothed?'. . . But seek ye first the kingdom of God, and his righteousness; and all these things shall be added unto you." (Matthew 6:31,33) The devotion and manner in which we in turn sow these inner seeds of love and truth on those around us will determine when "thy kingdom comes" in the world.

Discussion

The Success-Driven Self is so named because, more flagrantly than any other personality type, it seeks to substitute an image for the reality of "Who

I am." Therefore, transformation of the Success-Driven Self often brings a profound and soul-wrenching experience of repentance, or metanoia. Salvation, as it is understood by religion, always implies a change of mind about "who I am." Thus the transformed Success-Driven Self, now the Spiritual Warrior, may become deeply and zealously committed to the salvation of humanity. Spiritual Warriors are particularly effective at this task because of their inherent optimism, dynamism, and ability to function practically in the world. They are skilled at adapting their message to the understanding or biases of the real-life people they encounter. These "sowers" have the knack of finding fertile ground on which to sow their seeds of salvation and will even create that ground if need be. The heart of the Spiritual Warrior coordinates numerous and complex tasks through love, while focusing single-mindedly on its spiritual goals.

One of Buddhism's major branches is Mahayana Buddhism. The highest ideals of Mahayana are exemplified by the *bodhisattva* (one whose essence, or sattva, is perfected wisdom, or bodhi). The *bodhisattva* is a being who reaches the brink of nirvana, or enlightenment, then voluntarily returns to the world to help others reach nirvana and end suffering. He or she may stay on this mission of compassion for age after age. The Goddess of Mercy is the most beloved of the *bodhisattvas* throughout Asia. The following passage from *Buddhist Scriptures* describes the *bodhisattva's* spiritual mission of infinite compassion:

> A Bodhisattva resolves: I take upon myself the burden of all suffering. . . . I do not turn or run away, do not tremble, am not terrified, . . . do not turn back or despond.
>
> And why? . . . I have made the vow to save all beings. . . . The whole world of living beings I must rescue, from the terrors of birth-and-death, from the jungle of false views. . . . My endeavors do not merely aim at my own deliverance. . . . I must rescue all these beings from the stream of Samsara. . . . And I must not cheat beings out of my store of merit. I am resolved to abide in each single state of woe for numberless aeons; and so I will help all beings to freedom, in all the states of woe that may be found in any world system whatsoever.
>
> And why? Because it is surely better that I alone should be in pain than that all these beings should fall into states of woe.[7]

The Apostle Paul could be considered the quintessence of the "Christian *Bodhisattva*." His truth-conversion, or metanoia, on the road to Damascus changed him from a persecutor of believers into an emissary of salvation. Scottish historian W.H.C. Frend states, "Paul is one of the few individuals in history who merit the title "religious genius."[8] He describes the effectiveness of Paul's approach to such diverse listeners as the Hellenistic Jews of the Dispersion (Jewish community outside Palestine) and the Roman adherents of various mystery cults. By tailoring his approach ingenuously to each audience, Paul effectively spread the message of salvation as he understood it throughout the Roman Empire. His gospel was imbued with love and propelled by love. No more beautiful tribute to love was ever written than in his first epistle to the Corinthians, Chapter 13, which ends, "And now abideth faith, hope, and charity, these three; but the greatest of these is charity." (I Corinthians 13:13) So profound was Paul's influence that the early Christian Church became in effect the "Church of Paul" and continues so to this day.

In reference to Paul's missionary journeys, which began in Cyprus in 46 A.D. and ended with his death in Rome in 62 A.D., Frend states: "It is a record of astonishing activity. The energy required for such a program ending with imprisonment, and preaching even in his semicaptivity at Rome, was enormous." [9] In a second letter to the Corinthians, Paul writes of the overwhelming hardship he faced:

> Of the Jews five times received I forty stripes save one. Thrice was I beaten with rods, once was I stoned, thrice I suffered shipwreck, a night and a day I have been in the deep; in journeyings often, in perils of waters, in perils of robbers, in perils by mine own countrymen, in perils by the heathen, in perils in the city, in perils in the wilderness, in perils in the sea, in perils among false brethren; in weariness and painfulness, in watchings often, in hunger and thirst, in fastings often, in cold and nakedness. Beside those things that are without, that which cometh upon me daily, the care of all the churches. (2 Corinthians 24-28)

The *bodhisattva* cares little about his own flesh and blood apart from its use as an instrument for the salvation of human souls. Such was Paul in his transformation from dishonest religious egotist to mighty spiritual warrior.

Transformation, Expansion, and Regression

When the Success-Driven Self, transforms into the Spiritual Warrior it moves toward its core virtues of truthfulness and in so doing it begins to develop compassion and empathy for others. It becomes more connected to its inner life of true feelings and thoughts, balancing outer-directedness with inner-directedness. It supports and encourages others, overcoming the fear of intimacy and personal encounter. It is committed and consistent in embracing higher values and ideals in action. The Spiritual Warrior expands in the yang direction by becoming supportive of others' success and developing the service motivation of divine enterprise in place of the need to prove oneself. Yin expansion involves optimism, sensitivity to others' positions and needs, and connecting deeply with being.

When the Success-Driven Self resists transformation it becomes more deceitful, becomes self-loathing and engages in self-defeating behavior. Overwhelming feelings of hostility lead to impaired action and function. It may dissociate from all feelings and shuts down, becoming slovenly and inactive.

The energetic trends above are consistent with Enneagram personality type three.

Soul Type: Heroic

Separated Self	Transforming Principles	Transformed Self
The Success-Driven Self	Principle of Cause and effect Principle of Belief	The Spiritual Warrior

---

Exercise for The Success-Driven Self: "Thy kingdom come"

Close your eyes, breathe deeply.

Imagine yourself standing in front of an empty yet fertile field ready to receive seeds to grow. See yourself holding a precious cup of seeds in your hands. Imagine as you stand in front of the field, your angry self appears and attempts to steal your seeds and plant them. What grows?

Change the scene and imagine your fearful self coming to you and stealing your seeds to plant them. What grows?

Now one last time imagine your sorrowful self coming and stealing your cup of seeds to plant them. What grows?

Taking a deep breath, allow the Christ Self to come to your side, become your loving self and plant your own seeds. What grows now?

You can repeat this exercise for anything you'd like to sow in the garden of your life. Always become your loving self and allow the Christ light to guide you!

THE SPIRITUAL WARRIOR
"Thy kingdom come"

PRINCIPLE OF CAUSE AND EFFECT
PRINCIPLE OF BELIEF

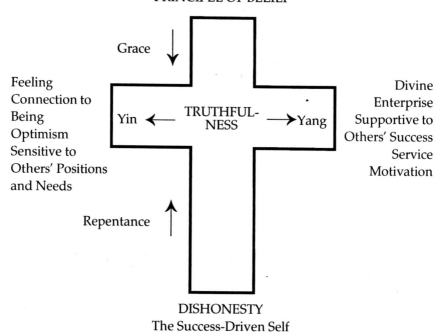

Grace

Feeling
Connection to
Being
Optimism
Sensitive to
Others' Positions
and Needs

Yin ← TRUTHFUL-NESS →Yang

Divine
Enterprise
Supportive to
Others' Success
Service
Motivation

Repentance

DISHONESTY
The Success-Driven Self

CORE VICE – ENVY
PERSONALITY EXPRESSION OF THE PRODIGAL SON:
THE MELODRAMATIC SELF

Instruction: "Thy will be done in earth, as it is in heaven."

Examples: Parable of the Children in the Marketplace,
    Parables of the Mustard Seed and the Growing Seed

> Whereunto then shall I liken the men of this generation? and to what are they like? They are like unto children sitting in the marketplace, and calling one to another, and saying, "We have piped unto you, and ye have not danced; we have mourned to you, and ye have not wept."
> For John the Baptist came neither eating bread nor drinking wine; and ye say, "He hath a devil." The Son of man is come eating and drinking; and ye say, "Behold a gluttonous man, and a winebibber, a friend of publicans and sinners!" But wisdom is justified of all her children. (Luke 7:31-35)

> The kingdom of heaven is like to a grain of mustard seed, which a man took, and sowed in his field: which indeed is the least of all seeds: but when it is grown, it is the greatest among herbs, and becometh a tree, so that the birds of the air come and lodge in the branches thereof. (Matthew 13:31-32)

> So is the kingdom of God, as if a man should cast seed into the ground; and should sleep, and rise night and day, and the seed should spring and grow up, he knoweth not how. For the earth bringeth forth fruit of herself; first the blade, then the ear, after that the full corn in the ear. But when the fruit is brought forth, immediately he putteth in the sickle, because the harvest is come. (Mark 4:26-29)

Lesson: The Principle of Equilibrium, The Principle of Continuity

Nothing about Jesus disturbed the sanctimonious religious leaders of that day more than Jesus' divine *ordinariness*. Like children sitting in the marketplace, they piped a tune of religious expectations, but Jesus did not dance to it. They mourned with proper solemnity, and he celebrated life instead. Jesus did not even satisfy their image of a proper religious layperson, much less a messiah. He did not deny himself, or strictly regulate, food and drink according to any arbitrary legalistic standards of religion. Even worse in their eyes, he dared to relax and enjoy himself in the company of "publicans and sinners" and all manner of social pariahs. When this "ordinary" teacher did perform a miracle, his enemies accused him of doing so by the power of Beelzebub, "the prince of devils." (Matthew 12:24)

Jesus lived according to the Principle of Equilibrium, which states that the perfect equilibrium and balance of Spirit is maintained in creation through the interchange between opposite poles. To obey the Principle of Equilibrium is to respect the nature of creation's design. Healthy and creative manifestations on the earth plane cannot be achieved without following this basic Principle. A respect for the Principle of Equilibrium implies respect for one's own being; to eat what the body needs when hungry, to drink when thirsty, to work when inspired, to rest or play when tired, to pray and serve alone and together, to think, feel and act in harmony, to balance animus and anima. The Principle of Equilibrium must be followed intuitively, not logically or according to a rigid formula. One must "know thyself," because what brings one person into perfect balance at a given time might throw another person into a tailspin. Sometimes a transient extreme is necessary to achieve stability, as a hurricane or volcanic eruption restores calm to nature.

The Parable of the Mustard Seed shows how the Father's Will in heaven can be brought to earth by obeying the Principle of Equilibrium. When the tiny mustard seed is planted in good ground and receives the proper balance of air, water, and sunlight, it grows imperceptibly a day at a time into "the greatest among herbs," with branches so large that birds can nest on them. In the same manner, the tiniest seed of truth in one's heart can manifest powerfully as divine will when it is nurtured by the "four elements" of earth (the physical body), water (the emotions), air (thought), and fire (love).

The Parable of the Growing Seed, as well as that of the Mustard Seed, illustrate the Principle of Continuity. It is known on the physical level as the Principle of Thermodynamics and states that energy can be neither created nor destroyed, but only changed in form according to the properties of the physical system it enters. For example, the energy of a fire may flow into a block of ice, changing this solid state to the liquid state of water, and finally emerging in the gaseous state of steam. When a guitar string and a harp string are plucked in exactly the same manner, a unique and reproducible sound, or harmonic, is produced by each. A seed, nurtured by the right balance of elemental forces, will transmute energy and grow according to its own nature, eventually ripening to the point where the plant may be harvested. Seed is again planted, maintaining the continuity of cyclic change and growth. Through these cycles Spirit manifests creatively in the world.

The Principle of Continuity also applies to emotional, mental, and spiritual levels of reality. It is a metaphysical law that energy follows thought, which is to say that energy enters whatever entity or system on which we place our attention. This energy resonates within us as a particular quality of experience and without as a particular manifestation. A given amount of attention on sex, career, feelings, or philosophy produces particular, corresponding inner experiences and outer results. Absolute Beingness, however, is within every diverse element of creation, so it follows in turn that full attention on anything can also produce a spiritual experience. This experience of beingness, or true connection with the Source, can only occur with full attention in the present moment, because the only crack in time to eternity is now. It is only in the present that all the mortal and eternal aspects of our lives can be brought into the perfect equilibrium and harmony of Spirit. This is the reason that Jesus said, "Take no thought for the morrow: for the morrow shall take thought for the things of itself. Sufficient unto the day is the evil thereof." (Matthew 6:34) Moment by moment, we pray, may "thy will be done in earth, as it is in heaven."

Discussion

Every separated personality type has a tendency to become unbalanced and disharmonious in one way or another. The Melodramatic Self, as the name indicates, does so by creating intense emotional experiences as a substitute for the experience of being. Through a sense of missing and longing for some unobtainable or lost love object, the Melodramatic Self loses awareness of what he or she has now. All of this focus on what is *not* present or *not* happening now can lead to particularly strong imbalances in the personality, a sense of teetering on the edge, and the loss of the grounding necessary to manifest creative inner drives externally.

The solution is to regain balance and harmony by rediscovering the magic in the present moment and the extraordinary nature of the ordinary. If we nurture the tiniest inner seeds of truth daily in a balanced and attentive way, Spirit can manifest monumental creative works through us that we ourselves can't fathom. As multidimensional beings, we may be called to serve on any level of our existence from the densest physical to the highest spiritual. We can bring the greatest possible joy to ourselves and others by discovering the particular "frequency" on which to bring the will of God to earth. This discovery, as well, can only be made intuitively in the present moment.

Siddhartha Gautama, the Buddha, discovered through experience the futility of fleshly self-indulgence as well as ascetic self-denial. As a result he established the principle of the Middle Way, giving the body what it needs to function optimally, but no more. The Middle Way was appealing to the pragmatic Chinese, to whom Buddhism eventually spread from India. China's indigenous Taoism exerted a strong influence on Buddhism, yielding a sect of Buddhism known as Ch'an. Ch'an spread to Japan, where it became known as Zen and has exerted a profound influence on Japanese culture through the centuries.

Zen attempts to find satori, or enlightenment, in the simplest of daily activities by being fully present. The highest form of meditation in Zen is called za-zen, or "just sitting." The Lay Disciple Ho captures the spirit of Zen in the following verse:

> My daily activities are not different,
> Only I am naturally in harmony with them.
> Taking nothing, renouncing nothing,
> In every circumstance no hindrance, no conflict. . . .
> Drawing water; carrying firewood,
> This is supernatural power, this the marvelous activity.[10]

Master Rinzai also praises the potential of ordinary life in this verse:

> You have only to be ordinary with nothing to do.
> Defecating, urinating, putting on clothes, eating
> food, lying down when tired. Fools laugh at me,
> but the wise man understands.[11]

Master Rinzai is also known for the saying, "Wherever you are, you are the Master."[12] Whatever time and place one occupies is the center of reality and potential circumstance of enlightenment. "Where is my attention now?" becomes the most balancing question a Melodramatic Self in transformation can ask. Centered in balance and equanimity, doing nothing, this transformed personality becomes paradoxically the visionary builder of the new heaven and the new earth of prophecy. (Revelation 21:1)

Transformation, Expansion, and Regression

When the Melodramatic Self is transformed into the Visionary Builder it moves toward its core virtue of balance and equanimity. In so doing it develops objectivity about self, especially its emotional reactions and those of others. It achieves a balanced lifestyle, with less attraction to extremes. It chooses selfless service to ideals and their actualization as well as self-actualization. It becomes self-reliant, independent, consistent, and emotionally disciplined. Expansion in the yang direction brings fulfillment in the present, satisfaction in service, and discovery of the magic in everyday life through divine connection. Yin expansion brings simplicity and completeness of being.

When the Melodramatic Self resists transformation it entrenches more deeply in its core vice of envy. It develops doubts about its own desirability and worthiness to be loved. It fears abandonment and manipulates to hold on to significant others. It becomes dependent and demanding of attention. Its high ideals about love are followed by disappointment.

The energetic trends above are consistent with Enneagram personality type four.

Soul Type: Heroic

Separated Self	Transforming Principles	Transformed Self
The Melodramatic Self	Principle of Equilibrium	The Visionary Builder
	Principle of Continuity	

Exercise for The Melodramatic Self: "Thy will be done in earth, as it is in heaven."

Exercise for discovering and planting the inner gifts:

Close your eyes, breathe deeply.

Imagine your guardian angel taking you to a beautiful garden. This garden is like the Garden of Eden—a place of love, sweetness and infinite beauty. Fill yourself with the splendor, light, and specialness of this place. The Christ awaits you in a temple and says, "You have never left that which you truly are, but you have gone away in your awareness from it." He takes you to an altar and there are the many gifts that you are to bring into the world. These gifts are in golden boxes and contain your talents, abilities, and qualities as a human being.

Allow yourself to open at least three of them and to choose one which you would like to bring into the world. Return in your visualization to your own home and plant this gift like a seed in your garden. Ask your guardian angel to assist you in discovering which steps you need to take in thought, feeling and action to manifest this divine gift and plan of your soul.

Return to the garden of your heart (Garden of Eden). Ask as much as you like to restore your power, love, and intent to manifest this project on earth.

THE VISIONARY BUILDER
"Thy will be done in earth, as it is in heaven"

PRINCIPLE OF EQUILIBRIUM
PRINCIPLE OF CONTINUITY

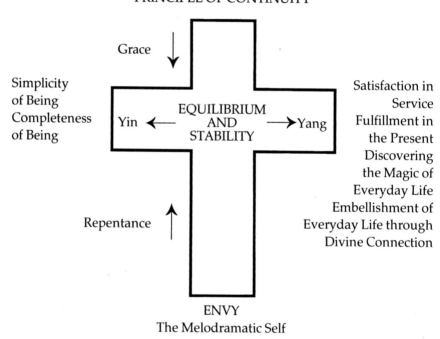

Grace

Simplicity
of Being
Completeness
of Being

EQUILIBRIUM
AND
STABILITY

Yin ←   → Yang

Satisfaction in
Service
Fulfillment in
the Present
Discovering
the Magic of
Everyday Life
Embellishment of
Everyday Life through
Divine Connection

Repentance

ENVY
The Melodramatic Self

CORE VICE –GREED
PERSONALITY EXPRESSION OF THE PRODIGAL SON:
THE ISOLATED SELF

Instruction: "Give us this day our daily bread."

Examples: The Feeding of Five Thousand,
Parable of the New Cloth on an Old Coat

He (Jesus) departed thence by ship into a desert place apart: and when the people had heard thereof, they followed him on foot out of the cities. And Jesus went forth, and saw a great multitude, and was moved with compassion toward them, and he healed their sick. And when it was evening, his disciples came to him, saying, "This is a desert place, and the time is now past; send the multitude away, that they may go into the villages, and buy themselves victuals."

But Jesus said unto them, "They need not depart; give ye them to eat."

And they say unto him, "We have here but five loaves, and two fishes."

He said, "Bring them hither to me." And he commanded the multitude to sit down on the grass, and took the five loaves, and the two fishes, and looking up to heaven, he blessed, and brake, and gave the loaves to his disciples, and the disciples to the multitude. And they did all eat, and were filled: and they took up of the fragments that remained twelve baskets full. And they that had eaten were about five thousand men, beside women and children. (Matthew 14:13-21)

No man putteth a piece of new cloth unto an old garment, for that which is put in to fill it up taketh from the garment, and the rent is made worse. Neither do men put new wine into old bottles: else the bottles break, and the wine runneth out, and the bottles perish: but they put new wine into new bottles, and both are preserved. (Matthew 9:16-17)

Lesson: The Principle of Abundance, The Principle of Nonattachment

Jesus said, "I am come that (you) might have life, and that (you) might have it more abundantly." (John 10:10) The Principle of Abundance states that the universe is inherently bountiful and that its abundance is available to anyone who has learned how to receive it with gratitude. The abundance of one's life springs ultimately from that endlessly renewable source of the most pure, absolute, and divine order of energy—the Christ Self within. The presence of the Christ Self offers the final assurance of the inexhaustible supply of energy needed to sustain eternal life. Even now the Christ Self, being antecedent to Mind, is one source of energy we can access to renew the etheric vitality which energizes the physical body.

Etheric vitality, the energy of the body's etheric template, is "our daily bread," according to Daskalos.[13] Etheric energy may be obtained from such diverse sources as food, water, sunlight, and meditative visualizations. Mental techniques are among the most useful, as the etheric body is fundamentally "condensed mind" vibrating at a particular frequency. Jesus demonstrated the abundance of these unseen sources of universal energy by the apparently miraculous feat of feeding the five thousand people. Even now various spiritual masters are reportedly able to materialize and dematerialize physical substances by working consciously with etheric energy according to principles of natural law.

While very few of us have learned to access universal energies in such sophisticated and direct ways, it is still not necessary to live in the state of scarcity and lack that permeates so much of our mass consciousness. To receive the abundance that Jesus promised, however, we must first learn what receiving is. Truly receiving anything is to fully take it into one's being out of a sense of gratitude rather than grasping it out of a sense of addictive neediness. Receiving with gratitude increases the capacity for receiving even more. As Jesus said in "The Parable of the Talents," "Unto every one that hath shall be given, and he shall have abundance." (Matthew 25:29)

The Principle of Abundance is closely linked with The Principle of Nonattachment, which states that one must not hold on to anything if one is to experience life to the fullest. Jesus told his disciples, "Freely ye have received, freely give." (Matthew 10:8) One cannot give what he or she does not have. To give freely and hold onto nothing implies a sense of plenty. Giving and receiving, correctly understood, are mirror images of each other, just as abundance and nonattachment are two forms of the same basic principle. To truly give, one must truly receive, and vice versa. Giving and receiving imply a continuous flow of energies in and out of a person. Blockage of either the inflow or the outflow prevents the experience of abundance.

The "Parable of the New Cloth on an Old Coat" shows the problems that result when the Principle of Nonattachment is broken. If one holds on to an old coat and tries to patch it with new cloth, the new cloth shrinks and tears the coat even worse. If one clings to an old wineskin and pours new wine into it, then the skin breaks and the wine as well as the skin is lost. A sense of scarcity and lack, paradoxically, is only intensified when one holds on to anything that has served its purpose and is not benefitting us, whether it be a possession, relationship, job, or creed. There comes a time to let go and move on, both individually and collectively.

Advancing knowledge and wisdom in society requires changes in educational institutions. The spiritual progress of a society requires corresponding expansion of religious definitions and forms to accommodate and further stimulate this progress. Failure to make the necessary adjustments in the forms and belief systems, or "wineskins," of our institutions weakens both the institutions and their missions. It is regrettable when the truth in tradition is weakened by unthinking traditionalism and truth in scriptures is diluted by clinging to rigid, dogmatic interpretations from another era that no longer serve a useful purpose.

Discussion

The Isolated Self separates out of the illusion of lack—lack of time, space, energy, goods—and protectively clutches the little it believes it has. It barricades and isolates itself to protect its endangered resources, learns to get by with very little, and retreats to the safety of mental activity. This type of retreat is sometimes called *detachment* as opposed to nonattachment. This detachment may foster a particular breadth of objectivity and perspective in the Isolated Self, but at the price of being powerless to influence the world with its knowledge and being unable to experience life to the fullest. The solution to this problem is to reconnect with the neglected physical and emotional parts of oneself, then discover the joy of sharing life's abundance with others. The Isolated Self in transformation takes the following advice of Jesus to heart:

> Ye are the light of the world. A city that is set on an hill cannot be hid. Neither do men light a candle, and put it under a bushel, but on a candlestick; and it giveth light unto all that are in the house. Let your light so shine before men, that they may see your good works, and glorify your Father which is in heaven. (Matthew 5:14-16)

Daskalos describes God's nature as Divine Wisdom, Divine Power, and Divine Love. Whereas "civilized" man tends to emulate Divine Wisdom, native peoples of the earth tend to be most attracted to the experience of Divine Power. The word *wakan*, in the language of the Oglala Sioux tribe of Native Americans, means sacred, but implies power and is sometimes even translated directly as power. *Wakan-Tanka* is the Great Spirit.[14] Those who live close to the elemental forces of nature generally appreciate the sacredness of life in the natural world. Their sacred traditions emphasize harmony with nature, giving to her and receiving "daily bread" from her in a spirit of

gratitude and respect. Rituals are designed to invoke a bodily-felt sense of
the sacred and build power.

Inipi, the Oglala Sioux rite of purification, is commonly known as "the
sweat lodge ceremony." Black Elk describes the purpose of this well-known
rite:

> The rite of the *onikare* (sweat lodge) utilizes all the Powers of the
> universe: earth, and the things which grow from the earth, water, fire, and
> air. The water represents the Thunder-beings who come fearfully but
> bring goodness, for the steam which comes from the rocks, within which is
> the fire, is frightening, but it purifies us so that we may live as *Wakan-Tanka*
> wills, and He may even send to us a vision if we become very pure.
>
> When we use the water in the sweat lodge we should think of *Wakan-Tanka*
> who is always flowing, giving His power and life to everything; we
> should even be as water which is lower than all things, yet stronger even
> than the rocks. . . .
>
> These rites of the *Inipi* are very wakan and are used before any great
> undertaking for which we wish to make ourselves pure or for which we
> wish to gain strength; and in many winters past our men, and often the
> women, made the *Inipi* even every day, and sometimes several times in a
> day, and from this we received much of our power.[15]

The native healers among the world's indigenous peoples are known as
shamans. While the form of their work varies considerably from one region
or country to another, their basic approach to healing is the same everywhere. The shaman typically heals by extracting etheric "power disturbances" while in an altered, often ecstatic, state of consciousness. The
shaman may perceive strange creatures and entities as very real while in
this state; yet these same entities would be considered nonsense or fantasy
to one in the ordinary, "rational" state of consciousness. Anthropologist
Michael Harner calls this altered state the "Shamanic State of Consciousness." A deep emotional connection between healer and patient, accompanied by a strong commitment to heal, are other key components of effective
shamanic healing.[16]

Jesus apparently wanted his apostles to develop shamanic healing
powers as part of their spiritual mission, as evidenced by the following
verses:

> And when he had called unto him his twelve disciples, he gave them
> power against unclean spirits, to cast them out, and to heal all manner of
> sickness and all manner of disease. . . . These twelve Jesus sent forth, and
> commanded them, saying, "Go . . . to the lost sheep of the house of Israel.

And as ye go, preach, saying, 'The kingdom of heaven is at hand.' Heal the sick, cleanse the lepers, raise the dead, cast out devils." (Matthew 10:1,6-8)

The Isolated Self in transformation may never become a shaman or participate in Native American rites. Yet the consciousness of shamanic healing and sacred native traditions can effectively show it the direction to proceed in its own path from detached mentation to the fullness of life. With no need to hide and nothing to hold on to, the nonattached Magus has the power to share the light of his or her knowledge and experience with the world, so that others may "see their good works and glorify the Father which is in heaven."

Transformation, Expansion, and Regression

When the Isolated Self is transformed into the Magus it moves in the direction of its core virtue of nonattachment and it becomes self-confident and capable of acting without fear, developing strong leadership capacity. It is able to take in life without withdrawing from experience. Yang expansion brings confident self-expression and leadership, resourceful action, and the ability to celebrate life and share it with others. Yin expansion leads to strong connection with feeling, embracing abundance, reaching out for intimacy, and the experience of truth as a bodily-felt sensation.

When the Isolated Self resists transformation it regresses more deeply into its core vice, greed, and it becomes impulsive and scattered, makes mistakes repetitively, and is easily distracted from life goals and purposes.

The energetic trends above are consistent with Enneagram personality type five.

Soul Type: Philosophic

Separated Self	**Transforming Principles**	**Transformed Self**
The Isolated Self	The Principle of Abundance	The Magus
	The Principle of Nonattachment	

Exercise for The Isolated Self: "Give us this day our daily bread."

Close your eyes. Breathe deeply.

Imagine yourself traveling into a beautiful garden. There in the garden is a beautiful white-domed temple structure. As you enter it, feel yourself surrounded by peace and tranquility. In the center of the circular room is a golden-yellow fire in an altar.

Look down at your energy hands and create a fiery golden sun-like sphere between the palms of your hands with a beautiful chalice cup in the center. Look into the cup and ask that as you send this chalice cup within the golden sphere into the golden-yellow flames, that the energy of light and love that is returned multiply a hundred-fold. After receiving the cup, once again send it into the light several more times and again receive and behold the abundance of the Christ's unconditional love for you.

Comment: Daskalos once said that an elemental is often the size of a pinhead and when held in a positive manner (i.e., positive thought-desire) in the spiritual eye center, it continues to build momentum and power to manifest. Yet, unless it is surrendered, it can't draw back the gifts of God. To wish for something, but hold it tightly to oneself never gives it a chance to be planted to grow.

THE MAGUS
"Give us this day our daily bread"

PRINCIPLE OF ABUNDANCE
PRINCIPLE OF NONATTACHMENT

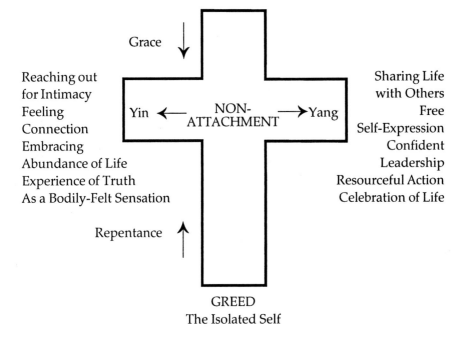

Grace

Reaching out
for Intimacy
Feeling
Connection
Embracing
Abundance of Life
Experience of Truth
As a Bodily-Felt Sensation

Yin ← NON-ATTACHMENT → Yang

Sharing Life
with Others
Free
Self-Expression
Confident
Leadership
Resourceful Action
Celebration of Life

Repentance

GREED
The Isolated Self

CORE VICE –FEAR
PERSONALITY EXPRESSION OF THE PRODIGAL SON:
THE DOUBTFUL SELF

Instruction: "And forgive us our debts, as we forgive our debtors."

Example: Parable of the Two Debtors

And one of the Pharisees desired him that he would eat with him. And he went into the Pharisee's house, and sat down to meat. And, behold, a woman in the city, which was a sinner, when she knew that Jesus sat at meat in the Pharisee's house, brought an alabaster box of ointment, and stood at his feet behind him weeping, and began to wash his feet with tears, and did wipe them with the hairs of her head, and kissed his feet, and anointed them with the ointment.

Now when the Pharisee which had bidden him saw it, he spake within himself, saying, "This man, if he were a prophet, would have known who and what manner of woman this is that toucheth him: for she is a sinner."

And Jesus answering said unto him, "Simon, I have somewhat to say unto thee."

And he saith, "Master, say on."

"There was a certain creditor which had two debtors: the one owed five hundred pence, and the other fifty. And when they had nothing to pay, he frankly forgave them both. Tell me therefore, which of them will love him most?"

Simon answered and said, "I suppose that he, to whom he forgave most."

And he said unto him, "Thou hast rightly judged." And he turned to the woman, and said unto Simon, "Seest thou this woman? I entered into thine house, thou gavest me no water for my feet: but she hath washed my feet with tears, and wiped them with the hairs of her head. Thou gavest me no kiss: but this woman since the time I came in hath not ceased to kiss my feet. My head with oil thou didst not anoint: but this woman hath anointed my feet with ointment. Wherefore I say unto thee, 'Her sins, which are many, are forgiven; for she loved much: but to whom little is forgiven, the same loveth little."

And he said unto her, "Thy sins are forgiven. . . . Thy faith hath saved thee; go in peace." (Luke 7:36-48,50)

Lesson: The Principle of the Mercy of God

The oldest Jewish traditions viewed Yahweh primarily as a stern God of justice who demanded strict adherence to the law that regulated Jewish life. Jesus, in alignment with the teachings of later prophets such as Isaiah, set out to reveal a God whose primary attributes are love and mercy. The touching story above is a good illustration of that divine quality of mercy which Jesus revealed. Likewise, the highest morality for any of us as individuals is an expression of mercy rather than judgment.

Divine mercy might be considered applied love, that attitude behind divine forgiveness. It is often experienced as the time lag between the transgression of a divine Principle and the consequences of that transgression. This time lag gives one the opportunity to erase the "karmic debt" altogether in the eyes of God through repentance, or metanoia. Genuine repentance arises from love, not fear of punishment. The depth of assurance that one has been forgiven by God's infinite mercy is proportionate to the extent one has forgiven one's own "debtors." This capacity to accept divine forgiveness as well as to forgive others is a genuine measure of the love in one's heart.

Discussion

Fear is ultimately the source of all failure to forgive. The Doubtful Self holds the conviction that a threat of annihilation lurks everywhere. This pervasive fear is a direct barrier to forgiveness, because it blocks the ability to perceive the light of Christ within others and merge with that light. This is the reason that forgiveness presents such a direct challenge to the Doubtful Self. Valor, the core virtue of this personality in transformation, is a measure of the consistency and degree of one's forgiveness, one's ability to perceive others in oneness rather than separation.

The Apostle John said, "Perfect love casteth out fear." (1 John 4:18) Guru Nanak had a transcendent experience of divine and perfect love that cast all religion-based fear out of his heart in a profound manner. Nanak was born in 1469 A.D. into a Hindu family of the Punjab region of northwest India. At this time Muslim invaders were in firm control of the Punjab and enmity between Hindu and Muslim was great. Around the year 1500 Nanak mysteriously disappeared while bathing in a river. When he reappeared three days later, he said: "Since there is neither Hindu nor Muslim, whose path shall I follow? I will follow God's path. God is neither Hindu nor Muslim, and the path I follow is God's."[17] He explained that in his three-day absence he had been taken to God's court, where he was given a cup of nectar and told:

> This is the cup of the adoration of God's name. Drink it. I am with you. I bless you and raise you up. Whoever remembers you will enjoy my favor. Go, rejoice in my name and teach others to do so also. Let this be your calling.[18]

The Sikhs (literally disciples) are followers of Guru Nanak's divine revelation. Out of Sikhism arose a theologic synthesis of Hinduism and Islam. The Sikh community took shape under a lineage of ten gurus, and not surprisingly, has been under heavy assault during much of its history. The Tenth Guru, Gobind Singh, founded the Khalsa, or Pure Order, for those prepared to commit their lives to the faith. All dressed in a particular way for protective as well as symbolic purposes. Uncut hair in a turban shielded the skull while tying in with the yogic belief that uncut hair conserves vitality. A comb symbolized cleanliness and order. A steel bracelet provided a small shield, while at the same time "shackling" its wearer to God as a reminder that hands should always be in God's service. Undershorts meant that one was always dressed for action. The dagger, originally needed for self-defense, symbolizes the fierceness invoked in the defense of the truth. At the same time Gobind Singh extended his name Singh, literally lion, to all members of the order.[19]

That distinguishing mark of Sikhism, the courage of a lion, originated in the perfect forgiveness of Guru Nanak's holy vision. The unlikely syncretism, or religious synthesis, of Hinduism and Islam, two bitter rivals, was the theologic expression of the vision. Still this loyal, lion-hearted, and heavily outnumbered lineage of Guru Nanak defends the noble truth that "God is neither Hindu nor Muslim, and the path I follow is God's."

Transformation, Expansion, and Regression

When the Doubtful Self is transformed into the Defender of Truth, it moves toward its core virtue of valor and becomes adaptable, intuitive, and self-confident, flowing through unknown life situations with faith and trust. It becomes accepting and supportive of others, especially the underdog. Yang expansion brings the ability to trust others and appreciate their differences, to encourage others to empower themselves by being themselves, and to take charge. Yin expansion brings tolerance, optimism, confidence, defenselessness, and the ability to trust oneself.

When the Doubtful Self resists transformation it becomes even more fearful and it develops feelings of inferiority, free-floating anxiety, and worry, while missing its own authentic feelings. It retaliates to punish others whom it feels or perceives has hurt it.

These energetic trends are most consistent with Enneagram personality type six.

Soul Type: Philosophic

Separated Self	Transforming Principle	Transformed Self
The Doubtful Self	Principle of the Mercy of God	Defender of the Truth

---

Exercise for The Doubtful Self: "And forgive us our debts, as we forgive our debtors."

Close your eyes and breathe deeply.

Allow yourself to travel to a beautiful garden. There in the center of the garden is a temple of light. As you enter the temple, your guardian angel greets you and asks you to take a seat. A video/movie camera runs scenes from your life of people and situations where you have felt wronged or hurt and have not forgiven them. Then another film is run for you where you have been the aggressor, hurting others and feeling blame for them.

When the film is over, imagine the people that have hurt you and that have not been forgiven stand on stage. The Christ Self comes to your side and offers you a stone to throw. He says to you, "Has anyone among you not sinned? Choose the power of forgiveness and let go of your hatred and fear."

Then see yourself standing on stage with those you've hurt in the audience. Become your loving self and let go of your blame of them and receive the light of forgiveness.

DEFENDER OF THE TRUTH
"And forgive us our debts, as we forgive our debtors"

PRINCIPLE OF THE MERCY OF GOD

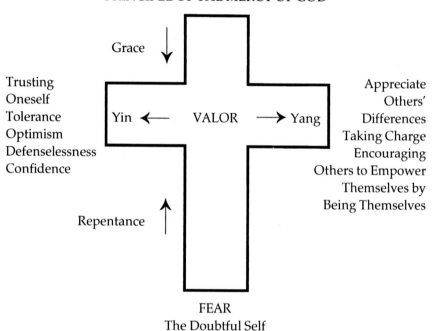

Grace

Trusting
Oneself
Tolerance
Optimism
Defenselessness
Confidence

Yin ← VALOR → Yang

Appreciate
Others'
Differences
Taking Charge
Encouraging
Others to Empower
Themselves by
Being Themselves

Repentance

FEAR
The Doubtful Self

CORE VICE –GLUTTONY
PERSONALITY EXPRESSION OF THE PRODIGAL SON:
THE PLEASURE-SEEKING SELF

Instruction: "Lead us not into temptation, but deliver us from evil."

Examples: Parable of the Prodigal Son (see Chapter 8), Parable of the Good Samaritan

A certain man went down from Jerusalem to Jericho, and fell among thieves, which stripped him of his raiment, and wounded him, and departed, leaving him half dead. And by chance there came down a certain priest that way: and when he saw him, he passed by on the other side. And likewise a Levite, when he was at the place, came and looked on him, and passed by on the other side.

But a certain Samaritan, as he journeyed, came where he was: and when he saw him, he had compassion on him, and went to him, and bound up his wounds, pouring in oil and wine, and set him on his own beast, and brought him to an inn, and took care of him. And on the morrow when he departed, he took out two pence, and gave them to the host, and said unto him, 'Take care of him; and whatsoever thou spendest more, when I come again, I will repay thee. (Luke 10:30-35)

Lesson: The Principle of Commitment and Right Action

The Parable of the Prodigal Son was discussed in the previous chapter as it applies universally. This parable also serves as a particular example of the above instruction from the Lord's Prayer. The Prodigal Son, tempted and ensnared by the cravings of physical pleasure, found these brought him only suffering and disillusionment. Like so many of us, he discovered the value of sobriety in response to the pain his self-indulgence brought him. His sober-minded view of reality ("When he came to himself") is demonstrated by his decision to return to his father and work as a lowly hired servant. This difficult decision brought him solidly into alignment with the Principle of Commitment and Right Action, which says that our own consistent choices and right actions are essential for spiritual progress, or "deliverance from evil." God does not deliver us magically from the evil of our own making. Spirit, however, will unfailingly show us the way back to true happiness if we are willing to do the holy work involved—day after day, week after week, year after year.

The Parable of the Good Samaritan tells the story of a man who lives by the guidance of the Principle of Commitment and Right Action. The priest

and the Levite, who came before him, were unwilling to help a fellow
human being in need. Perhaps they were too caught up in the requirements
of the law or preoccupied with too many "important" activities, or simply
didn't care. The Samaritan, in contrast, showed an unrestrained commitment to his labor of love and saw it through to the end. His actions far
surpassed any societal, or even religious, expectations of duty. Again, the
highest ethical behavior is shown to result from the spontaneous and
committed impulses of love.

Discussion

The Pleasure-Seeking Self, always concerned about missing out on
something, scatters its energies here and there in its futile search for satisfaction and self-validation. Sustained commitment to a way of truth is difficult
for this personality type to make, because in separation, it doesn't understand the nature of truth. It may believe truth demands sacrifice of pleasure
or is boring. When the pain of aimless pleasure-seeking finally leads the
Pleasure-Seeking Self to face reality and look for a better way, he or she
starts making interesting discoveries: Truth is endlessly fascinating; it is
unique, radical, and often defies conventional wisdom. Holy work is a
source of continuing delight, both to oneself and others. Sobriety does not
bring dullness, but rather the joy of being fully alive. Responsibility and
commitment do not bring a type of incarceration, but the highest order of
freedom. Letting go of cravings for physical pleasure makes real pleasure
possible at every dimension of life, including the physical.

The Buddha's Dharma, or Way of Truth, is focused above all else on
helping to end the universal experience of suffering. The Buddha speaks
intimately to the Pleasure-Seeking Self, whose path back to love so directly
involves suffering as a consequence of its attempt to *escape* suffering. In the
following statement he emphasizes the necessity of committed action and
initiative to achieve "deliverance from evil" and union with God:

> "If this river . . . were full of water . . . and a man with business on the
> other side . . . standing on this bank, should invoke the further bank, and
> say, 'Come hither, O further bank! come over to this side!'
>
> "Now what think you? Would the further bank . . . by reason of that
> man's invoking and praying and hoping and praising, come over to this
> side?
>
> ". . . In just the same way . . . do the Brahmans (priestly caste), omitting
> the practice of those qualities which really make a person (noble) and
> adopting the practice of those qualities which really make people (ig-

noble), say thus: 'Indra we call upon . . . Brahma we call upon!' (The thought that) they, by reason of their invoking and praying and hoping and praising, would, after death . . . become united with Brahma (God)—verily such a condition of things can in no wise be." [20]

The Buddha's Fourth Noble Truth reveals the way to end suffering and reach that opposite bank. This way is the Eightfold Path of right views, right intent, right speech, right conduct, right livelihood, right effort, right mindfulness, and right concentration.

The Indians take delight in tales of unusual behavior by saints and sages whose commitment to right action for its own sake is uncompromising. One example of such "holy madness" is the story of a yogi who saw a scorpion fall into the Ganges as he sat meditating. He scooped it out, only to have it sting him. The scorpion fell back into the river and the yogi once more scooped it out, again getting stung. This sequence was repeated twice more. Finally, a bystander asked the yogi, "Why do you keep rescuing that scorpion when its only gratitude is to sting you?" The yogi replied, "It is the nature of scorpions to sting. It is the nature of yogis to help others when they can." [21]

The Pleasure-Seeking Self in transformation, having made the difficult commitment to a way of truth and sobriety, becomes the master of right action and a minister of joy. He or she is unconcerned about appearances and is rarely lured into self-righteous behavior or empty ritualism. If radical commitment to holy work makes him or her the "holy fool," then so be it. Better than anyone else, this "closet philosopher" understands these words of the Apostle Paul: "The foolishness of God is wiser than men." (1 Corinthians 1:25)

Transformation, Expansion, and Regression

When the Pleasure-Seeking Self is transformed into God's Divine Fool, it moves toward its core virtue of commitment and learns to dedicate itself to a course of action and focus on a single direction. It digs deeply into activities rather than skimming the surface. It finds purpose in sharing with others with joy. It becomes consistent in purpose and direction. Yang expansion results in the commitment to a steady course of action and sacred work, expanding one's possibilities within a single-minded focus. Yin expansion brings focused attention, sobriety, and the ability to embrace one's shadow.

When the Pleasure-Seeking Self resists transformation, it regresses more deeply into its vice of gluttony and in so doing it becomes resentful and controlling. It tries to anchor scattered energy through obsessive thinking and compulsive actions.

These energetic trends are consistent with Enneagram personality type seven.

Soul Type: Philosophic

Separated Self	Transforming Principle	Transformed Self
The Pleasure-Seeking Self	Principle of Commitment and Right Action	God's Divine Fool

---

Exercise for The Pleasure-Seeking Self: "Lead us not into temptation, but deliver us from evil."

Close your eyes, breathe deeply.

Imagine your guardian angel taking you to a marketplace of your desires. All your gluttonous fantasies and passions line the street like merchants selling their goods. The street is lined with golden steps and at the other end of the market stands a luminous being with outstretched arms.

As you walk toward this light, also feel which of the merchants of desire entice you to stop and lose your direction and commitment to your goal and purpose. When you feel you've gotten stuck or off track, ask yourself what gets you hooked by the desire and why you have made this desire more important than your true Self—the Spirit-ego-self.

Allow your guardian angel to assist you until you reach the radiant figure of light at the end of the path. Who is it? Your Spirit-ego-self, the Christ within you, of course!

Merge with this love in joy.

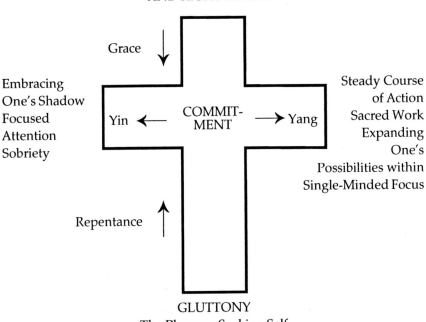

GOD'S DIVINE FOOL
"Lead us not into temptation, but deliver us from evil"

PRINCIPLE OF COMMITMENT
AND RIGHT ACTION

Grace

Embracing
One's Shadow
Focused
Attention
Sobriety

Yin ← COMMIT-MENT → Yang

Steady Course
of Action
Sacred Work
Expanding
One's
Possibilities within
Single-Minded Focus

Repentance

GLUTTONY
The Pleasure-Seeking Self

CORE VICE –LUST
PERSONALITY EXPRESSION OF THE PRODIGAL SON:
THE CONTROLLING SELF

Instruction: "For thine is the kingdom, and the power, and the glory, for ever."

Examples: Cleansing the Temple, Parable of the Tares

And they come to Jerusalem: and Jesus went into the temple, and began to cast out them that sold and bought in the temple, and overthrew the tables of the moneychangers, and the seats of them that sold doves; and would not suffer that any man should carry any vessel through the temple. And he taught, saying unto them, "Is it not written, My house shall be called of all nations the house of prayer? but ye have made it a den of thieves."

And the scribes and chief priests heard it, and sought how they might destroy him: for they feared him, because all the people was astonished at his doctrine. (Mark 11:15-18)

"The kingdom of heaven is likened unto a man which sowed good seed in his field: but while men slept, his enemy came and sowed tares among the wheat, and went his way. But when the blade was sprung up, and brought forth fruit, then appeared the tares also. So the servants of the householder came and said unto him, 'Sir, didst not thou sow good seed in thy field? from whence then hath it tares?'

"He said unto them, 'An enemy hath done this.'

"The servants said unto him, 'Wilt thou then that we go and gather them up?'

"But he said, 'Nay; lest while ye gather up the tares, ye root up also the wheat with them. Let both grow together until the harvest: and in the time of harvest I will say to the reapers, Gather ye together first the tares, and bind them in bundles to burn them: but gather the wheat into my barn.". . .

Then Jesus sent the multitude away, and went into the house: and his disciples came unto him, saying, "Declare unto us the parable of the tares of the field."

He answered and said unto them, "He that soweth the good seed is the Son of man; The field is the world; the good seed are the children of the kingdom; but the tares are the children of the wicked one; the enemy that sowed them is the devil; the harvest is the end of the world; and the reapers are the angels. As therefore the tares are gathered and burned in the fire; so shall it be in the end of this world. The Son of man shall send forth his angels, and they shall gather out of his kingdom all things that offend, and them which do iniquity; and shall cast them into a furnace of fire: there shall be wailing and gnashing of teeth. Then shall the righteous shine forth as the sun in the kingdom of their Father. Who hath ears to hear, let him hear." (Matthew 13:24-30,36-43)

Lesson: The Principle of Relational Opposites, The Principle of Surrender

The life and teachings of Jesus offer as great a lesson in the exercise of divine power and as in divine wisdom and love. Those who are drawn in sentimentality to an image of a "gentle Jesus, meek and mild" have usually lost sight of the fact that Jesus "swam with sharks" that were bent on his destruction during most of his public ministry. Regrettably, these "sharks" came primarily from the ranks of the day's religious elite, though the Roman civil authorities also watched Jesus closely for any signs of threat to their rule.

Jesus could not have functioned so effectively in such hostile surroundings without a keen sensitivity to the fluctuating power influences around him and the ability to modify his actions quickly and intuitively, yet truthfully, to counter them. Insensitivity to authority, even one tactless confrontation, would have been the undoing of his ministry. Had he been intimidated, on the other hand, the sprouts of his fledgling spiritual work would have been choked off by this "field of tares" immediately.

Jesus' absolute confidence in the power of the Almighty within him gave him no need to personally control his surroundings or battle with his adversaries to protect himself. His divine assurance was the source of his genuine innocence, which sometimes manifested as the gentleness of a lamb. If circumstances required, Jesus could just as easily and naturally assert his inner strength openly. The story of "Cleansing the Temple" above is perhaps the best example to be found. In a spontaneous burst of indignation toward the greedy commercialism occurring at the Jerusalem temple at Passover, Jesus amazed the people by an open physical confrontation with his enemies at this center of their world. That same week he delivered his final address in the temple that included the memorable denunciation, "Woe unto you, scribes and Pharisees, hypocrites!" (Matthew 23)

While Jesus might have taught and lived indefinitely among his enemies, these "tares," and gone unscathed, his ministry had been nearly completed and it was time to return to the Father. He chose to end his work in a mighty display of spiritual power: In the innocence of divine certitude, he permitted his body to be crucified as a "lamb of God," then rose from the dead to demonstrate the eternal and unassailable nature of our true life as sons and daughters of God.

At this time of spiritual harvest, the work of Jesus and his disciples, the "wheat," was separated from the efforts of his adversaries, the "tares." The children of "the wicked one" (egotism), were thrown by the "angels" (their own souls) into the "furnace of fire" (the suffering of subconscious living) to attempt once again to gain consciousness in the school of life. The followers of Jesus who had awakened to love "shined forth as the sun in the kingdom of their Father" as they went "into the world and preached the gospel to every creature." (Mark 16:15) In spite of the mistakes of some of its leaders, Judaism itself continued to be a potent spiritual force throughout the Roman Empire, even after the fall of Jerusalem to Titus in 70 A.D. and the destruction of the temple.[22]

In the same manner, we cannot allow virtues and "unclean spirits" to function on and on together in our personalities. Eventually the "unclean spirits," or "tares," of our psyches must be consumed by the fires of spirit as their corresponding virtues arise to "shine forth as the sun."

The Parable of the Tares, and Jesus' own example, teach important and universal lessons about the nature of power and how to exercise it wisely. The Principle of Relational Opposites says that nothing in creation exists apart from its relationship to its opposite, or "that which it is not." "High" has meaning only in relationship to "low," "big" in relationship to "little," laughter in relationship to tears, etc. A middle, or neutral, zone exists between the two polarities as well. The world of form is a world of relativity, i.e., relationships among diverse expressions of Spirit's unity. The Principle of Relational Opposites is in essence the application of the Principle of Oneness to the world of form, an expression of universality in the universe.

Power is one primal, universal principle which takes various expressions in the worlds of time and space. It has an active, or yang, dimension, which Jesus demonstrated in the cleansing of the temple and his denunciation of the scribes and Pharisees. It has a yielding, or yin, dimension, which Jesus, for his own purposes, expressed when he permitted his arrest and crucifixion. There is also a neutral position, or "balance of power," between the two polarities, in which one acts in awareness of power influences around oneself, but is neither actively projecting power nor yielding. Jesus' teaching in parables was an example of this neutral position, where he neither yielded to his enemies' pressure to go away, nor confronted them directly with his teachings. To use power wisely and effectively requires that one draw on its true Source within, then become facile in all dimensions of its expression under spirit guidance.

The Principle of Surrender says that the greater the effort expended to control a person or situation, the less effective the effort. Anything truly worth changing in the world can be accomplished with Spirit guidance and support. Regardless of the strict quantity of time and energy expended, one's exertions are carried along by a sense of ease when in alignment with Spirit. In contrast, the greater the sense of struggle, the more likely the effort being made by the present-day personality is in isolation from Spirit. The separated personality, attempting to get what it thinks it wants by its own efforts, must draw exclusively on its own reservoir of physical and etheric energy. The harder it pushes and forces an illusory agenda of separation onto its surroundings, the more resistance the surroundings tend to put up to maintain equilibrium. Eventually the personality exhausts itself. The world has witnessed the fall of many dictatorships by this process.

Jesus, in alignment with the Principle of Surrender, changed the course of human history in only a few years. He lived the simplest of lifestyles and claimed no authority but God's. His enemies, out of alignment with this Law, found that the harder they struggled against him to maintain their control, the more rapidly their actual influence over the people slipped away. When they eventually managed to gather together their dwindling resources and have him killed by the Roman authorities, he arose, and their misadventures collapsed into abject failure. In the end they salvaged nothing, returning to their subconscious illusions with "wailing and gnashing of teeth."

Discussion

The Controlling Self, in separation, believes it must overcome, possess, and consume the world around it to compensate for its feelings of vulnerability. It is angry about its lost innocence and its need to dominate everything to feel safe. The greater its efforts to control, the greater the resistance the environment puts up. Its life becomes a losing battle. Failure and rejection eventually result from this confusion of weakness with strength.

The Controlling Self in transformation finds true power and protection in God, then learns to surrender to this Higher Power innocently and intelligently. Having "let go and let God," he or she lives in ease, simplicity, and security, extending the grace and protection of beneficent leadership to his or her surroundings.

The prophet Mohammed had a great deal to say about "the kingdom, and the power, and the glory of God." He taught absolute surrender to Allah (literally, The God). The word Islam, in fact, is best translated as surrender (to Allah). By his own account, this illiterate prophet received the holy book of Islam, the Koran, from the Archangel Gabriel. Over a 23-year period in

Saudi Arabia, he received a total of 114 chapters, or *surahs*.[23] The opening to the first *surah*, given below, admonishes believers to follow the straight path in surrender to Allah:

> In the Name of God, the merciful Lord of mercy.
> Praise be to God, the Lord of all being,
> The merciful Lord of mercy,
> Master of the Day of Judgment.
> You alone we serve and to You alone we come for aid.
> Guide us in the straight path,
> The path of those whom You have blessed,
> Not of those against whom there is displeasure,
> Nor of those who have gone astray.[24]

The following passage from the Koran extols the nature of God:

> All that is in the heavens and in the earth magnifies God. He is the all-strong, the all-wise. To Him belongs the kingdom of the heavens and of the earth. He gives life and He brings on death and He is omnipotent over all things. He is the first and the last, the manifest and hidden, and has knowledge over all things. It is He who created the heavens and earth in six days and then assumed his Throne. He knows all that permeates the ground and all that issues from it, what comes down from the heaven and what ascends thither. He is with you wherever you are. God is aware of all you do. His is the kingdom of the heavens and of the earth and to Him all things return. He makes the night to give way to the day and the day to the night and He knows the innermost heart.[25]

Transformation, Expansion, and Regression

When the Controlling Self transforms into the Beneficent Leader it moves toward its core virtue, surrendering to higher will, and becomes trusting, empathetic, supportive of others, open to giving and receiving love without control. It begins to value softness and sensitivity as strength and becomes vulnerable to expressing love and kindness. Yang expansion results in right use of will, tough love, wise projection of power, and conscious leadership for service. Yin expansion brings the ability to yield intelligently and embrace innocence, vulnerability, gentleness, and softness.

When the Controlling Self resists transformation it entrenches more deeply in its vice of lust and becomes suspicious, mistrustful, and isolated, withdrawing from feelings. It controls its space rigidly. It feels loneliness and open hostility toward everyone.

The energetic trends above are consistent with Enneagram personality type eight.

Soul Type: Angelic

Separated Self	Transforming Principle	Transformed Self
The Controlling Self	Principle of Relational Opposites	The Beneficent Leader
	Principle of Surrender	

Exercise for The Controlling Self: "For thine is the kingdom, and the power, and the glory, for ever."

Close your eyes and breathe deeply.

Allow your guardian angel to take you into the spiritual garden in your heart. See him/her guiding you along a path into a sacred sanctuary. Call on the Christ Self there, and allow him to come to you. Feel his love, presence and wisdom. Feel his total balance and energy of healing.

Ask him these questions: "What am I controlling in my life that I need to let go of to find inner peace and freedom from struggle and conflict? What must I give up to take my next step spiritually and know love in a greater way?"

If you are ready to surrender this situation, attitude, or issue in yourself, then offer it to him, giving it to him in all trust and faith that he can take it from you. Receive his love and support as it replaces the burden you have given up to him.

THE BENEFICENT LEADER
"For thine is the kingdom, and the power, and the glory for ever"

PRINCIPLE OF RELATIONAL OPPOSITES
PRINCIPLE OF SURRENDER

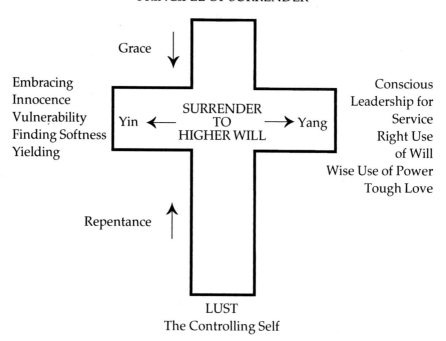

Working with Elementals in Daily Life

Daskalos once asked Nick Demetry, "Do you consider yourself a Greek or an American?" Nick replied that he wasn't sure. Daskalos responded that he considered himself a human being. Even though most spiritual traditions tend to focus on contemplation of God, meditation, and elevation of consciousness, we've chosen exercises to disengage from negative elementals of the human personality, allowing the natural flow of spiritual energies throughout every level of one's being.

Sri Hari Poonjaji, in the tradition of Ramana Maharshi, says, "Enlightenment in simple; we just have to get out of the way." According to Poonjaji, our cravings and identification with the world are our sources of suffering and blockage of self-realization. Poonjaji eloquently describes the enlightenment process through the image of a person walking through a thick forest that is slowly burning. As each tree burns, so does a desire that blocks us from realization of Self. The trees continue to burn until only one remains; this is the lust for freedom itself. This desire we must too burn.

Spiritual paths are sometimes seen as fostering escapism, dissociation, and the desire to be free of one's current conditions. Therefore, we have chosen to use exercises which assist the student in disengaging association from those elementals which veil him/her from the spiritual light within. This light may then unfold naturally out of the simple intention of growing toward it.

Numerous masters have taught that the challenge is not to learn but to unlearn our personalities' habits of thought, feeling, and action which block the natural flow of spirit. When Daskalos was once asked about exercises to develop paranormal abilities, he replied, "Have patience, for as your consciousness evolves through purification of the personality, these abilities unfold in service to love." The "casting out of demons," or deenergizing negative elementals we have created, is a potent way to approach this necessary unlearning process. "Seek ye first the kingdom of God, and his righteousness; and all these things shall be added unto you." (Matthew 6:33)

Daskalos encouraged his students to do daily introspection exercises to clear the mirrors of the mind and emotions for spiritual growth and development. Based on his inspiration and our own experiences, we offer a few exercises and observations about beginning your work on elementals.

Daily Introspection Exercise

- Every night review the day and identify problematic experiences.
- Ask yourself, "What spiritual principles have I ignored?"

- Ask. "What choice might I have made to align myself with the spiritual principles?"
- Reframe the experience in accordance, with the principle broken.
- Bring in the Beloved One and become your loving Self.
- Replay the experience in accordance with the spiritual principles.

In working with these exercises you will see progressive disengagement from elementals over time. This happens in the following stages:

1. When you feel totally identified with the elemental you feel justified in criticizing, blaming, and feeling victimized by recurrent patterns in your life.

2. You recognize the existence of the elemental, that it is playing itself out through you.

3. You become aware of when the elemental is coming, i.e., you recognize its presence before it expresses itself through your thoughts, feelings, and behavior. Still, you feel driven and can't stop its effects.

4. You know it's coming, how it plays itself out, you know you are doing it yet the power of your observer is stronger. You watch yourself doing it, yet you still can't stop it. This stage may go on for some time.

5. You know it is coming like in the stage #4 above, but you go through with it with one added variable. You reframe the situation. For example, imagine you have a fight with your boss, a recurring issue. You sensed it was coming, it starts happening, you are watching yourself beginning to feel victimized, but as you shut the door, you realize it has nothing to do with the boss. It's you! At this point you come back through the door and replay in your reality what you did in your exercise at night. Once you've begun to do this, you begin manifesting a positive elemental, surrendering your will to it instead of the negative one.

6. When you sense it coming, you feel the choice to enact it or not and have more power to keep your own perspective rather than buying into it (i.e., the negative elemental and behavior).

7. When it presents itself, you feel the freedom from it and you're able to laugh about it.

In East Indian spirituality the first stages are equivalent to the play of *Maya*, the illusion that this happening is really outside oneself. In the next stage, which the Indians call *laya*, outer perceptions are recognized as projections of inner states and there is movement toward unity consciousness as awareness expands. In traditional psychological terms, the process of getting out of illusion involves first a movement from self-justification and blame to self-judgment. The danger of this stage, where a little observational ability has been gained, lies in the possibility of creating guilt and negativity and getting stuck there. The final stage is the stage of forgiveness, where one accepts what he or she goes through without either guilt or blame of others. At this point, one reaches compassion and recognizes that the elemental really wants to be transformed and attracted home by love.

Be cautioned that there are triggers for these elementals to be reactivated as you work with them. When an elemental returns to draw on your energy, it generally remains in the periphery of your energy field, waiting for a doorway to be opened into a chakra of corresponding vibration. Some key word or behavior on the part of someone, based on their own security, relationship, or social issues, opens the door; your distress over what's happening eats up enough etheric vitality to weaken your field. The negative elementals "hunt" for any such weakness to gain entry. By analogy, the physical body harbors many viruses and bacteria. It cannot be harmed until the immune system is weakened by some stressor. Disease then can occur.

In the Lord's Prayer Jesus said, "Lead us not into temptation, but deliver us from evil." Indeed worry and emotional reaction tempts us to leave open the door. It is important to recognize that our elementals are our own creations and operate primarily through the Principle of Cause and Effect. Remember the Parable of the Sower, and that "what you sow, that shall ye also reap."

A Visualization Exercise to Aid Introspection

- Get in a comfortable position.
- Close your eyes and take a deep breath.
- Center attention on the heart.
- Visualize a full-length mirror in front of you.
- As you look on yourself in the mirror, bring to mind a situation that exemplifies one of the nine core vices or a related negative elemental.
- Imagine that elemental vice stands behind the mirror in whatever form it presents itself.
- Call it forth into full view and look into its eyes.
- Ask:
  (a) How do you sabotage me and those I love?
  (b) Why do I hold onto you?
  (c) What are you teaching me as I suffer?

- Say:
  (d) I no longer need you.
  (e) I no longer choose to see you as myself.
  (f) I choose to become my loving Self.
- Envelop the vice in flames of amber-golden light and allow it to be consumed.
- Out of the flames allow your beloved Self to emerge in a halo of this amber light.
- Receive this reflection of yourself into your heart.

The nine transformational meditations given previously may be helpful in uncovering core issues that need more focused attention.

The visualization exercise to aid introspection given above may be used to support the healing of these issues.

The two introspective exercises may, on the other hand, lead one to work more intensively with a given separated self. Therefore, all of the exercises in this chapter may be used naturally in conjunction with one another.

VIII

MEDITATIONS FOR AWAKENING LOVE

Instructions for the Meditations

The following series of nine meditations flow naturally from the meditative exercises presented in the previous chapter. They are designed to promote deeper healing in the personality through more focused soul intention. The chakras are cleared one by one of obstructing elementals, allowing love to awaken gently and naturally within all the chakra centers.

These healing meditations have been utilized in various forms in Europe and in the U.S., successfully bringing deep insight and positive changes to our seminar participants. The complete series is available for purchase.

We suggest that these meditations be done in the morning upon awakening or at bedtime. If you don't have the c.d.s you can do the meditations most easily with a partner reading them aloud. Relaxing music in the background may be helpful. We find the best results come to individuals when they dedicate a period of time to each meditation, ideally a week or longer, repeating it as many times as necessary to receive their Christ light fully and deeply.

The meditations can also be used in a group format.

Don't be concerned if you encounter difficulties staying with the meditation process in some sections. The healing will still take place so long as your intent is to remain open to it through spirit. Once entering the healing

149

temples, you may be led to follow an agenda other than the instructions given you. If so honor this experience.

Finally, enjoy and have a happy fulfilling journey home!!

Meditation #1

Basic daily meditation for alignment and protection.

I *Find a comfortable place to sit. Close your eyes. Breathe deeply. Relax your body.*

II *Visualize a white ball of light at the bottom of your feet. As you breathe, visualize and feel the white light moving up your feet into your legs, thighs and hips. As you continue to breathe, feel the light growing brighter and brighter. Feel the light progressing into your pelvic area, abdomen, chest and heart. Feel the light moving over your shoulders, down your arms into your hands and fingers. Feel and see the light moving into your neck, head and face.*

III *Look down at your healing hands of light and on the ground before you. Create a circular disc several times your size in white light and upon it build a white dome structure. This is your healing temple for balancing and aligning your energies and three bodies.*

IV *Step into the temple going to its center. As you stand there look down and you will see that you are standing in the center of an equilateral cross.*

V *On your right side and flowing toward the right side of your body is a Red Flame of Light representing the element of fire, heat, metabolism and the healing force for your physical body and will. Breathe in the Red Flames of Light and ask that your will be strengthened for your life's journey.*

VI *Next put your attention on your left side. Flowing toward the left side of your body is a Violet-purple Flame of Light representing the air element and the healing force for your mind and thoughts. Breathe in the Violet-purple Flames of Light and ask that your mind and thoughts be put into clarity, harmony, and order for your life's journey.*

VII *Now, place your attention along your back side and feel and see a beautiful Blue Flame of healing light flowing over your body from behind you and breathe in this light. This Blue Flame of Light represents the water element, and is the healing force for your emotional body. As you breathe in the Blue Flames ask that your emotional body and heart be cleansed and that you receive joy and courage for your life's journey.*

VIII *Now looking directly in front of you and flowing toward the front of your body is a Silver-White Flame of Light symbolizing the force of integration, balance, harmony and alignment of your three bodies. Breathe in these flames of Silver-white light and ask for harmony and peace to be with you on your life's journey.*

IX *Once again breathing slowly pay attention to your body and feel yourself returning from the journey with the light. Honor the light within you and give thanks for the healing you have received. With your hands of light, dissolve the dome of light that you have created and slowly be more aware of your surroundings. Gently open your eyes. You are ready to receive your blessing for the day!!*

Meditation #2

Basic daily meditation for spiritual reconnection.

I *Find a comfortable place to sit. Close your eyes. Breathe deeply. Relax your body.*

II *Visualize a white ball of light at the bottom of your feet. As you breathe, visualize and feel the white light moving up your feet into your legs, thighs and hips. As you continue to breathe, feel the light growing brighter and brighter. Feel the light progressing into your pelvic area, abdomen, chest and heart. Feel the light moving over your shoulders, down your arms into your hands and fingers. Feel and see the light moving into your neck, head and face.*

III *Visualize a path of golden light along a forest floor.*

IV *Walk along the path until you come to the gates of a beautiful garden.*

V *On the garden gate is a golden-red six-pointed star with a cross in the center.*

VI *Place your hands on the symbol and ask that the healing force awaken your heart to love.*

VII *Go through the garden gate into a beautiful rose garden. Explore the beauty, harmony and loving expressions of nature there. Enjoy all.*

VIII *Somewhere within the garden you will discover a radiant golden fiery flame of light in the shape of the sun. Walk toward this light. From its center emerges your Christ Self in a Golden Robe of Light.*

IX Go to Him. Take His hands and look into His eyes. Contact his Divine Love and Humility. Hear Him speak the words, "Step into My heart my beloved."

X Step into His Radiant Light Body and look through His eyes.

XI Hear Him say to you: "My light is your light, My body is your body of power and action, My eyes are your eyes of truth and vision, My heart is your heart of love, My hands your healing hands."

XII Now create a ball of golden light between the palms of your hands and feel it growing brighter with every breathe you take. Place someone that needs your love into this golden ball of light. See them with the eyes and love of the Christ Self. Visualize the perfection of their physical, emotional and mental bodies. Ask that this healing love reach them and work for their highest good, for their growth and development spiritually, mentally, emotionally and physically.

XIII Now, letting go of the ball of light, create a new ball of golden-light and place yourself in it. See and feel the same Christ Love as before, seeing the perfection of your physical, emotional and mental bodies. Ask that this healing love touch you and work with you for the highest good of your being spiritually, mentally, emotionally and physically. Place the ball of light into your heart.

XIV Walk back through the rose garden and out of the gate. See the symbol of the six-pointed star at the doors of the gate. Give thanks for the healing you have received. Honor the Christ presence in you and in every human being. Very slowly put your attention on your physical body and gently open your eyes and return from the healing meditation journey.

Instructions for meditations #3 – 10
Taking a Spiritual Inventory

I Take a piece of note book paper and place it lengthwise in front of you. Draw three vertical lines on it equally spaced to create 4 columns.

On the far left column write the following categories:

1 Survival (Root Chakra):
  a money
  b homeplace
  c possessions
  d health

2 *Relationships (Sacral Chakra):*
  a *friendship*
  b *partnership/sexuality*
  c *children*
  d *parents*
  e *other significant people*
3 *Work / Career (Solar Plexus Chakra):*
  a *social relationships*
  b *Job position*
  c *Leadership roles*
4 *Love-understanding (Heart Chakra):*
  a *Inner feelings / outer circumstances*
  b *Gratitude*
  c *Service*
5 *Communication / Listening (Throat Chakra)*
6 *Spiritual vision / Goals / Wisdom about life / Forgiveness (Brow Chakra)*
7 *Purpose in Life (Crown Chakra)*

II *On the column next to that write at the top:* **Past**—*Old patterns, attitudes, feelings and conditions of past years. Fill in all these past patterns, etc., for all seven chakra domains listed.*

III *On the third column at the top write:* **Present**—*current patterns, attitudes, feelings and conditions. Fill in all the current patterns, etc., for all seven chakra domains.*

IV *On the far right side column at the top write* **Future**. *Here you can write down what you'd like to create in the future—new patterns, attitudes feelings and conditions that can best support your life in all seven domains of experiences.*

Meditation #3
Healing the Root Chakra

Enhancing your self-worth and overcoming insecurity.

I *Find a comfortable place to sit. Close your eyes. Breathe deeply. Relax your body.*

II *Visualize a white ball of light at the bottom of your feet. As you breathe, visualize and feel the white light moving up your feet into your legs, thighs and hips. As you continue to breathe, feel the light growing brighter and brighter. Feel the light progressing into your pelvic area, abdomen, chest and heart. Feel the light moving over your shoulders, down your arms into your hands and fingers. Feel and see the light moving into your neck, head and face.*

III *Look down at your healing hands of light and on the ground before you. Create a circular disc several times your size in white light and upon it build a white dome structure. This is your healing temple for balancing and aligning your energies and three bodies.*

IV *Step into the temple going to its center. As you stand there look down and you will see that you are standing in the center of an equilateral cross.*

V *On your right side and flowing toward the right side of your body is a Red Flame of Light representing the element of fire, heat, metabolism and the healing force for your physical body and will. Breathe in the Red Flames of Light and ask that your will be strengthened for your life's journey.*

VI *Next put your attention on your left side. Flowing toward the left side of your body is a Violet-purple Flame of Light representing the air element and the healing force for your mind and thoughts. Breathe in the Violet-purple Flames of Light and ask that your mind and thoughts be put into clarity, harmony and order for your life's journey.*

VII *Now, place your attention along your back side and feel and see a beautiful Blue Flame of healing light flowing over your body from behind you and breathe in this light. This Blue Flame of Light represents the water element, and is the healing force for your emotional body. As you breathe in the Blue Flames ask that your emotional body and heart be cleansed and that you receive joy and courage for your life's journey.*

VIII *Now looking directly in front of you and flowing toward the front of your body is a Silver-White Flame of Light symbolizing the force of integration, balance, harmony and alignment of your three bodies. Breathe in these flames of Silver-white light and ask for harmony and peace to be with you on your life's journey.*

IX *Go through the back side of the dome into a beautiful rose-garden.*

X *There in the garden you will see a suitcase that contains all the current possessions, conditions, patterns, thoughts and feelings of your root chakra, including any issues with self esteem and unworthiness.*

XI   *Lie down on your back next to your suitcase. Look up at the sky above you. Visualize a beautiful Ray of Light coming down from the Light Temple of your root chakra directly into the rose garden and connecting to your root chakra.*

XII   *Imagine yourself stepping out of your physical body into your energy body and with your suitcase in hand, feel yourself lifting into the ray of healing light. Feel yourself lifting lighter and freer, freer and lighter all the way to the garden gate of your root chakra center.*

XIII   *Enter the Garden and explore its beauty. Somewhere in the garden is your Healing Light Temple for your root chakra. Go to the entrance of your Temple with your suitcase in hand. Call on your Spiritual Guide to stand on your right side and call on your Guardian Angel to stand on your left side. Connect with their energies through your heart.*

XIV   *Ask your guide and guardian angel to open the suitcase and reveal to you any conditions or beliefs that promote in you feelings of insecurity, unworthiness or low self-esteem. Ask that these be projected on a big movie screen that opens up to your right side. Ask to be shown the origins of these feelings in your life or relationships. Maintain your focus in your heart and receive the images as a gift of your higher consciousness for your healing process. Gather these events, situations or beliefs together before you and say to them: "I am not you, you are not me. I have created you for my learning. I wish to be free of you now!"*

XV   *Ask your Guardian Angel and Spiritual Guide to transform the self-limiting thought patterns you carry in your suitcase into the new energies and conditions that you really need for the next part of your journey.*

XVI   *Return through the garden of your root center with these transformed energies and come down the Ray of Healing Light returning to the Rose Garden. Plant these new energies like seeds and watch the new patterns, conditions and attitudes grow.*

XVII   *Return through the Dome Temple and give thanks for all the divine guidance and assistance you have received.*

XVIII   *Once again, breathing slowly, pay attention to your body and feel yourself returning from the journey with the light. Honor the light within you and give thanks for the healing you have received. With your hands of light, dissolve the dome of light that you have created and slowly be more aware of your surroundings. Gently open your eyes. You are ready to receive your blessing for the day!!*

Meditation #4
Healing the Sacral Chakra

Awakening love, forgiveness, and intimacy.

  I *Find a comfortable place to sit. Close your eyes. Breathe deeply. Relax your body.*

 II *Visualize a white ball of light at the bottom of your feet. As you breathe, visualize and feel the white light moving up your feet into your legs, thighs and hips. As you continue to breathe, feel the light growing brighter and brighter. Feel the light progressing into your pelvic area, abdomen, chest and heart. Feel the light moving over your shoulders, down your arms into your hands and fingers. Feel and see the light moving into your neck, head and face.*

III *Look down at your healing hands of light and on the ground before you. Create a circular disc several times your size in white light and upon it build a white dome structure. This is your healing temple for balancing and aligning your energies and three bodies.*

 IV *Step into the temple going to its center. As you stand there look down and you will see that you are standing in the center of an equilateral cross.*

  V *On your right side and flowing toward the right side of your body is a Red Flame of Light representing the element of fire, heat, metabolism and the healing force for your physical body and will. Breathe in the Red Flames of Light and ask that your will be strengthened for your life's journey.*

 VI *Next put your attention on your left side. Flowing toward the left side of your body is a Violet-purple Flame of Light representing the air element and the healing force for your mind and thoughts. Breathe in the Violet-purple Flames of Light and ask that your mind and thoughts be put into clarity, harmony and order for your life's journey.*

VII *Now, place your attention along your back side and feel and see a beautiful Blue Flame of healing light flowing over your body from behind you and breathe in this light. This Blue Flame of Light represents the water element, and is the healing force for your emotional body. As you breathe in the Blue Flames ask that your emotional body and heart be cleansed and that you receive joy and courage for your life's journey.*

VIII *Now looking directly in front of you and flowing toward the front of your body is a Silver-White Flame of Light symbolizing the force of integration,* balance, harmony and alignment of your three bodies. Breathe in these flames of Silver-white light and ask for harmony and peace to be with you on your life's journey.

IX Go through the back side of the dome into a beautiful rose-garden.

X As you enter your rose garden, find a comfortable place to lie down. Visualize a large column of orange-white light on your left side.

XI Think of the most important people in your life now that you find the most challenging in relationship. I.e. could be your partner, parents, friends, brothers, sisters, fellow workers, etc.

XII Now step out of your physical body into your energy body. You will see the people standing in the orange-white column of light.

XIII Feel yourself lifting together with them in the column of light, lifting lighter and freer, freer and lighter, traveling to the garden gate of the Light Temple of your sacral chakra.

XIV Go through the garden gate and open your heart to receiving the healing energy available in your garden.

XV Together with those individuals that have joined you step to the entrance of your healing temple.

XVI Call on your Spiritual Guide and Guardian Angel to surround you and the group you've come with. Ask your Guide and Guardian Angel to take you before an altar in the Temple.

XVII Look at each person that has come with you. See how they each mirror some part of yourself, and how the issues you hold and find with them are your own and are only being reflected back to you by them. Ask yourself what are the lessons you have to learn and understand and be grateful for their presence in your life. Forgive yourself, forgive them, and ask for their forgiveness for what has happened.

XVIII Feel your Guardian Angel and Spiritual Guide transforming your self-limiting thought patterns through flames of orange-golden-yellow light into the energy of love.

XIX Bring each individual into your heart and say to them: "I make a space for you in my heart, I give you thanks for all the lessons you've helped me with. I set you free!"

XX Walk out of the temple and through the garden of your sacral chakra to the garden gate. Give thanks for the support of your Spiritual Guide and

Guardian Angel. Step back into the column of light and slowly return to the Rose Garden. Gently pass through your dome temple and out of the front entrance.

XXI *Once again, breathing slowly, pay attention to your body and feel yourself returning from the journey with the light. Honor the light within you and give thanks for the healing you have received. With your hands of light, dissolve the dome of light that you have created and slowly, be more aware of your surroundings. Gently open your eyes. You are ready to receive your blessings for the day!!*

Meditation #5
Healing the Solar Plexus Chakra

Uncovering and manifesting personal empowerment.

I *Find a comfortable place to sit. Close your eyes. Breathe deeply. Relax your body.*

II *Visualize a white ball of light at the bottom of your feet. As you breathe, visualize and feel the white light moving up your feet into your legs, thighs and hips. As you continue to breathe, feel the light growing brighter and brighter. Feel the light progressing into your pelvic area, abdomen, chest and heart. Feel the light moving over your shoulders, down your arms into your hands and fingers. Feel and see the light moving into your neck, head and face.*

III *Look down at your healing hands of light and on the ground before you. Create a circular disc several times your size in white light and upon it build a white dome structure. This is your healing temple for balancing and aligning your energies and three bodies.*

IV *Step into the temple going to its center. As you stand there look down and you will see that you are standing in the center of an equilateral cross.*

V *On your right side and flowing toward the right side of your body is a Red Flame of Light representing the element of fire, heat, metabolism and the healing force for your physical body and will. Breathe in the Red Flames of Light and ask that your will be strengthened for your life's journey.*

VI *Next put your attention on your left side. Flowing toward the left side of your body is a Violet-purple Flame of Light representing the air element and the healing force for your mind and thoughts. Breathe in the Violet-*

purple Flames of Light and ask that your mind and thoughts be put into clarity, harmony and order for your life's journey.

VII *Now, place your attention along your back side and feel and see a beautiful Blue Flame of healing light flowing over your body from behind you and breathe in this light. This Blue Flame of Light represents the water element, and is the healing force for your emotional body. As you breathe in the Blue Flames ask that your emotional body and heart be cleansed and that you receive joy and courage for your life's journey.*

VIII *Now looking directly in front of you and flowing toward the front of your body is a Silver-White Flame of Light symbolizing the force of integration, balance, harmony and alignment of your three bodies. Breathe in these flames of Silver-white light and ask for harmony and peace to be with you on your life's journey.*

IX *Go through the back side of the dome into a beautiful rose-garden.*

X *As you enter your Rose Garden, find a comfortable place to lie down. Visualize a large column of Golden-Ruby-Red Light on your left side. Think of your profession and conditions of your work place. Identify problematic issues with your job and the part of yourself that struggles to achieve success, that feels somehow unrecognized for your efforts. Allow your thoughts to manifest two figures before you: a controlling self that drives you and holds you to the task and a helpless struggling self that doesn't feel good enough and at the same time is unrecognized for your efforts.*

XI *Imagine stepping out of your physical body into your energy body and into the golden-ruby-red light with these two aspects of yourself. Feel yourself lifting to the gate of your solar plexus chakra garden. Go to your healing temple.*

XII *As you step into the entrance see and feel your Spiritual Guide on your right side and the Holy Spirit of creation as a flame of golden-ruby-light on your left. Connect with their energies through your heart.*

XIII *As you enter the temple, face both aspects of yourself. Place your hands on their hearts and see more deeply the lessons you are to learn with them. Ask yourself why you need them in your life. Keep asking until you find a true answer that touches your heart with the full understanding of your lessons. Let the Holy Spirit of Creation and your Spiritual Guide transform these self-limiting thought patterns into truth, wisdom, and power for you.*

Bring the transformed energies into your solar plexus as a ball of light asking it to grow within you.

XIV *Return to your rose garden by passing out of the garden gate of your temple, coming down the column of light. Plant these new energies and let them continue to grow. Return to your dome temple and give thanks for your journey.*

XV *Once again, breathing slowly, pay attention to your body and feel yourself returning from the journey with the light. Honor the light within you and give thanks for the healing you have received. With your hands of light, dissolve the dome of light that you have created and slowly, be more aware of your surroundings. Gently open your eyes. You are ready to receive your blessings for the day!!*

Meditation #6
Healing the Heart Chakra

Building divine love in relationships.

I *Find a comfortable place to sit. Close your eyes. Breathe deeply. Relax your body.*

II *Visualize a white ball of light at the bottom of your feet. As you breathe, visualize and feel the white light moving up your feet into your legs, thighs and hips. As you continue to breathe, feel the light growing brighter and brighter. Feel the light progressing into your pelvic area, abdomen, chest and heart. Feel the light moving over your shoulders, down your arms into your hands and fingers. Feel and see the light moving into your neck, head and face.*

III *Look down at your healing hands of light and on the ground before you. Create a circular disc several times your size in white light and upon it build a white dome structure. This is your healing temple for balancing and aligning your energies and three bodies.*

IV *Step into the temple going to its center. As you stand there look down and you will see that you are standing in the center of an equilateral cross.*

V *On your right side and flowing toward the right side of your body is a Red Flame of Light representing the element of fire, heat, metabolism and the healing force for your physical body and will. Breathe in the Red Flames of Light and ask that your will be strengthened for your life's journey.*

VI Next put your attention on your left side. Flowing toward the left side of your body is a Violet-purple Flame of Light representing the air element and the healing force for your mind and thoughts. Breathe in the Violet-purple Flames of Light and ask that your mind and thoughts be put into clarity, harmony and order for your life's journey.

VII Now, place your attention along your back side and feel and see a beautiful Blue Flame of healing light flowing over your body from behind you and breathe in this light. This Blue Flame of Light represents the water element, and is the healing force for your emotional body. As you breathe in the Blue Flames ask that your emotional body and heart be cleansed and that you receive joy and courage for your life's journey.

VIII Now looking directly in front of you and flowing toward the front of your body is a Silver-White Flame of Light symbolizing the force of integration, balance, harmony and alignment of your three bodies. Breathe in these flames of Silver-white light and ask for harmony and peace to be with you on your life's journey.

IX Standing in the center of your domed temple, call on the 4 flames of the elements—red on the right, violet-purple on the left, blue on your back and silver-white in front of you to support your journey.

X Go through the back side of the dome into a beautiful rose-garden.

XI Lie down in a comfortable place and look up at the sky above you. Visualize a beautiful pink-rose ray of light coming down to your heart chakra from the light temple of your own heart chakra.

XII Imagine stepping out of your physical body into your energy body and lift into the ray of the healing light and travel to the gate of the garden of your heart chakra. On the garden gate you will see a six-pointed golden star with a cross in the center.

XIII Place your hands on the symbol and receive the healing energy into your heart.

XIV Step into the garden and go to the temple entrance. Connect with your Spiritual Guide and the Holy Spirit of Mercy and enter your temple.

XV Ask them to bring forth your perfect male and female aspects and energies (as in the Garden of Eden).

XVI Together with them, walk out of the temple through the garden and out the gate, down the ray of rose-pink light back to the rose garden. See the perfect *male and female energies of your soul transformed into the wounded male and female aspects and energies of your personality.*

XVII   *Look into their eyes. What are they feeling, thinking? What holds them apart from love and union?*

XVIII *Choose the one that needs the healing most at first. What old belief or attitude keeps it isolated and separated from love? What happened within your own family or life experience that made you mistrust love and close your heart down? (pause). What are the lessons you must learn to regain your trust in love? Are you ready to let go of all pain and suffering and embrace forgiveness? If not, ask to be shown why and how can you work on it.*

XIX   *Look at your other aspect and ask what belief and attitude has impacted your capacity for love and union? What happened within your own family or life experience that made you mistrust love and close your heart down? (pause) What are the lessons you must learn to regain your trust in love? Are you ready to let go of all pain and suffering and embrace forgiveness? If not ask to be shown why and how can you work on it.*

XX   *Place your hands on their hearts and become your loving self, feeling the support of the Holy Spirit of Mercy and your Spiritual Guide.*

XXI   *Together with the male and female aspects of your wounded personality lift into the rose-pink ray of light and lift to the garden gate of your light temple of your heart chakra. Enter the garden and proceed to your healing temple*

XXII   *Enter the temple and find your perfect male and female aspects again. Call on the Divine Father of Creation for the healing of your male, by asking Him to blend your perfect male-self with your wounded male-self, blessing you and healing the wounds through love and deep understanding of the truth. See the light flowing all the way from your heart, passing through all your lower chakras and upper chakras. See how important it is to have the bridge of your heart center always open and connected to the light of God within you.*

XXIII   *Ask the Divine Mother of Love for the healing of your female. Allow her to merge with your perfect female-self and your wounded female-self and pour over you the capacity to love unconditionally. See the wounds being healed and your female aspect become open to receive and understand all forms of love, without judgment or criticism.*

XXIV *See the light flowing all the way from your heart, passing through all your lower chakras and upper chakras. See how important it is to have the bridge of your heart center always open and connected to the light of the God within you.*

XXV *Take this energy deep into your heart and ask yourself to remember this healing and the love you feel right now in every time, place or situation where you may feel your heart is closing down again.*

XXVI *Walk out of the temple and through the garden of your heart chakra to the garden gate. Give thanks for the support of your Spiritual Guide and the Holy Spirit of Mercy. Step back into the column of light and slowly return to the Rose Garden. Gently pass through your dome temple and out of the front entrance.*

XXVII *Once again, breathing slowly, pay attention to your body and feel yourself returning from the journey with the light. Honor the light within you and give thanks for the healing you have received. With your hands of light, dissolve the dome of light that you have created and slowly, be more aware of your surroundings. Gently open your eyes. You are ready to receive your blessings for the day!!*

Meditation #7
Healing the Throat Chakra

Manifesting your spiritual path and life goals.

I *Find a comfortable place to sit. Close your eyes. Breathe deeply. Relax your body.*

II *Visualize a white ball of light at the bottom of your feet. As you breathe, visualize and feel the white light moving up your feet into your legs, thighs and hips. As you continue to breathe, feel the light growing brighter and brighter. Feel the light progressing into your pelvic area, abdomen, chest and heart. Feel the light moving over your shoulders, down your arms into your hands and fingers. Feel and see the light moving into your neck, head and face.*

III *Look down at your healing hands of light and on the ground before you. Create a circular disc several times your size in white light and upon it build a white dome structure. This is your healing temple for balancing and aligning your energies and three bodies.*

IV *Step into the temple going to its center. As you stand there look down and you will see that you are standing in the center of an equilateral cross.*

V *On your right side and flowing toward the right side of your body is a Red Flame of Light representing the element of fire, heat, metabolism and the healing force for your physical body and will. Breathe in the Red Flames of Light and ask that your will be strengthened for your life's journey.*

VI *Next put your attention on your left side. Flowing toward the left side of your body is a Violet-purple Flame of Light representing the air element and the healing force for your mind and thoughts. Breathe in the Violet-purple Flames of Light and ask that your mind and thoughts be put into clarity, harmony and order for your life's journey.*

VII *Now, place your attention along your back side and feel and see a beautiful Blue Flame of healing light flowing over your body from behind you and breathe in this light. This Blue Flame of Light represents the water element, and is the healing force for your emotional body. As you breathe in the Blue Flames ask that your emotional body and heart be cleansed and that you receive joy and courage for your life's journey.*

VIII *Now looking directly in front of you and flowing toward the front of your body is a Silver-White Flame of Light symbolizing the force of integration, balance, harmony and alignment of your three bodies. Breathe in these flames of Silver-white light and ask for harmony and peace to be with you on your life's journey.*

IX *Go through the back side of the dome into a beautiful rose-garden and find a comfortable place to lie down.*

X *Call on the color light ray that can best support the healing of your throat chakra. Feel and see it connecting to your throat chakra from the healing light temple of your own throat chakra center.*

XI *Imagine stepping out of your physical body into your energy body. Step into the ray of light and feel yourself lifting to the gate of the garden of your throat center. Enter through the garden gate and go to the entrance of the temple of your throat chakra center.*

XII *Call your Spiritual Guide and the violet-purple flames of the air element, the healing force of your mind, to come to you. Connect with their energies through your heart.*

XIII *Walk into the temple and go to its holy altar. Ask your guide and the violet flame to bring forth old energy thought patterns (elementals) from the past that are blocking your communication, your vision of the future.*

XIV *Ask your guide to show you who and/or what incident from the past set this old elemental pattern in motion.*

XV *Look at this pattern and find out why you need it in your life. How has it served you? Why do you choose to keep it? What is the true hurt/pain you are trying to hide from yourself? Go deeper asking questions until you find the truth that speaks so loudly in your heart that you feel the breakthrough of the old energy within you and the light shining through your throat chakra. Speak (dialogue) with the elemental: "I am not you and you are not me." Tell it how it made you suffer, how it has hurt the ones you love. Say to it: "I created you, I have learned from you and I am ready to let you go."*

XVI *Face those involved, and say to them: "I can't carry this for you any longer. I need to set you free and I need to be free."*

XVII *Ask your guide and the violet-purple flame to transform these self-limiting thought patterns in the transformational fire of love and return them to you as a new energy for creation and manifestation.*

XVIII *With the violet-purple flames on your left and your spiritual guide on your right, visualize what you would like to create and manifest in your next phase of life.*

XIX *Walk to the entrance of the temple and through the garden to the garden gate. At the gate visualize the violet flame becoming the blue flame of the water element for the healing of your emotional body. As you breathe in this healing energy bring your new vision and goals for the future into your heart. Feel the strength of directed emotions, love and desire to manifest your vision and goals.*

XX *Go through the garden gate and down the ray of light back to the rose garden. Feel your guide on your right and feel and see the red flame of the fire element, the healing force for your physical body and will on your left. Breathe it in deeply.*

XXI *Visualize and draw your vision for manifestation from your heart center into your solar plexus center. Focus your movement of energy out of your solar plexus and into the world through a ball of light containing your vision. Ask that this vision be manifested for your highest good and the highest good of humanity and the planet. See it manifested now!*

XXII *Once again, breathing slowly, pay attention to your body and feel yourself returning from the journey with the light. Honor the light within you and give thanks for the healing you have received. With your hands of light, dissolve the dome of light that you have created and slowly, be more aware of your surroundings. Gently open your eyes. You are ready to receive your blessings for the day!!*

Meditation #8
Healing the Brow Chakra

Opening new vision and understanding.

Note: For meditations #8 and 9 we have changed the color light flames for the different healing forces of the elements, you can elect to use the ones given before.

I *Find a comfortable place to sit. Close your eyes. Breathe deeply. Relax your body.*

II *Visualize a white ball of light at the bottom of your feet. As you breathe, visualize and feel the white light moving up your feet into your legs, thighs and hips. As you continue to breathe, feel the light growing brighter and brighter. Feel the light progressing into your pelvic area, abdomen, chest and heart. Feel the light moving over your shoulders, down your arms into your hands and fingers. Feel and see the light moving into your neck, head and face.*

III *Look down at your healing hands of light and on the ground before you. Create a circular disc several times your size in white light and upon it build a white dome structure. This is your healing temple for balancing and aligning your energies and three bodies.*

IV *Step into the temple going to its center. As you stand there look down and you will see that you are standing in the center of an equilateral cross.*

V *On your right side and flowing toward the right side of your body is a Royal-Blue Flame of Light representing the element of fire, heat, metabolism and the healing force for your physical body and will. Breathe in the Royal-blue Flames of Light and ask that your will be strengthened for your life's journey.*

VI *Next put your attention on your left side. Flowing toward the left side of your body is a Emerald-green Flame of Light representing the air element* and the healing force for your mind and thoughts. Breathe in the Flames of Emerald-green Light and ask that your mind and thoughts be put into clarity, harmony and order for your life's journey.

VII Now, place your attention along your back side and feel and see a beautiful white-crystal Flame of healing light flowing over your body from behind you and breathe in this light. This white-crystal Flame of Light represents the water element, and is the healing force for your emotional body. As you breathe in the white-crystal Flames ask that your emotional body and heart be cleansed and that you receive joy and courage for your life's journey.

VIII Now looking directly in front of you and flowing toward the front of your body is a golden-ruby-red Flame of Light symbolizing the force of integration, balance, harmony and alignment of your three bodies. Breathe in these flames of golden-ruby-red light and ask for harmony and peace to be with you on your life's journey.

IX Go through the back side of the dome into a beautiful rose-garden and you will see a path of golden light before you. On the right side of the path you will find all the people you have blamed or judged or misunderstood. Let your guardian Angel awaken your heart to see each of them as mirrors for you. Forgive yourself and ask for forgiveness.

X On the left side of the path see all the people that have judged you. See how you have been a mirror for them. Ask their guardian angels to appear for them and to assist them in realizing how you have mirrored their own faults. Forgive them.

XI Ask the guides to lift both groups to the healing light.

XII See a beautiful amethyst ray of healing light coming down into your rose garden. Imagine stepping out of your physical body into your energy body. Step into this ray of light and travel to the gate of the garden of the light temple of your brow chakra. On the gate you will see a golden triangle of light. Place your hands on it and charge your energies with its light.

XIII Pass through the gate and go to your temple. As you stand in the entrance connect with your guardian angel on your left and your spiritual guide on your right.

XIV Ask them to take you before your altar and reveal to you any old thoughts or negative energy patterns that block and hold back your vision, clarity and understanding.

XV   *See them both step forth and surround these self-limiting thought patterns in the palm of their hands with violet flames of healing light, transforming them into the energies of clarity, understanding, compassion and objectivity.*

XVI   *Receive this light into your spiritual eye center and return through the garden of your temple, down the ray of the amethyst light to your rose garden. Plant this new seed of understanding into your garden and look at your life with new eyes. Return through the domed temple and give thanks for the love and the new awakening you have received.*

XVII   *Once again, breathing slowly, pay attention to your body and feel yourself returning from the journey with the light. Honor the light within you and give thanks for the healing you have received. With your hands of light, dissolve the dome of light that you have created and slowly, be more aware of your surroundings. Gently open your eyes. You are ready to receive your blessings for the day!!*

Meditation #9
Healing the Crown Chakra

Discovering your spiritual purpose and renewing your connection to joy and inspiration.

I   *Find a comfortable place to sit. Close your eyes. Breathe deeply. Relax your body.*

II   *Visualize a white ball of light at the bottom of your feet. As you breathe, visualize and feel the white light moving up your feet into your legs, thighs and hips. As you continue to breathe, feel the light growing brighter and brighter. Feel the light progressing into your pelvic area, abdomen, chest and heart. Feel the light moving over your shoulders, down your arms into your hands and fingers. Feel and see the light moving into your neck, head and face.*

III   *Look down at your healing hands of light and on the ground before you Create a circular disc several times your size in white light and upon it build a white dome structure. This is your healing temple for balancing and aligning your energies and three bodies.*

IV   *Step into the temple going to its center. As you stand there look down and you will see that you are standing in the center of an equilateral cross.*

V *On your right side and flowing toward the right side of your body is a Royal-Blue Flame of Light representing the element of fire, heat, metabolism and the healing force for your physical body and will. Breathe in the Royal-blue Flames of Light and ask that your will be strengthened for your life's journey.*

VI *Next put your attention on your left side. Flowing toward the left side of your body is a Emerald-green Flame of Light representing the air element and the healing force for your mind and thoughts. Breathe in the Flames of Emerald-green Light and ask that your mind and thoughts be put into clarity, harmony and order for your life's journey.*

VII *Now, place your attention along your back side and feel and see a beautiful white-crystal Flame of healing light flowing over your body from behind you and breathe in this light. This white-crystal Flame of Light represents the water element, and is the healing force for your emotional body. As you breathe in the white-crystal Flames ask that your emotional body and heart be cleansed and that you receive joy and courage for your life's journey.*

VIII *Now looking directly in front of you and flowing toward the front of your body is a golden-ruby-red Flame of Light symbolizing the force of integration, balance, harmony and alignment of your three bodies. Breathe in these flames of golden-ruby-red light and ask for harmony and peace to be with you on your life's journey.*

IX *Go through the back side of the dome into a beautiful rose-garden. See a beautiful violet flame on your right and a white-crystal flame on your left. Connect with the healing light of these flames.*

X *Standing before you is your Guardian Angel, kneel down before Him. Look up into His eyes and say to Him: "I surrender whatever is blocking me from my higher purpose."*

XI *Feel your Guardian Angel placing his healing hands on your Crown chakra and dissolving this block of energy.*

XII *As you look up see directly behind your angel a white column of light. Imagine stepping out of your physical body into your energy body. Step into the column of light and lift to the gate of the garden of your crown chakra. There on the garden gate is a beautiful arch in rainbow colored light. Feel the light as a shower, flowing down and cleansing you. Enter your garden and go to your light temple entrance.*

XIII *Connect with your Guardian angel on your left and your Spiritual Guide on your right. Go before your altar and ask to be shown the old patterns and energies blocking you from your spiritual purpose on the planet earth.*

XIV *Through the eyes of your Guardian angel look at all those patterns and ask why do you need these blocks? What do they represent to you? What do you gain by keeping them and what do you lose? What is the main emotion behind your patterns? What is your lesson? (pause and receive).*

XV *When you feel you have gotten the answer that really touches your heart, look at these elementals and tell them; "I am not you and you are not me. I want to know my true purpose and awaken my spiritual inspiration and joy."*

XVI *Ask your Guide and Guardian Angel to transform these self-limiting thought patterns into the virtue of unconditional love and renewed purpose by placing them in a white-crystal flame of light. Take your virtues back into yourself, placing them into your heart. Walk through the garden to the gate and enter the column of white light, returning from your journey into the rose garden. Walk through the domed temple and give thanks for the spiritual support that accompanies your life.*

XVII *Once again, breathing slowly, pay attention to your body and feel yourself returning from the journey with the light. Honor the light within you and give thanks for the healing you have received. With your hands of light, dissolve the dome of light that you have created and slowly, be more aware of your surroundings. Gently open your eyes. You are ready to receive your blessings for the day!!*

Meditation #10
Transforming Vices into Virtues for
Your Enneagram Personality Type

The previous exercises may be adapted to transform the core vice of your Enneagram personality type into its corresponding virtue at each of the seven chakra levels in this meditation.

I-IX *Go through steps I-IX as in meditation #3 (Healing the Root Chakra).*

X *Visualize a beautiful ray of white light coming down from the light temple of the specific chakra you are transforming directly into the rose garden and connecting to your same chakra.*

XI   *Imagine yourself stepping out of your physical body into your energy body and feel yourself lifting into the ray of healing light. Feel yourself lifting all the way to the garden gate of your _____ chakra.*

XII *Enter the garden and go to the entrance of your healing temple. Call on your Guardian Angel and Spiritual Guide to be with you.*

XIII *Imagine the core vice of your Enneagram personality type standing before you in whatever form it presents itself.*

   • *Ask*
     (a) How do you sabotage me and those I love?
     (b) Why do I hold on to you?
     (c) What are you teaching me as I suffer?

   • *Explore these questions using the inventory categories for the respective chakra exercise you are doing on pp. 152-153.*

   • *Say*
     (a) I no longer need you.
     (b) I no longer choose to see you as myself.
     (c) I choose to become my virtuous self.

XIV *Call on the angel of your virtue to stand behind you, touching your shoulders with energetic support and strength. Envelop the vice in flames of amber-gold light and allow it to be consumed and transformed.*

XV   *Out of the flames allow your virtuous energy to emerge and concentrate it into a ball of light between the palms of your hands. Charge it through breath, visualization, and feeling and take it into your corresponding chakra center. As you breathe, feel the energy filling all your chakras.*

XVI *Now create it again into a ball of light in your hands and send it to envelop your personal home space and work space as a positive elemental virtue to support your development.*

XVII *Walk out of your temple and through the garden, giving thanks for the new gift you've received. With these transformed energies come down the ray of healing light, returning to the rose garden.*

XVIII *Return to your dome temple and give thanks for all the divine guidance and assistance you have received. Dissolve the temple and return to your surroundings.*

IX

PRIVATE INTERVIEW WITH DASKALOS ON LOVE AND NONATTACHMENT

Nick

Daskalos, you have talked a lot about love. What is the difference between unconditional love and the conditional love that most people struggle with?

Daskalos

First of all we must understand that love is love. And I call it unconditional love. And this unconditional love should be directed as a reflection of the love of God coming to us, and the means of reflection is our heart. He is asking us not to contaminate his love which is reflected from our heart. So, this is first of all his love, and we don't have the right to color it. Our hearts should be the crystal clear mirror to reflect his love which is the unconditional love.

Towards whom do we reflect this love? We say in the prayer before starting our lesson, "to reflect your love towards you." To love him unconditionally does not mean to ask him in ignorance for that and that and that, to give it to us. His mercy is such as Joshua (Jesus) told us, "Ask and it will be given to you, knock and it will be opened to you, to one who is asking it will be given." It is the greatest expression of mercy from God the Father. He might say:

172

You unaware creatures, I have given you everything. A perfect body, which is perfect and can remain perfect provided you don't ruin it by your irreverent way of living. I have given you everything so that in this body, you may live in it happily. You're destroying it. What else can you ask of me? Favors, temporary things which are passing? I have given you everything! The body, the sun, all these things. Everything that I have created that you need to keep your gross material body alive and in good health. Food, water, everything. I have given to you within your body your lungs to breathe my vitality and myself in them. You are breathing, and taking in food and liquids and everything else I have given to you, so you can keep your material body in perfect health. I have given to you now apart from your body, on your body your senses, sight. You can see and enjoy the sun, and everything in nature that I have created. I enjoy them through them and through you. Why don't you enjoy them? For I have not done them for you but you can enjoy everything with your senses. Now everything is mine. I have created it, from my own self, from my own mind super-substance. And you are in the body, which is not yours. It is mine. He which eats my flesh, the logos supersubstance, is making it his flesh. What is my blood? In your bodies is my blood. So what do you expect me to give you? More? So do you give me at least thanks if not your love to me? Even thanks do you give me? No. Who is giving thanks to God?

Nick

Where is the gratitude?

Daskalos

"And all the time you ask for what? For what I have created? You live on the planet. I have given you the opportunity to enjoy it by seeing it? And instead you take the attitude of insolence toward me. To call it yours? My house, my property, mine, mine, mine, all mine. What were you going to ask of me as God which isn't mine and that you call it yours. I gave it to you! Before asking, I give you everything. What else? So, if you see what human beings are asking from God, it is imaginary and ignorant because everything is given already. And you don't even thank me and recognize that I am, and I am existing. So in giving a reflection of my unconditional love to me from you, you have not succeeded."

Now what is conditional love? We will study that. You have created in your personality, time and place petty self, in the body you are living, in my body that I have given you to live and that I sustain, a demon in reality. Why? Hating my other life reflections, my fellow man? Hating them, you hate me. I am in them. This is what Joshua has taught. Whatever you do, good or bad to any human being around me, you are doing it to me! All of you are in my oneness. You are injuring me, or you are just doing something good to me. Yet, we don't see that.

What do you call conditional love apart from love given to God? What do we ask from human beings and what are we giving other human beings, to our wives, to our husbands, to our children, to our parents? What is it? Study it. Satisfaction of our stupid egoism? Do you love the others as they are or as you think they should be? Why, who gave you that right? Each fellow is on the scale of his evolution. So what is love towards human beings? To a wife, to a husband, to children, to parents, to friends? All around us. What you call conditional love for me is just ingratitude to God and to the human beings. What is conditional love? Kneel before me and satisfy my desires, sexual or not sexual. If you serve this interest of mine, you love me. Otherwise you don't love me, and therefore, why should I love you? The conditional love you mention for me, what can I call it? Insolence is a very mild word. Insolence to God, because in every human being is God.

So, the first principle of Christianity which Joshua had taught, love the Lord your God in you. Your being self, your spirit being self, with what I have given you to love it, loving me! Because I am in you also. You're in my oneness. With all the heart I have given you, with all the soul I have granted you, with all your intelligence, your mind. I gave you the right to use my mind supersubstance. It's clear what Joshua has given. And love your fellow man—all your fellow human beings—your fellow man not less than you love yourself.

Nick

Daskalos, as well as you have shared it and embodied that love, too, very few people at this time on the planet really know perfect love. Does one have to reach into theosis in oneself to really know love?

Daskalos

Definitely.

Nick

Can it be achieved in different ways, not only through practice in daily life, but through exosomatosis and reaching in and beyond? Or can people do it through loving service to others?

Daskalos

Now Joshua has spoken clearly. If you are living in darkness, in a dark place, can you avoid stumbling? And he said, "If the light is in you, what will be the darkness for you then?" When we ask something from God, does he hear us? Definitely, before even the idea comes in your head and the thought, he knows it, that it is coming in your head. And if we ask him for something, see his great tolerance. For material things? He will give it! Definitely, he will give it, and he will give what is good for you. Because no father will give a snake when his child is asking him for a fish to satisfy his hunger. He will give it. And whatever is asked in his name, his name means becoming such as you have inside you, the Christhood, he will give it!

People are still asking for material things. Things are illusions, chimera, coming and going. Why ask God for that? God has given you everything. The material body, a father, a mother, loving, your heart, your mind, everything you need to keep your body alive, the holy archangels working in your body. They sustain it and keep it alive. What else can I ask? Even the kingdom of the heaven is within. I don't ask for anything! I have it, it's in me, I know it, I found it. Why should I ask for something that I have already found? Let us rather say, "Thank you for having it!"

Nick

Ah, that's the attitude. That's the correct way!

Daskalos

Ask for something I have already in me? Or thank you for having it! So, what shall I ask? "My Beloved, forgive me for not loving you, for minimizing you in the dimensions of my heart, putting you there. Forgive me for not being able to give you more love, but allow me only to love you, that's enough for me. I don't ask for anything else. Everything is given to me." What do I ask from my beloved one? Offering him a little of the unconditional love and not asking for anything, because in loving and asking, it's not unconditional love.

Nick

Love is the only reality.

Daskalos

The kingdom of heaven is in the spirit-soul-ego-self. Now, human beings are asking for a house, a car, a bicycle, a radio, etc. What are all these things? Illusions. What do I mean, illusions? These illusions are depriving me of everything good, because I'm concentrated only on what I call mine. For example, in reality all flowers in the world in the gardens of all people are mine! I see them, and from presentations I have them within the kingdom of the heavens within me as representations. I can see them, love them, enjoy them. Those things (objects) will decay after a time, because the Law in the gross material world is the rapid change of everything. Having it in me in the kingdom of the heavens, I must have my treasures permanently. Seeing a flower, loving it, I can close my eyes, not materialize it but substantializing it in me, seeing it in the light of the heaven, I can bring it forward any moment I like in my memory. Who can take it away from me?

Nick

So one lacks nothing, there is no lack, and so there should be no attachment—only nonattachment!

Daskalos

Definitely. Yes, you transform gross matter into something more real—the forms, the colors, the shapes. For the mind is more real than its expressions. Yes, "nonattachment." Loving each thing separately, I attach myself. But loving everything is "dis-attachment" (dis-identification), so "dis-attachment" is needed even in the kingdom of the heaven in us. Because one of the kingdoms of the heavens within us is the psychical body and the psychical plane. The noetical body and the noetical plane. Why should I attach myself and not be in the whole, i.e., expansion, superconsciousness, many places and many conditions at the same time? I go beyond the illusions of time. I enter in your omnipresence, Beloved, and I can love you everywhere. In everything I can love you. By expansion I don't lose you, my Beloved. I'm gaining more of you! More of love, more of your even human appearance as Joshua. But I can find you in everything I love.

This is unconditional love for me.

Strovolos, Cyprus
March 30, 1994

APPENDIX
1

SUMMARY OF ENNEAGRAM
PERSONALITY TYPES

THE SEPARATED SELVES

Type 8 - The Controlling Self

GENERAL PERSONALITY TRAITS

-confronts conflict directly
-fearless in the face of adversity
-intense interchanges and interactions with no let up
-protective of those that are perceived as weak
-energy often perceived as strong, confrontational, direct

PERSONALITY STRENGTHS OF EIGHT

-direct, truthful
-strong and just
-fearless
-powerful
-protective of allies and those less fortunate

PERSONALITY WEAKNESSES OF EIGHT

-overbearing, aggressive, insistent, forceful, leading to loss of relationships and isolation
-controlling, dominating, insisting on others changing
-vindictive over perceived injustices
-angry and blaming

EIGHT REGRESSES TO FIVE'S PERSONALITY WEAKNESSES

-becomes isolated, withdraws from feelings
-loneliness and open hostility toward everyone
-controls their space rigidly
-suspicious and mistrustful

EIGHT EXPANDS TO TWO'S PERSONALITY STRENGTHS

-open to giving and receiving love without control
-trusting, empathetic, supportive of others
-values softness, sensitivity as strength
-vulnerable to expressing love and kindness

Chart 1

THE ENNEAGRAM OF PERSONALITY TYPES
The Separated Selves

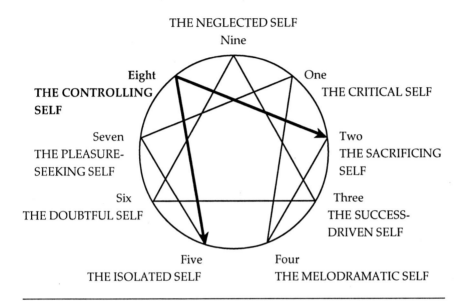

THE NEGLECTED SELF
Nine

Eight
THE CONTROLLING
SELF

One
THE CRITICAL SELF

Seven
THE PLEASURE-
SEEKING SELF

Two
THE SACRIFICING
SELF

Six
THE DOUBTFUL SELF

Three
THE SUCCESS-
DRIVEN SELF

Five
THE ISOLATED SELF

Four
THE MELODRAMATIC SELF

Type 9 - The Neglected Self

GENERAL PERSONALITY TRAITS

-holds to harmony and comfort
-avoids conflict
-merges with energy of others
-spaces out easily; dissociates
-can withdraw into passive-aggressive stance and stubbornness when
  overwhelmed
-difficulty saying NO or taking self-initiative
-excellent at motivation for "other" rather than self
-sensitivity to the needs of others

PERSONALITY STRENGTHS
OF NINE

-supportive of others
-honest, responsible
-yielding
-multifaceted talents and
  abilities, adaptability
-sharing

PERSONALITY WEAKNESSES
OF NINE

-numb to their real needs
-passive-aggressive
-stubborn when pushed or when
  yields too much for too long
-references to others' situations,
  energies to the point of losing sight
  of their own motivations, identity,
  personal space
-procrastination, putting off until
  the last moment for completion
-avoids expressing anger

NINE REGRESSES TO SIX'S
PERSONALITY WEAKNESSES

-confusion, ambivalent
  to taking right action
-paralysis and self-sabotage
-afraid of worst-case scenarios
-amps up fear and external
  conditions to overwhelming
  proportions

NINE EXPANDS TO THREE'S
PERSONALITY STRENGTHS

-shows self-initiative and right
  action in life situations
-present and self-motivated to
  developing themselves
-expresses their strengths, talents
  and abilities
-individuality grows

Chart 2

THE ENNEAGRAM OF PERSONALITY TYPES
The Separated Selves

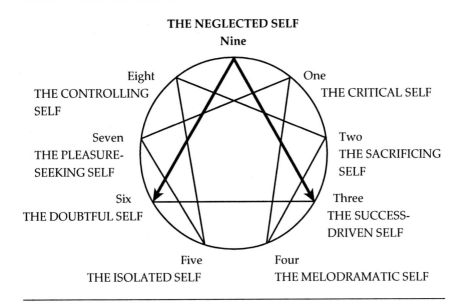

THE NEGLECTED SELF
Nine

Eight
THE CONTROLLING
SELF

One
THE CRITICAL SELF

Seven
THE PLEASURE-
SEEKING SELF

Two
THE SACRIFICING
SELF

Six
THE DOUBTFUL SELF

Three
THE SUCCESS-
DRIVEN SELF

Five
THE ISOLATED SELF

Four
THE MELODRAMATIC SELF

Type 1 - The Critical Self

GENERAL PERSONALITY TRAITS

-seeks perfection in order not to be rejected or thought badly of
-stymied by compulsive need to get it perfect
-strives for superiority through comparison
-self-blame when mistakes are made
-suppresses own needs, withholds pleasure from self
-high expectations for excellence leads to rigidity and "this is the only
  way to be or do"
-under stress of personal error, anger at self may get displaced on others,
  i.e., self-righteous anger, blame

PERSONALITY STRENGTHS OF ONE

-truthfulness
-idealism
-wants progress
-proper action
-committed
-industrious
-responsible
-standard of excellence

PERSONALITY WEAKNESSES OF ONE

-gets stymied by absorption in
  specific details — leads to
  immobilization
-bodily felt tension conceals angry
  feelings
-under stress, throws self-judgment
  out on others as self-righteous
  blame
-gets absorbed in self-criticism
  leading to worry and low self-worth
-chronic withholding of angry
  feelings

ONE REGRESSES TO FOUR'S PERSONALITY WEAKNESSES

-becomes disillusioned
  with ideals
-becomes depressed and
  self-destructive
-anger with life as it is
-feels different—like a misfit
-envious of those who appear
  to be fulfilled

ONE EXPANDS TO SEVEN'S PERSONALITY STRENGTHS

-more playful
-optimistic
-inventive, creative
-more productivity
-relaxes more and begins to enjoy life
-accepts reality with its necessary
  imperfections

Chart 3

THE ENNEAGRAM OF PERSONALITY TYPES
The Separated Selves

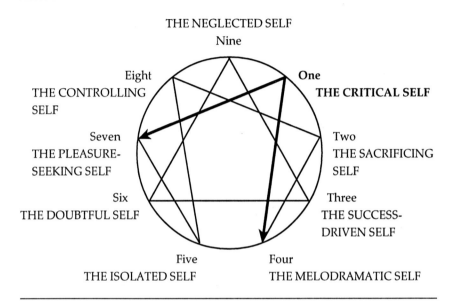

THE NEGLECTED SELF
Nine

Eight
THE CONTROLLING
SELF

One
THE CRITICAL SELF

Seven
THE PLEASURE-
SEEKING SELF

Two
THE SACRIFICING
SELF

Six
THE DOUBTFUL SELF

Three
THE SUCCESS-
DRIVEN SELF

Five
THE ISOLATED SELF

Four
THE MELODRAMATIC SELF

Type 2 - The Sacrificing Self

GENERAL PERSONALITY TRAITS

-strives for recognition from those they consider significant and important
-alters themselves to fulfill the needs of others
-keeps their attention off themselves, thereby neglecting their own needs
-manipulative tendencies in relationships to create likability,
  attractiveness
-likes affiliation to people they deem significant or important
-encourages and supports the growth and success of others.
-tends to avoid conflict in relationships, striving for harmony and good
  feelings
-gains a sense of self-value through fulfilling the needs of others
-pride in being indispensable

PERSONALITY STRENGTHS
OF TWO

-resourceful
-romantic
-generous and supportive
-care-giving
-enthusiastic
-capable and attentive

PERSONALITY WEAKNESSES
OF TWO

-difficulty placing limits on others'
 demands
-holds back disclosing their real needs
-preoccupation with relationships
 creates fear of losing significant
 others
-struggles with dependency vs.
 independence issues
-identifying and merging with others
 makes autonomy difficult
-over-extending their giving leads to
 stress and eruption of anger
-can become dependent demanding
 attention
-manipulative

TWO REGRESSES TO EIGHT'S
PERSONALITY WEAKNESSES

-eruption of angry feelings over
 unfulfilled needs
-vindictive and revengeful

TWO EXPANDS TO FOUR'S
PERSONALITY STRENGTHS

-accepts their real needs as valid
-feels worthy to receive love
-authenticity and true self-expression

-aggressive responses to underlying feelings of helplessness,
fear
-self-sabotages opportunities to
really receive from others
-tendency toward psychosomatic
disorders as indirect way to
express stress and non-fulfillment
-feeling dominated, struggles over
dependency vs. freedom,
autonomy
-giving to excess
-manipulates in attempt to get return
for love given to significant others
-attention seeking, demanding for
a sense of being valued, secure,
cared for

-stops their drive to constantly
self-sacrifice
-autonomous, creative, unique in
their expression

Chart 4

THE ENNEAGRAM OF PERSONALITY TYPES
The Separated Selves

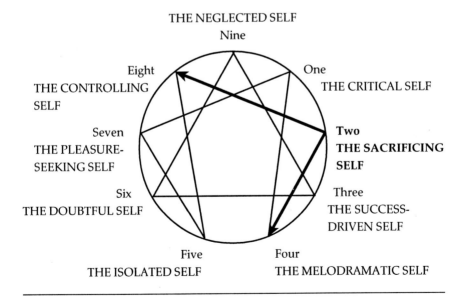

THE NEGLECTED SELF
Nine

Eight   One
THE CONTROLLING   THE CRITICAL SELF
SELF

Seven   Two
THE PLEASURE-   THE SACRIFICING
SEEKING SELF   SELF

Six   Three
THE DOUBTFUL SELF   THE SUCCESS-
                            DRIVEN SELF

Five   Four
THE ISOLATED SELF   THE MELODRAMATIC SELF

Type 3 - The Success-Driven Self

GENERAL PERSONALITY TRAITS

-identifies with the image of success
-seeks position, power, importance, leadership
-deceives self into believing they are what they do and what they are
   portraying
-keeps feelings suspended to get job done
-efficient, practical
-constantly active, avoids feelings from surfacing, especially unpleasant
   ones

PERSONALITY STRENGTHS OF THREE

-optimistic
-hopeful
-active, constructive
-efficient
-leadership
-future oriented
-building
-practicality

PERSONALITY WEAKNESSES OF THREE

-impatience when things slow down
-work-wise, may jump to new tasks
   prematurely
-workaholic
-difficulty relaxing
-drives forward to accomplish tasks
   and then quickly moves on to new
   projects
-cuts corners, softens the truth

THREE REGRESSES TO NINE'S PERSONALITY WEAKNESSES

-engages in self-defeating
   behavior
-overwhelming feelings of
   hostility lead to impaired action
   and function, dissociates
   from all feelings and shuts down;
   becomes slovenly, inactive
-self-loathing

THREE EXPANDS TO SIX'S PERSONALITY STRENGTHS

-develops compassion, empathy
   for others
-becomes more connected to the
   inner-life of their true feelings and
   thoughts
-balances outer directedness with
   inner directedness
-overcomes the fear of intimacy and
   personal encounter
-supports and encourages others
-committed and consistent in
   embracing higher values and ideals
   in action

Chart 5

THE ENNEAGRAM OF PERSONALITY TYPES
The Separated Selves

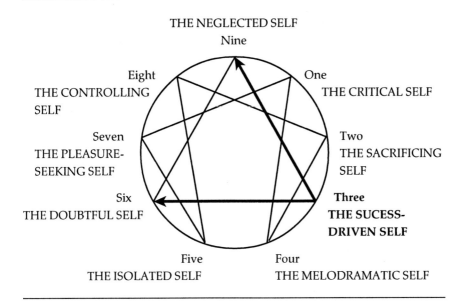

THE NEGLECTED SELF
Nine

Eight
THE CONTROLLING
SELF

One
THE CRITICAL SELF

Seven
THE PLEASURE-
SEEKING SELF

Two
THE SACRIFICING
SELF

Six
THE DOUBTFUL SELF

**Three
THE SUCESS-
DRIVEN SELF**

Five
THE ISOLATED SELF

Four
THE MELODRAMATIC SELF

Type 4 - The Melodramatic Self

GENERAL PERSONALITY TRAITS

-past and future oriented
-the present is boring, uninteresting
-seeks the extraordinary in life, avoiding everyday ordinariness
-merges with the emotional moods of others
-stubborn to changing viewpoint

PERSONALITY STRENGTHS OF FOUR

-creative orientation
-intensely romantic and
  passionate
-appreciates specialness,
  uniqueness
-sensitivity to aesthetics,
  emotional realities of life
-good in crisis intervention
  situations when others are in
  need of support

PERSONALITY WEAKNESSES OF FOUR

-addiction to intensity in
  relationships
-self-absorption with own emotions,
  especially feelings of suffering
-envy—something is always missing
-negative self-image; feeling like
  special outcast, renegade
-drama, depression, "poor me"
  syndrome, i.e., look how you've hurt
  me
-over-does, over-extends
-difficulty sustaining appreciation,
  gratitude for what they have,
  especially in relationships

FOUR REGRESSES TO TWO'S PERSONALITY WEAKNESSES

-dependency, demanding
  attention
-high ideals about love, and
  then is disappointed
-fear of abandonment,
  manipulates to hold on to
  significant others
-doubts about their own
  desirability and worthiness
  to be loved

FOUR EXPANDS TO ONE'S PERSONALITY STRENGTHS

-objectivity about self, especially their
  emotional reactions and others
-self-reliant, independent
-balanced lifestyle, less attraction to
  extremes
-selfless service to ideals and their
  actualization
-self-actualization
-consistency and emotional discipline

Chart 6

THE ENNEAGRAM OF PERSONALITY TYPES
The Separated Selves

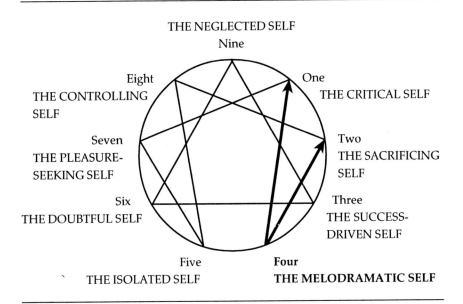

THE NEGLECTED SELF
Nine

Eight   One
THE CONTROLLING   THE CRITICAL SELF
SELF

Seven   Two
THE PLEASURE-   THE SACRIFICING
SEEKING SELF   SELF

Six   Three
THE DOUBTFUL SELF   THE SUCCESS-
          DRIVEN SELF

Five   **Four**
THE ISOLATED SELF **THE MELODRAMATIC SELF**

Type 5 - The Isolated Self

GENERAL PERSONALITY TRAITS

-tendency to withdraw from feelings, especially fear
-afraid of being entrapped by others' agendas
-minimizes their own needs
-attached to knowledge, substitutes it for direct experience of life
-controls activities by thinking them through in advance, thus
  minimizing the unexpected, i.e., avoids fearful unpredictable
  situations
-focused on ways to create privacy of space, time

PERSONALITY STRENGTHS
OF FIVE

-academically oriented
-calm
-knowledgeable (intellectually)
-simple
-ascetic
-reliant, trustworthy in friendship
-logical, objective

PERSONALITY WEAKNESSES
OF FIVE

-withholds, resists sharing
-withdraws from life, isolates self
  from others
-compartmentalizes their life
  activities, avoids spontaneity
-resists receiving from others, as
        something may be demanded of
  them later
-retreats into their thoughts; mental
  activity substitutes for real life
  experience

FIVE REGRESSES TO SEVEN'S
PERSONALITY WEAKNESSES

-distracted from life goals and
  purpose
-scattered, impulsive actions
-repetitive mistakes

FIVE EXPANDS TO EIGHT'S
PERSONALITY STRENGTHS

-acts without fear
-self-confident
-able to take in life without withdrawing from experience
-leadership

Chart 7

THE ENNEAGRAM OF PERSONALITY TYPES
The Separated Selves

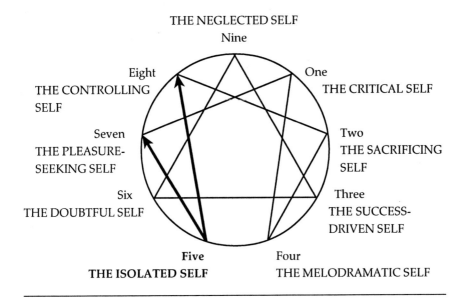

THE NEGLECTED SELF
Nine

Eight
THE CONTROLLING
SELF

One
THE CRITICAL SELF

Seven
THE PLEASURE-
SEEKING SELF

Two
THE SACRIFICING
SELF

Six
THE DOUBTFUL SELF

Three
THE SUCCESS-
DRIVEN SELF

Five
THE ISOLATED SELF

Four
THE MELODRAMATIC SELF

Type 6 - The Doubtful Self

GENERAL PERSONALITY TRAITS

-struggles with doubt, uses doubt to fuel fear
-phobic or counter-phobic stance to deal with perceived danger
-magnifies imagination to believe worst-case scenario will happen
-dutiful, protective of others less fortunate or those that are loved ones
-paranoid orientation to life experience

PERSONALITY STRENGTHS OF SIX

-dutiful, loyal
-sensitive, fair
-certainty and faith
-protective

PERSONALITY WEAKNESSES OF SIX

-self-sabotaging due to fear of
  exposure
-fear, worry, victimization orientation
-doubt, mistrust of others, especially
  authority figures
-looks to find hidden agendas behind
  all events, situations
-active imagination magnifies danger

SIX REGRESSES TO THREE'S PERSONALITY WEAKNESSES

-feelings of inferiority
-misses own authentic feelings
-free-floating anxiety, worry
-retaliates to punish others
  whom they feel or
  perceive have hurt them

SIX EXPANDS TO NINE'S PERSONALITY STRENGTHS

-adaptable, flows with life situations
  with trust
-self-confident
-accurate intuition, accepting and
  supportive of others, especially the
  underdog
-able to tolerate the unknowns of life
  with faith and trust

Chart 8

THE ENNEAGRAM OF PERSONALITY TYPES
The Separated Selves

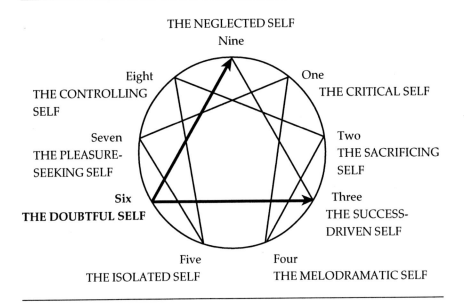

THE NEGLECTED SELF
Nine

Eight   One
THE CONTROLLING   THE CRITICAL SELF
SELF

Seven   Two
THE PLEASURE-   THE SACRIFICING
SEEKING SELF   SELF

Six   Three
THE DOUBTFUL SELF   THE SUCCESS-
                              DRIVEN SELF

Five   Four
THE ISOLATED SELF   THE MELODRAMATIC SELF

Type 7 - The Pleasure-Seeking Self

GENERAL PERSONALITY TRAITS

-strives to remain emotionally upbeat
-seeks thrills, high adventure
-driven to pleasure-seeking to avoid pain and fear
-maintains multiple options, many possibilities
-hard to pin down to commitment
-outgoing, cheerful disposition
-diligent, hard working until bored or interest fades
-tendency to rebel against sanctions of control, disregards or equalizes
  with authority figures
-narcissistic tendency

PERSONALITY STRENGTHS
OF SEVEN

-cheerful, optimistic
-highly energized and upbeat
-active, curious
-seeks enjoyment; enjoyable
    socially
-extroverted
-helpful and supportive of
  others with similar interests
-imagination, open to possibilities

PERSONALITY WEAKNESSES
OF SEVEN

-over-extending, scattered, loss
of direction
-avoidance of commitment
-avoids pain, discomfort
-unwilling to receive others' negative
feelings, suffering

SEVEN REGRESSES TO ONE'S
PERSONALITY WEAKNESSES

-resentment
-tries to anchor scattered
  energy through
  obsessive-compulsive thinking
-asserts control

SEVEN EXPANDS TO FIVE'S
PERSONALITY STRENGTHS

-makes commitment to a course of
  action, focuses on single direction
-digs deeply in activities rather than
  touching the surface
-finds purpose in sharing with others
  with joy
-becomes consistent in purpose and
  direction

Chart 9

THE ENNEAGRAM OF PERSONALITY TYPES
The Separated Selves

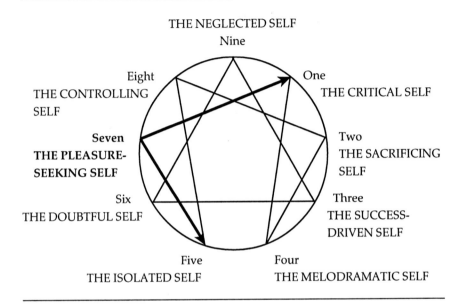

THE NEGLECTED SELF
Nine

Eight
THE CONTROLLING
SELF

One
THE CRITICAL SELF

Seven
THE PLEASURE-
SEEKING SELF

Two
THE SACRIFICING
SELF

Six
THE DOUBTFUL SELF

Three
THE SUCCESS-
DRIVEN SELF

Five
THE ISOLATED SELF

Four
THE MELODRAMATIC SELF

APPENDIX
II

CLINICAL CASE STUDIES

Etherikos Resilience Process—E.R.P.

Etherikos derives from the word *ether*, which refers to the subtle energy that governs life, and *Kos*, the birthplace of Hippocrates and site of his healing sanctuary that was dedicated to the god Asclepius. With its roots in the writings of the Greek physician Hippocrates and on to our modern scientific research into bio-energy, energy and healing go hand in hand with the repair of our spirit, mind, emotions and body. Resilience is our ability to fight back and rebound from the most aversive human conditions and grow as individuals. However, resilience is only possible through life energy. All healing begins with the activation, cleansing and rebalancing of our life-energy body (etheric soma). The scientific basis for the existence of the energy body will be considered in Appendix III.

During our development through childhood, we have accumulated memories of experiences that shape our beliefs, thoughts, feelings and actions. These thought patterns are stored in the energy body as charged emotion-thought complexes we have called elementals. Negative elementals influence our mind, emotions, and physical body unfavorably. Through the clearing of these "energy parasites," we activate our resilience and life energy for physical health, emotional joy and happiness, mental clarity and the spiritual presence of unconditional love.

Through the Resilience Process we learn to access the energy centers or chakras. As discussed in Chapter IV, these centers act as bridges for the flow of life energy between our spirit, mind, emotions and body. Each center activates at different periods of our development from childhood onward.

Each governs specific instincts and areas of psychological mastery ranging from survival/self preservation skills to intimacy and bonding in relationship to social/career abilities, and into higher virtues such as love, empathy and compassion. By clearing these centers of the elementals blocking them, we can access deeper experiences of our spiritual nature.

We believe that central to all healing that takes place in counseling and psychotherapy is the vital dialogue and relationship that takes place between the spirit-ego-self and our present-day personality as mediated through the human heart.

The Resilience Process involves seven basic steps summarized as follows:

1. The therapist induces the client into a trance state of consciousness.
2. The therapist finds the energy center involved in the issue at hand.
3. The therapist and the client uncover the emotional defense.
4. The therapist and the client unravel the story that created that defense.
5. The therapist and the client discover the faulty (self-limiting) elemental thought that fuels the emotional defense.
6. The therapist and the client complete the understanding, forgiveness and surrender process.
7. The therapist supplies positive affirmations for the client to repeat.

The interaction between therapist and client is like an alchemical dance of energy that requires constant presence and attention to subtle movements and changes within the client's energy field. During the sessions usually required to complete the healing process, the client may explore various altered states of consciousness, including biographical, perinatal, and transpersonal levels of awareness, so that complete healing occurs.

Case History 1

Jill is a bright middle-aged woman who reported having a stormy relationship with her parents since the early years of her life. Jill had lived away from her parents a good part of her adult life, but due to financial strain from the loss of her job and a broken leg, returned to live with them for a period of time. She had never married or engaged intimately on an emotional level in male-female partnership. She gave me a history of being rather guarded and mistrustful with both men and women, plagued by doubt, fear, and confusion. She came to me for psychotherapy with the desire to work out differences she was having with her mother, with whom she had not communicated openly for years.

After a guided visualization exercise, I began to scan her chakras within the etheric energy field of her aura. I immediately felt a disturbance in the sacral center (second chakra). We often find that a wounded chakra center will emanate a color and texture visible clairvoyantly and felt clairsentiently that can be communicated verbally to the patient as an emotional state or condition. Her sacral center appeared a ruddy burnt orange-red color and felt searing hot. The other center that felt primarily disturbed was the heart chakra. It appeared a greyish color, heavy, thick and molasses-like in texture.

I asked Jill if she often felt anger and resentment toward her parents. She answered affirmatively. She said she often felt a sorrowful, heavy feeling in her heart when interacting with her parents. As we began to dialogue about these matters, Jill spoke about events of her early teen years. She stated that her mother was troubled by her father's physical and emotional absence from home and the family. Jill's description of him was of a man dominated by his ruthless drive for power through career achievement and emotional (relational) control of others. I pondered to myself that it sounded like a strong solar plexus energy, that she had a modern-day Herod as a father! Jill began sharing that she had difficulty expressing her genuine feeling with him without being ignored or reprimanded. Her father had been highly successful in business and well-received by his social community, despite being very dictatorial at home.

Energetically, Jill revealed blocked and wounded second and third chakras due to the lack and non-allowance of intimate sharing (second chakra) in her family and a strong controlling, competitive attitude about life from her father (third chakra). As I uncovered the issues she was having about her mother, the heart (fourth chakra) became the primary focus of work. Jill related that her mother was needy for love from her father, yet constantly meeting with his rejection. She remembers her mother clinging to her emotionally for support and validation, and at the same while, projecting her own subconscious anger at her husband onto Jill. Jill and her dad had similar physical traits and mannerisms. This story about her parents unfolded as I worked on the heart center. I asked her to visualize the teenage girl standing between the mother and father. As she did so, she felt a tugging sensation in her heart and a pushing sensation against her sacral and solar plexus chakras. She could see within herself an energetic cord (hook) connecting this inner teenage girl to the mother and an image of her father's fist in her sacral/solar plexus centers.

I asked Jill to look within the eyes of the inner teenager and to tell me what she could see. She saw/felt sadness, anger, mistrust of both her parents. When I had her look into the eyes of the mother and then even deeper into the mother's inner child within herself, I asked her to ask the child if it had a message for her. The message was "I am weak and scared to be alone" (second chakra issue) and "I feel helpless to change my life." (third chakra issue) Jill suddenly recognized that in her relationship to her mother, she had taken on these two elementals subconsciously for her mother and had decided in response to these subconscious demands: "I must accept all the bad things that come to me," (fourth chakra) and "I feel responsible for the world," i.e., another's life.

At this point in the session, it became obvious to me that her mother had been very dependent upon Jill for self-validation and pulling on her for love and support. Jill had her own fears of abandonment and took upon herself a position of responsibility toward her mother and her mother's views of the father. Meanwhile our modern-day Herod (her father) was directing his dissatisfaction and anger at his wife through the daughter.

We had Jill dialogue extensively with both parents. She chose to break these subconscious contracts she had taken on with each of them to act as intermediary for their relationship and unfulfilled needs with each other. She began to release her pent-up emotions about this role she played with tears, waves of sadness and fluctuations of anger. What was left for her in this moment of release was a lonely, isolated, separated self (the teenage girl) standing in a wasteland (visually described as a desert). I asked Jill to reach to the teenager, as she needed reassurance and love. "Hold her Jill," I said, and "give her all the love she's missed. She's been waiting for someone to do it. You're the only one who can. Take her out of that place."

Jill looked within the eyes of the teenage girl and began to see a spark of joy and light within her. As she visualized herself touching the girl's heart and embracing her, a wave of love, indicating reconnection to her own Christ Self was beginning for her. Touching the girl's solar plexus brought a rush of warmth and the scene of a beautiful halo of golden energy and light surrounding Jill's body and solar plexus center. As Jill drew the teenage girl closer and deeper into her own heart, she experienced a deep feeling of peace and harmony.

This session was followed by several others to clarify and heal other age-specific blocks in her chakra centers. The overall results were life-changing for her. She reconciled many issues with her parents and began for the first time ever a warm, emotionally-connected relationship with a man. She no longer was willing to give in to the old elementals of "I must not love or I will be hurt" (fourth chakra) and "I can't trust anyone" (second chakra) and "I can't be myself in a relationship without hurting the other person," i.e., transfer of father's former sentiments toward the mother through Jill. She continues to improve her relationship with her mother and father and feels healthier psychological boundaries with them. Interestingly enough, her father became avidly involved in attitudinal healing work and her mother is now independent, with a career and much happier within herself.

I once asked Daskalos if one can destroy an elemental in therapy. He replied that one can never destroy an elemental, but an elemental can be discharged of its negative energy. In therapy I have repeatedly observed that once the life lessons and spiritual principles of an issue are learned and understood, the elemental will not return to hamper the individual. Like a teacher the elemental (a product of separation consciousness) is there to assist the individual to look within and through a process of introspection to clear the mirrors of the mind, emotions and physical body. When this is done, the Spirit-ego-self shines through the three bodies to reveal to the evolving personality its true nature and splendor as love. And so, love is awakened naturally and effortlessly within the individual. This love then builds the incentive for the expression of virtues and positive thought elementals that allow for growth and the manifestation of new opportunities in life.

Case History 2

Mary described herself as being seen by her parents to be a "perfect" child while growing up with them. She excelled as an athlete and gymnast and was popular at school. She came to me for resilience therapy because she was having a difficult time sustaining an intimate relationship with her husband. Mary described herself as being overly responsible and unable to easily relax and have fun. Nevertheless, she took satisfaction in her achievements and had the appearance of being a "normal, well-adjusted individual." Yet, within her inner world she had an empty, insecure, and uneasy feeling about herself, which she relieved through escape into hard work and external activities.

As the session opened, I scanned her chakra centers and contacted an emotion within her root center (first chakra) of deep unexpressed shame. Her sacral chakra (second center) was absent of life energy and her solar plexus (third center) was hot, congested, and overactive with energy.

We uncovered a memory of her as a child of three to four years of age, where she witnessed her father and mother both drinking heavily and fighting with one another. She looked into the young child's eyes and witnessed loneliness, fear and disappointment. When asked what she felt with her parents throughout her youth, she responded that she could never remember affectionate emotional sharing between them or with herself. She remembered very little physical touch between her parents and herself. She recalled them as being distant and self-absorbed in their problems and sorrows. She painfully recollected long periods of being left at home to do for herself. These memories brought a flood of tears to her eyes.

I suggested she embrace the young child with all the love she could give her and ask her what decision she made regarding her life and her parents. She realized that the only way she could ever receive any positive attention from them was to show them evidence of a job well done. Through this means she'd get the acknowledgment she deserved. As she dialogued more deeply with her inner child and her parents, she made a startling discovery. This child loved and honored her parents in such a way that she wanted to cover up for their imperfections socially, especially for their alcoholic tendencies, their emotional disturbances hidden from the public eye. Mary wanted to give the family a good name by excelling and setting up high standards of performance.

As she realized these things, another flood of tears came to her, she blushed deeply, and for a time couldn't speak about her experience. I gave her the time and space to be with her inner child. When she began to communicate, she revealed a deep realization. Her whole life had been a deep cover-up for shame she felt about her parents. The energetic connection to her parents was one of her carrying for them their guilt and shame. She worked on breaking their unhealthy contractual ties—verbally, subconsciously, and energetically.

She felt a deep peace come over her. I could feel within my hands an expanded feeling of her first chakra (shame issues) and third chakra (control and responsibility issues) dissolving and lightening up energetically. The earlier lack of energy within her second chakra was no longer evident. She realized that she could only feel real acknowledgment and validation by recognizing her intrinsic value as a spiritual being. She spoke directly with the inner child, saying that she didn't have to prove herself worthy of love by working hard for the approval of her parents and society. She didn't have to act perfectly to cover the shame she held for her parents.

As Mary held her inner child, she said, "I love you just the way you are. You don't have to prove anything to me. I see your joy, light, love." With this the image of her parents disappeared and the child stood radiant and free within her heart. The report I received thereafter from her was that the relationship issues with her husband began to clear up, she was taking more time for herself to relax and was enjoying life. Learning self-love was a path to improving the quality of her life and relationships.

Case History 3

(The following case study was offered by a student of the Etherikos Resilience Process.)

This 32-year-old single man with no children, working as a technician in a company, came to my office because he had authority problems with colleagues and felt troubled about his relationships with women. He had had a short relationship, but it ended because the woman did not like his low socioeconomic status. Besides his profession, he liked theater and was a member of a local well-known theater company.

I worked through most of his authority problems using body psycho-therapy (Core Energetics). Many of his issues originated from lacking emotional closeness to his father, who did not support the boy's needs for sexual identity. After having learned to claim his self-value, using me as a positive transference figure, he still had a deficit of self-value in relation to women.

During therapy he fell in love with two women at once in a manner that had all the attributes of adolescent love. He had well-grounded arguments as to why he wanted to enjoy both relationships at the same time and not be stopped by the moralistic objections his parents would have had. Neverthe-less, he suffered from guilt feelings. At this point I suggested to him an ERP session in order to let him look deeper into the origins of these feelings and help him resolve them.

In the ERP session the process was somewhat different from what I had expected. The solar plexus chakra was split. On its right side the energy was thick and blackish, and on the left it was light and brighter. The energy funnel above the third eye was reversed, with its tip up and the larger opening directed toward the forehead. Also, the second chakra did not have so much energy.

I decided to work on his third chakra first, then clean the sixth one. While opening his third chakra, he saw his uncle's face in the mirror. His eyes looked rigid and severe, expressing control and condemnation of the young boy's self-will as the boy stood there. My client was astonished to see this side of his uncle and remembered also the warmth and kindness his uncle showed him. I told my client that his uncle must have had both sides, which resulted in the energetic structure of the chakra. Then I asked him to look toward the background of his uncle's figure in the mirror to see if he could detect there the negative elemental of control which also governed his uncle. Surprisingly enough, a group of men appeared who were dressed in black uniforms like miners. What did they want from the uncle and— through his eyes—from the young boy?

The client realized that they were a group of conspirators, saying, "You have to follow our will, otherwise we will pull and put you down." There it was, the negative anguishing elemental of negative power and submission, which always caused the authority problems of the client. He analyzed that yielding to it had meant avoiding punishment, but also meant sacrificing the inner child's longing for autonomy and free will. Now he decided to release the negative elemental of this plot-group into the light. He looked very peaceful as the negative elemental left and the bright golden light of Christ streamed down into his solar plexus. He let the light move up into his heart, throat, and third eye, which I cleaned.

I asked him which words came up and what he wanted to affirm. He said, "I have free will where to go and where to stay." Then I let him say the sentence while looking at his uncle's face, adding, "And I like to be with you." Picking up the issue with the women from the last session, I encouraged him to say the same sentence of truth in the visualized presence of the two women, one after another.

After we had finished the session with a time of rest, he reported some important experiences. First, he had felt no strong commitment to either of the two women yet and that this was true for him. Second, he had had dreams of this obscure conspiracy group in the past. Third, he had seen an elemental over his forehead showing an iron cage with an imprisoned woman, coming and going as he rested; finally he could wipe it away. Fourth, he felt very tired but good after the session. I explained that this fatigue might be an exhaustion which was coming up after a subconscious life-long struggle for freedom and true self-will against negative elementals which had been denying this truthful claim of the soul.

APPENDIX
III

MIND WITHIN MATTER
The Anatomy of the Energy Body

Mind, Brain, and Consciousness

Western science has been dominated by the assumptions of British scientist Isaac Newton and French philosopher Rene Descartes for the past 300 years. Newton is best known for discovering the law of gravity and inventing calculus. Newton's universe is in essence a gigantic three-dimensional machine run by wholly predictable and unchangeable laws of God. In keeping with this model, science has traditionally assumed that the universe, like a machine, can be best understood by analyzing its individual parts and reduced to the sum of its parts. This philosophy is known as reductionism. Descartes, on the other hand, taught that there was an absolute dualistic separation between mind and matter, allowing the world to be objectively described by a neutral observer. This Newtonian-Cartesian model of reality has led to remarkable progress in the natural sciences and corresponding gain for humanity, even as it has begun to impose significant limitations on the modern world view.[1]

Today we are struggling to integrate the discoveries of modern physics, social science, and metaphysics into a more expansive reality without discarding the ongoing benefits of the older model. Some of the most perplexing challenges in this regard are arising in the field of cognitive, or neural, science, which explores the areas of mind/brain/consciousness and their relationship to human experience. Decades of intensive research have led to ever more sophisticated understanding of the close relationship between brain physiology and consciousness. Mechanistic neural science and psychology hold that new information can only be accessed through the five material senses or by recombining old data. They often postulate that art, religion, emotion, ethics and all forms of human intelligence are products of material brain function.[2]

Despite so much research and speculation, it has never been proven that the mind actually arises from the brain or that the brain in and of itself can think at all. In fact many commonplace human experiences, as well as modern science itself, challenge the materialistic paradigm deeply. Returning to the biblical story of "The Woman at the Well," Jesus demonstrates the ability to access information about a total stranger through means other than the five senses:

> Jesus saith unto her, "Go, call thy husband, and come hither."
> The woman answered and said, "I have no husband."
> Jesus said unto her, "Thou hast well said, 'I have no husband': For thou hast had five husbands; and he whom thou now hast is not thy husband: in that saidst thou truly."
> The woman then left her waterpot, and went her way into the city, and saith to the men, "Come, see a man, which told me all things that ever I did..." (John 4: 16-18, 28-29)

Some scientists might well dismiss this account as fictional or some religionists, as the unique action of a divine being, were it not for the fact that so many ordinary people acquire information commonly through such non-ordinary means. In modern terms some people might say that Jesus did a "psychic reading" on the Samaritan woman at the well. Non-ordinary means of perception, or extra-sensory perception, may be experienced as clairvoyance, clairaudience, clairsentience, shamanic journeying, unusual dreams, or merely telepathic knowing, among others.

There are those who would deny that they have ever acquired information through such natural but "paranormal" channels. Most people, however, have at least experienced meaningful but mysterious "coincidences" between their inner states and outer events from time to time. Psychologist Carl Jung postulated that there must be some acausal connecting principle which links our subjective states of mind with objective experience, yet is not explainable by mechanistic science. He termed this principle "synchronicity" and observed that synchronistic phenomena most often occur in the context of emotionally intense or transformational experiences.[3]

Carl Gustav Jung (1875-1961), Swiss founder of analytical psychology, became the most prominent member of Sigmund Freud's Viennese circle of students. Many psychologists would say that Jung's pioneering work pushed psychology as far ahead of Freud as Freud himself moved ahead of his own time. Jung was well aware that his discoveries and theories could not, like Freud's, be fully reconciled with the Newtonian-Cartesian world view. He came of age as the developments of quantum-relativistic physics were beginning to drastically alter scientific assumptions about reality. Einstein's model of the universe as a four-dimensional time-space continuum was rendering Newton's three-dimensional universe obsolete and only relatively valid. Jung had productive dialogue with several of the leading physicists of the early century.[4]

Jung also was unique in that he had a genuine interest in numerous mystical traditions and deep respect for the spiritual dimensions of human experience. While he was sometimes criticized for his tendency to "spiritualize" psychology, he believed that the spiritual aspect was a genuine, influential aspect of the psyche and was compatible with the expanding 20th Century world view. Unlike Freud, Jung had no difficulty accepting the nonrational, paradoxical, and mysterious as genuine facets of human experience.[5]

Jung was like Freud in that he focused his psychoanalytical work primarily on the unconscious mind as it relates to the conscious. Freud, however, viewed the unconscious mind exclusively as a repository of repressed personal memories and instinctual tendencies; this mind he termed the subconscious. Jung expanded Freud's concept of the unconscious mind to include a collective element, a cosmic Self or universal mind which links all personalities together at a deeper level. This collective unconscious is a central element of Jungian theory.[6]

Jung studied comparative religion and world mythology, as well as his own dreams and those of his patients to understand the collective unconscious. He discovered universal motifs and images that occurred all over the world and throughout history, but were expressed uniquely in different cultures and physical environments. These universal myth-creating patterns within the collective unconscious he termed archetypes. He showed how these archetypal forces within the individual contributed to mental health and illness and rejected the possibility that some of these patterns could result purely from biology or personal experience. He believed that the concept of synchronicity was compatible with modern physics and provided a reasonable framework in which to study events separated in time and space, yet linked through the collective unconscious.[7]

Even as a strict Freudian approach to psychoanalysis has become a bit archaic, Jungian theory has gained progressively wider acceptance the past

30 years. The unconventional research of psychiatrist Stanislav Grof has contributed significantly to this trend. Prior to 1967 Grof conducted thousands of sessions with LSD and other mind-altering substances in volunteers, both psychiatric patients and "normal" professionals. In his book *Beyond the Brain* Grof describes four categories of psychedelic phenomena derived from this research. He terms the fourth category the transpersonal, because this group of experiences gave the subjects the common feeling of expanding beyond ego boundaries and time-space limitations.[8] Such experiences violated some of the most basic rules of mechanistic science.[9]

Grof goes on to describe the surprisingly accurate insight of some of his subjects into phenomena about which they should have had no knowledge whatsoever. Their means of non-ordinary insight include the range of "psychic" phenomena noted earlier and the dynamic synchronistic connections between inner experience and the outer world as described by Carl Jung.[10] Out of this wealth of research, Grof established with others the discipline of transpersonal psychology in the late sixties. So closely does Grof's own research support Jungian theory that Grof has designated Jung "the first transpersonal psychologist."[11]

The Modern Dance of Science and Religion

Just as Carl Jung took an interest in modern physics, it is equally natural and all but inevitable that theoretical physicists would delve into the area of consciousness. Consider, for example, the implications of quantum theory. Quantum physics demonstrated early this century that subatomic particles such as electrons can manifest as waves and that wave forms such as visible light can manifest as particles. Subatomic phenomena are therefore termed quanta to identify their complementary wave/particle nature. According to Danish physicist Niels Bohr and German physicist Werner Heisenberg, the leading quantum theorists until 1950, quanta do not even manifest as particles, i.e. objective, "solid" reality, unless they are being observed. Quantum physics has therefore led to numerous interpretations from physics, psychology, and cognitive science that assume a central role of the mind in quantum reality. On the subatomic level, at least, there is no doubt but that Descartes' teaching of absolute mind-matter separation is invalid.[12]

The principles of modern physics cannot be automatically transferred to all areas of the natural sciences. Mechanistic, predictable aspects of the human body and behavior can be seen when viewed from certain vantage points. Still the evidence is compelling that human beings must be approached by science as more than biological machines and the mind as more than material brain function.[13] Science, like religion, now offers considerable support to the view of humans as multi-dimensional beings whose brains translate reality from an unseen dimension into a form suitable for function on the physical plane.

A revolutionary view of matter and consciousness has been formulated by David Bohm, a prominent theoretical physicist and former co-worker with Einstein at Princeton University. Based on research and interest in such areas as plasma physics, order and chaos, holography, and nonlocal aspects of quantum systems, he has proposed a model of the universe which blends in some respects with that of mystical and esoteric spiritual traditions. Whereas Einstein linked space and time into a continuum, Bohm has gone so far as to propose that everything in the universe is a continuum. All that can be identified or named by any means, including consciousness itself, is part of an explicate order which he terms the holomovement. The explicate order arises from a still, vast, underlying implicate order which pervades all time and space with the fullness of life itself. Since mind, or consciousness, arises from the implicate order, matter can ultimately be viewed as "condensed mind."[14] While skepticism of Bohm's model persists in the physics community, support comes from such leading theorists as Roger Penrose, creator of the modern theory of the black hole, and Brian Josephson, winner of the 1973 Nobel prize in physics. Josephson hopes that Bohm's concept of the implicate order may someday lead science to include God or Mind within its paradigm.[15]

Bohm's theory clearly gives credence to the paradigm of transpersonal psychology and more particularly to the teachings of Stylianos Atteshlis (Daskalos) regarding God, mind, and matter. Daskalos often refers to God as "Absolute Beingness." In *The Esoteric Teachings* he states:

> ABSOLUTE BEINGNESS, we would say, is a State of Self-aware Absolute Consciousness, in which everything IS and finds and draws upon the energy needed for its existence and expression. IT is the One and Only God, Who in Its Absolute Self-sufficiency thinks and expresses Itself. Everything, visible and invisible, above and below, takes as the source of being Its expression, the result of Its Divine Munificence.
>
> It is inconceivable that there is any part of the Infinite which does not contain within it ABSOLUTE BEINGNESS. However the Infinite is not God, nor does God confine Itself to the Infinite. God is beyond the concept of any sort of space. It is Life itself—the life which is the expression of ABSOLUTE BEINGNESS within itself, with special aspects which It creates for this very purpose. One of these special aspects is mind. With Mind, ABSOLUTE BEINGNESS expresses Itself as Multiplicity in the worlds of space-ness. . . .

So, Mind is a creation and not an immortal part of ABSOLUTE BEINGNESS as are the Holy Monads, both before and after their expression. Let us not confuse Mind, then, even in its state of supersubstance with the Holy Spirit, because Mind is not the Holy Spirit. . . .

Everything is Mind, in differing degrees and frequencies of vibration. . . .

We can say of Mind that it is the first cause, the first expression of Divine Thought. However, we find it in different frequencies of vibration and gross matter is solidified Mind.[16]

Likewise, Bohm has said, "The ability of form to be active is the most characteristic feature of mind, and we have something that is mindlike already with the electron."[17] If Absolute Beingness can be seen as equivalent to Bohm's implicate order, Daskalos' teachings express Bohm's ideas eloquently in sacred rather than scientific language. Their philosophies are monistic rather than reductionistic, in that they profess the oneness of all creation and a belief that no part can be understood except in relationship to the whole.

Many cultures and spiritual traditions recognize the presence of an active, "mindlike" form which envelopes and pervades the physical body. This form is most often called the "aura" or "subtle energy field." Some of these traditions recognize the presence of layers, or subtle bodies, within this field. Most commonly these bodies are known as the etheric body; the astral, or emotional, body; the mental body and the causal body. Daskalos uses a slightly different nomenclature. He recognizes the etheric layer as a sort of energy blueprint, or "double", of the physical body rather than a distinct subtle body. He recognizes the astral body as the first subtle body, but calls it the "psychonoetic" body or "psychic" body. He recognizes a third body which he terms the "noetic" body. The noetic body functions on lower or higher planes that correspond roughly to the mental and causal bodies of Indian literature.[18]

The Christ Self, which Daskalos calls the "Spirit-ego-self" or "Holy Monad," is the individuated aspect of Absolute Beingness which indwells us as the Son of God and establishes our truest and ultimate identity. The Holy Monad works in partnership with the human personality to build the eternal soul, even as the free will of the human partner reigns supreme. As discussed in Chapter IV, the multiple dimensions and forms of the individual personality are connected through the energy vortices called chakras.

While recognizing that multiple layers of form exist within and beyond the physical body, it generally is not helpful to try to distinguish them while working with subtle energies on a therapeutic level. For this reason many therapists refer to all subtle levels of energy from the etheric and beyond as the energy body of the individual. Daskalos, in the manner of Bohm, would note as quoted above that all multiplicity of form from the physical to the noetic is ultimately illusory, for all these forms are only the supersubstance of Mind manifesting at different frequencies of vibration.

"As Above, So Below": The Creations of God and Man

Bohm describes the consciousness-matter continuum, or holomovement, according to the principles of holography. In this model any independent "thing" is an abstraction, because it arises from the wholeness of the implicate order. Bohm calls "things," including individual human beings, "relatively independent subtotalities" that contain the fabric of the entire implicate order.[19] This order, however, is hidden from view, or "enfolded," as it manifests in the holomovement. This is a way of saying, as countless mystics have asserted, that every part of the universe is a microcosm, or sort of miniature, of all creation.

Daskalos again reflects Bohm's scientific theory in the language of the sacred:

> "As above, so below." As the Macrocosm is, so is the Microcosm. As are ABSOLUTE BEINGNESS, the CHRIST LOGOS, the HOLY SPIRIT and the Universes, so is the Holy Monad, the Self-Aware Soul of Human Beings, the Permanent Self-Aware Personality and its bodies.
>
> We are an image and a likeness of the LORD. In quality alike, but certainly not in quantity. We differ as far as overlordship is concerned, but not in the sense which we usually give to that term.
>
> By knowing the Microcosm, we know the Macrocosm. By knowing Man, we know GOD. By knowing the material, the psychic and the noetic bodies, we know the Universes. By knowing Mind, in the way humanity uses it (elementals of desire-thoughts and thought-desires), we know Mind as Substance and Supersubstance, as the means of maintaining the Universes, which is used by the CHRIST LOGOS and the HOLY SPIRIT.
>
> It is impossible to study the universes until we know ourselves. Once we know ourselves, we shall know ABSOLUTE BEINGNESS. That part of us that resonates with ABSOLUTE BEINGNESS is our Innermost Self, the Holy Monad. . . .[20]

Just as the universe arises from Mind in response to the munificence of Absolute Beingness,[21] our personal universes are constructed through personal choice as a web of psychonoetic entities called elementals. These elementals, while composed of "mindstuff," beget our experience of the physical realm just as surely as that of the emotional and mental realms. A study of these elementals—how they are created, energized, and de-energized—can give us insight not only into ourselves, but into the very means God creates on a grand scale. In so doing we discover the astonishing power of our thoughts. Our present-day personalities, according to Daskalos, are the sum total of all the elementals we have created or attracted by resonance from the mass consciousness.[22] "For as he thinketh in his heart, so is he." (Proverbs 23:7)

Most of us create elementals subconsciously in a reflexive response to material cravings. These desire-thoughts, or negative elementals, serve the ego's desires by creating the conditions for satisfaction at the expense of genuine happiness. In so doing these "unclean spirits" bind the present-day personality to the material plane as its slave, creating the conditions for suffering.[23] The elementals that dominate the subconscious mind were discussed in Chapter V.

NOTES

Chapter One

[1] Stylianos Atteshlis, *The Symbol of Life,* Nicosia, Cyprus: The Stoa Series, 1998, pp. 70, 202.

Chapter Two

[1] Stylianos Atteshlis, *The Esoteric Teachings* (self-published, printed in Cyprus by IMPRINTA LTD., Nicosia, Cyprus), p. 122.

[2] Atteshlis, adapted from *The Esoteric Teachings*, pp. 101-106.

[3] Ibid., pp. 144-145.

[4] Ibid., p. 98.

Chapter Three

[1] Andreas Ebert, from "Are the Origins of the Enneagram Christian After All?" *The Enneagram Monthly,* January 1996, pp. 14-15.

[2] Ibid.

[3] Richard G. Geldard, *The Travelers' Key to Ancient Greece*, New York: Alfred A. Knopf, Inc., 1989, pp. 71-72.

[4] Ibid., p. 72.

[5] Ibid., p. 73.

[6] Ibid., pp. 74-75.

[7] Ibid., pp. 72.

[8] Stylianos Atteshlis, adapted from *The Esoteric Teachings*, pp. 36, 66.

[9] Michael Trout, *The Infant-Parent Institute Newsletter*, Champaign, Illinois, September 1992.

[10] John Bowlby & James Robertson, from "What Price Separation?" *Mothering,* Summer 1992.

Chapter Four

[1] Selma Fraiberg, *The Magic Years: Understanding and Handling the Problems of Early Childhood*, New York: Charles Scribner's Sons, 1959, pp. 35-38.

[2] Ibid., pp. 45-47.

[3] Ibid., pp. 56-66.

[4] Ibid., pp. 91-95, 107-108.

[5] Ibid., pp. 133-135.

[6] Ibid., pp. 168-176.

[7] Erik H. Erikson, *Childhood and Society*, New York: W.W. Norton and Co. Copyright 1950, (c) 1963 by W.W. Norton & Company, Inc., renewed (c) 1978, 1991 by Erik H. Erikson. Used by permission of W.W. Norton & Company, Inc.

[8] Fraiberg, *The Magic Years*, pp. 160-168.

[9] Ibid., pp. 189-192.

[10] Ibid., pp. 242-244.

[11] W.H.C. Frend, *The Rise of Christianity*, Philadelphia: Fortress Press, 1984, p. 67.

[12] Ibid., p. 18.

[13] Erikson, *Childhood and Society*, p. 259.

[14] Ibid., pp. 260-261.

[15] Stephen Mitchell, trans., *Tao Te Ching: A New English Version*, New York: Harper and Row, 1988, p. 44.

[16] Erikson, *Childhood and Society*, p. 261.

[17] Ibid., pp. 261-262.

[18] Ibid., pp. 262.

[19] Frend, *The Rise of Christianity*, pp. 24-25.

[20] Ibid., pp. 25-26.

[21] Stephen Mitchell, ed., *The Enlightened Mind: An Anthology of Sacred Prose*, New York: Harper Collins, 1991, p. 3.

[22] Ibid., pp. 51, 215.

[23] Erikson, *Childhood and Society*, pp. 263-264.

[24] Mitchell, *Tao Te Ching*, p. 19.

Chapter Six

[1] James Hillman & Michael Ventura, *We've Had a Hundred Years of Psychotherapy and the World's Getting Worse*, New York: Harper San Francisco, 1992, p. 6.

[2] Ibid., pp. 17-21.

[3] Ibid., p. 152.

[4] Ibid., p. 29.

[5] Stylianos Atteshlis, *The Esoteric Teachings*, p. 167.

Chapter Seven

[1] Huston Smith, *The World's Religions*, New York: Harper San Francisco, 1991, pp. 83-86.

[2] J.G. Bennett, *Enneagram Studies,* York Beach, Maine: Samuel Weiser, Inc., 1983, p. 132.

[3] Mir Valiuddin, ed. and trans., *Love of God,* Farnham, Surrey (England): Sufi Publishing Co. LTD., 1972, p. 196.

[4] Ibid., pp. 197-198.

[5] Stephen Mitchell, trans., *Tao Te Ching: A New English Version,* New York: Harper and Row, 1988, pp. 2, 45.

[6] Stephen Mitchell, ed., *The Enlightened Mind: An Anthology of Sacred Prose,* New York: Harper Collins, 1991, pp. 88-89.

[7] Pancavimsatisahasrika, quote in Philip Novak, ed., *The World's Wisdom,* Edison, New Jersey: Castle Books, 1994, pp. 80-81.

[8] W.H.C. Frend, *The Rise of Christianity,* Philadelphia: Fortress Press, 1984, p. 91.

[9] Ibid., pp. 96-97.

[10] Huston Smith, quoted in *The World's Religions,* New York: Harper San Francisco, 1991, p. 138.

[11] From *Zen Word, Zen Calligraphy* by Eido Tai Shimano and Kogetsu Tani. 1990, 1995 by Theseus Verlag, Zurich, Munich. Reprinted by arrangement by Shambhala Publications, Inc., Boston, p. 49.

[12] Ibid., p. 151.

[13] Stylianos Atteshlis, *The Esoteric Teachings,* p. 31.

[14] Black Elk, *The Sacred Pipe,* Norman: University of Oklahoma Press, 1953, pp. 3-4, recorded and edited by Joseph Epes Brown.

[15] Ibid., pp. 31, 43.

[16] Michael Harner, *The Way of the Shaman,* New York: Bantam Books, 1980, pp. xii-xvi.

[17] Smith, quote in *The World's Religions,* pp. 75-76.

[18] Ibid., p. 75.

[19] Ibid., pp. 76-77.

[20] Novak, ed., quoted in *The World's Wisdom,* p. 63.

[21] Smith, *The World's Religions,* p. 40.

[22] Frend, *The Rise of Christianity,* pp. 125-126.

[23] Smith, *The World's Religions,* pp. 231-233.

[24] Novak, ed., quoted in *The World's Wisdom,* p. 283.

[25] Ibid., p. 289.

Appendix Three

[1] Stanislav Grof, *Beyond the Brain,* Albany, NY: State University of New York Press, 1985, pp. 18-19.

[2] Ibid., pp. 21-23.

[3] Ibid., p. 70.

[4] Ibid., p. 174.

[5] Ibid., pp. 174, 188-189.

[6] Ibid., p. 188.

[7] Ibid., pp. 188-189.

[8] Ibid., p. 41.

[9] Ibid., p. 44.

[10] Ibid., pp. 58-59.

[11] Ibid., p. 174.

[12] Ibid., pp. 58-59.

[13] Ibid., pp. 73-74.

[14] Michael Talbot, *The Holographic Universe*, New York: Harper Perennial, 1991, pp. 46-50.

[15] Ibid., p. 54.

[16] Stylianos Atteshlis, *The Esoteric Teachings*, pp. 18, 32, 34.

[17] Talbot, *The Holographic Universe*, p. 50.

[18] Atteshlis, *The Esoteric Teachings*, pp. 89-92.

[19] Talbot, *The Holographic Universe*, p. 49.

[20] Atteshlis, *The Esoteric Teachings*, pp. 54-55.

[21] Daskalos uses the word "munificence" as the best English translation of the Greek *euareskeia*. He called *euareskeia* "God's pleasure in creativeness." From *The Esoteric Teachings*, p. 166.

[22] Atteshlis, *The Esoteric Teachings*, pp. 101-102.

[23] Ibid., pp. 104-105.

GLOSSARY

Alternative Spirituality — A term used to denote eclectic modern spiritual trends that fall outside the context of the mainstream religions; the spirituality of the "New Age."

Anima, Animus — The female and male archetypes, as termed by Jung. These are equivalent to the yin and yang principles of Chinese theory. See "Jungian Psychology."

Atonement — Conscious, sustained awareness of the "at-one-ment" that exists between one's higher Self and all creation. Atonement manifests as a state of permanent, universal, and consistent forgiveness toward all beings. It is known as "enlightenment" or "unity consciousness" in Eastern circles and termed "theosis" or "Self-superconsciousness" by Daskalos.

Chakra — A Sanskrit word meaning "wheel." The chakras of the human personality are circular energy vortices which form an energetic connecting link between the Christ Self and the mental, emotional, and physical bodies at particular levels of experience.

Christ Self — The individualized spirit of divinity which indwells each of us, establishing our true identity as a son or daughter of God. The Bible refers to this spirit as "the true light which lighteth every man that cometh into the world." (John 1:9) Daskalos refers to the Christ Self as the "Holy Monad" or "Spirit-ego-self." Alternative spirituality often uses the term "Higher Self."

Consciousness — As used in this book, consciousness is the stage of psychospiritual transformation in which one awakens from the spiri-

216

tual sleep of subconsciousness and separation. Consciousness is initiated by salvation and is marked by the longing to return to the Source. It occurs largely in the realm of chakras 4-5.

Ego — The self-identity that arises from one's observation of his or her own human nature. This capacity for self-observation distinguishes the human being from the animal kingdom.

Egotism — The ego's identification with the inner network of negative elementals, leading to separation and suffering.

Elementals — A term used by Daskalos to denote entities, or forms, within the human energy field that are created by thought.

Negative elementals are emotional thought forms which are created subconsciously to satisfy material cravings and serve the ego's desires. The creation of negative elementals is the process of addiction and binds the personality to the material plane as its slave, creating the conditions for suffering. The Bible refers to negative elementals as "unclean spirits," or "demons." Daskalos also calls negative elementals "desire-thoughts." They exist in inflated forms, termed "ego strengths," and deflated forms, termed "ego weaknesses."

Positive elementals are pure thought forms, or virtues, created by the higher mind under the inspiration of Spirit. Daskalos also calls positive elementals "thought-desires." Virtues purify the reflecting function of the mind, allowing the Christ Self to be reflected more clearly into awareness. A positive elemental may appear similar to an inflated negative elemental, or "ego strength," as it manifests in a person's outer behavior. Its actual reality is determined by the motivations of its creator.

Enlightenment — See "Atonement."

Enneagram — A nine-pointed star diagram that can be used to describe nine different personality types and their interrelationships.

The Fall — The loss of awareness of one's divine nature, leading to exclusive identification with an isolated ego form. The term arises from the biblical story of Adam and Eve, which may be seen as an allegory of this process of separation in awareness from God that we all experience.

Forgiveness — The direct spiritual perception of the divine nature, or Christ Self, within oneself or another person. Forgiveness implies that one sees past human error in the process.

Grace — The unconditional extension of love.

Hell — The suffering and fear that results inevitably from egotism.

Holy Monad — See "Christ Self."

Holy Spirit — In Christian theology, the third person of the Holy Trinity. According to Daskalos, this is the aspect of divinity which expresses the infinite power of God through the creation of the universe.

Identify, Dis-identify

To *identify* with an inner experience is to relate to it with the conviction that "this is an aspect of the real me."

To *dis-identify* from an inner experience is to react to it with the conviction that "this which is within me is not the real me."

Jungian Psychology — A post-Freudian depth psychology which is based on the theory of Carl Jung. Jung expanded Freud's concept of the unconscious to include a *collective unconscious*. The collective unconscious holds *archetypes*, or myth-creating patterns, that bind the individual to all humanity and the cosmos.

Mandala — A symbolic visual representation of the flow of spiritual energies, generally associated with Tibetan Buddhism.

Mind — According to Daskalos, mind is the "supersubstance" from which all universe reality below the level of spirit is constructed.

Pan-ecumenism — The principle and practice of acknowledging and promoting the essential spiritual unity of all the major world religions along with alternative spiritual practices which lead to progress.

Permanent Personality — A term used by Daskalos to refer to one's eternal and unchanging identity, divinely bestowed.

Present-day Personality — The unevolved image of one's permanent personality. It is defined by Daskalos as the sum total of one's elemental creations of mind.

Psychospiritual Transformation — The change that occurs in the personality as it progresses toward spiritual awakening; the process of healing.

Repentance — The process of bringing the blind spots of awareness, the shadow, into the light of spirit for healing. This process is most accurately called psychotherapy in modern times. It results in *metanoia*, translated from Greek as a "change of mind" (about who I am).

Salvation — The awakening to the awareness of the inner Christ Self; the experience of being "born again."

Self-consciousness — A term used by Daskalos to denote the stage of psychospiritual transformation in which one directly perceives oneself and others as the Christ Self. It is the realm of forgiveness and final resignation to the truth. It occurs largely within the sixth chakra domain. Self-consciousness holds on to a dualistic me-you perception and therefore is a step short of the unity consciousness of Self-super-consciousness.

Self-superconsciousness — See "atonement."

Separation — The loss of the awareness of one's connection to God and the inner Christ Self; the experience of being spiritually "lost." See "The Fall."

The Shadow — A term coined by Carl Jung to describe the blind areas in one's awareness. The shadow is experienced through egotism. The "inner Judas," as used in this book, is equivalent to the shadow.

Son of God — One's divine nature. See "Christ Self."

Son of Man — One's human nature.

Soul — The progressing, multidimensional entity produced by the interaction between the divine nature (the Son of God) and the human nature (the Son of Man).

Spirit — The highest and most direct manifestation of deity.

Spirit-ego-self — A term for the Christ Self used by Daskalos to emphasize its individualized nature. See "Christ Self."

Subconscious Mind — A term used by Sigmund Freud to describe the repressed personal memories and instinctual tendencies which unconsciously govern behavior. Daskalos describes the subconscious as the "home of the present-day personality," because it contains that complex of negative elementals which govern and satisfy the egotism of the unevolved personality. The subconscious resides primarily in the domain of chakras 1-2-3.

Theosis — See "Atonement."

Transpersonal Psychology — A modern discipline established in the late 1960s which emphasizes spirituality and transcendental needs as intrinsic aspects of human nature.

The Unconscious — The aspects of one's inner life which lie outside of conscious awareness.

RESOURCES

Etherikos International School
of Energy Healing and Spiritual Studies

Awakening Love has been translated into German, Hungarian, Icelandic, and Portuguese and will soon be available in these languages.

For information on seminars, training programs, CDs, and healing sessions:

U.S.A.:   Nicholas C. Demetry, M.D.   Edwin L. Clonts, M.D.
           2823 Regents Park Lane   P.O. Box 5614
           Marietta, GA 30062   Hopkins, MN 55343
           Phone: (770) 435-0180
           Fax: (770) 956-9949
           Web: www.etherikos.com

Germany: Birgitta Kaessmann   Joachim G. Vieregge
          Hochgratstrabe 323   Tratfeldstrabe 21
          D- 88179 Oberreute/Allgau   D-83646 Bad Tolz, Germany
          Phone: 08387-3282 or 1297   Phone: 08041-8851
          Fax: 08387-2394   Fax: 08041-75293

Hungary: Erica Miklody
1021 - Budapest, Hungary
Kuruclesi u– 47-B
Phone/Fax: 0361-200-2903

Iceland: Solbjort Gudmundsdottir   Hrafnaildur Juliusdottir
Skarphedinsgata 18   Huldubraut 60
105 Reykjavik, Iceland   200 Kopavogur, Iceland
Phone: 0354-552.4545   Phone: 0354-554.2021
Fax: 0354-872.1945
e-mail: solbjort@ismennt.is

Islenk Heilsa Ehf
Gauja Litla
Brautarholt 8
105 Reykjavik, Iceland

Brazil: Maria Cristina Zeppelini - Despertar
Av. Rio Branco, 78 – Jd. Esplanada
Sao Jose dos Campos, Sao Paulo, SP. Brasil 12242-800
Phone/Fax: 011-55-12-322.8767
e-mail: despert@netvale.com.br

INDEX

ABOUT THE AUTHORS

Nicholas Demetry, MD, is a holistic psychiatrist dedicated to the journey of self-realization. He has studied with several spiritual teachers, healers, and shamans, and has integrated techniques and methods of both traditional and alternative therapies. He received his MD degree from Emory University School of Medicine. After completing his medical training, he continued his studies at the University of Hawaii, specializing in general psychiatry and trans-cultural studies. He is currently in private practice in Atlanta, Georgia.

Dr. Demetry is the director of the Etherikos International School of Energy Healing and Spiritual Development located in Atlanta, which has offered programs and classes in the United States, Germany, Brazil, Norway, Iceland and Hungary. He has studied the Enneagram with Helen Palmer and currently teaches it. He has studied Christian mysticism and healing with Stylianos Atteshlis (Daskalos) of Strovolos, Cyprus.

Dr. Edwin L. Clonts received his MD degree from the University of Tennessee Center for the Health Sciences. He completed a family practice residency through a University of Minnesota affiliated program and is an associate clinical professor with the University of Minnesota Department of Family Practice. He practices conventional allopathic medicine in the Twin Cities area, with an emphasis on prevention.

Dr. Clonts is a long-time student of *The Urantia Book* and *A Course in Miracles*. He studied with Stylianos Atteshlis, who inspired him by embodying the spirit and teachings of these great works. Using the life and teachings of Jesus as a guide, he has sought to develop a model which illustrates the fundamental spiritual unity of the world's religions.